THE PURITANS ON PRAYER

JOHN PRESTON
The Saint's Daily Exercise

NATHANIEL VINCENT
The Spirit of Prayer

SAMUEL LEE
Secret Prayer

Soli Deo Gloria Publications
...for instruction in righteousness...

Soli Deo Gloria Publications
P.O. Box 451, Morgan, PA 15064
(412) 221-1901/FAX 221-1902

The Puritans on Prayer
is © 1995 by Soli Deo Gloria.
Printed in the United States of America

*

ISBN 1-877611-77-8

Editor's Note

In the process of editing these classic works on prayer by the venerable authors, I became aware that often, when they referred to Scripture, it would be from memory rather than an exact biblical quotation. I have decided to leave the Scriptures as they appear in the original manuscripts, whether cited from memory or paraphrased, rather than correcting them to exact quotations from Scripture passages.

John Preston's work is, arguably, the classic Puritan work on prayer. The other two works by Vincent and Lee fit so nicely with it that Soli Deo Gloria is offering them as a trilogy on this most vital subject for today's church. Preston calls us to prayer and defines it. Vincent tells us to pray continually and gives instruction how to do that. Lee gives us the sweetness of secret prayer, then adds a section on sudden, spontaneous prayers. Combined, these three treatises give us encouragement and instruction in the duty and privilege of prayer, that "holy breathing of the soul."

May God use this book to encourage your heart to greater communion with Himself in prayer.

Rev. Don Kistler
Editor
Soli Deo Gloria Publications

Contents

Secret Prayer Successfully Managed, by Samuel Lee

The Saints' Daily Exercise

A
Treatise
Concerning
the Whole Duty of Prayer

Delivered in Five Sermons Upon
1 Thessalonians 5:17

by the late Faithful and
Worthy Minister of Jesus Christ

John Preston

Doctor in Divinity, Chaplain to His Majesty,
Master of Emmanuel College in Cambridge,
and sometimes Preacher of Lincoln's Inn

"The effectual fervent prayer of a righteous
man availeth much." James 5:16

"If I regard iniquity in my heart, the Lord
will not hear my prayer." Psalm 66:18

To The Reader

Courteous Reader,

To discourse of the necessity and use of this piece of spiritual armor after so many learned and useful treatises upon this subject may seem superfluous, especially considering that there is so much spoken to this purpose for your satisfaction in the ensuing treatise. Besides unfolding the nature of this duty (which is the saint's daily exercise) and strong enforcement to it, there is contained herein an endeavor to give satisfaction in the most incidental cases, lack of clearing whereof is usually a hindrance to the cheerful and ready performance thereof. In all of this, what has been done by this reverend and worthy man we would rather should appear in this treatise itself to your indifferent judgment than to be much in setting down our own opinion. We do not doubt that, by reason of the spiritual and convincing manner of handling this argument, it will win acceptance with many, especially considering that it is of that nature wherein, though much has been spoken, yet much more may be said with good relish to those who have any spiritual sense. For it is the most spiritual action wherein we have nearer communion with God than we do in any other holy performance, and whereby it pleases God to convey all good to us, their performance whereof Christians find most backwardness and indisposedness, and from thence, most dejection of spirit. In these times, this is also most necessary wherein, unless we fetch help from heaven this way, we see the church and cause of God likely to be trampled under foot.

Only remember that we let these sermons pass forth as they were delivered by himself, in public, without taking that liberty of adding or detracting which, perhaps, some would have thought good. For we thought it best that his own meaning should be expressed in his own words and manner, especially considering that there is little which, perhaps, may be superfluous to some, but may, by God's blessing, be useful to others. It would be a good prevention of many inconveniences in this kind if able men would be persuaded to publish their own works in their lifetime, yet we think it is a good service to the church when that defect is supplied by giving some life to those things which otherwise would have died of themselves. The blessings of these labors of his we commend unto God, and the benefit of them unto you, resting

Yours in our Lord Jesus Christ,

Richard Sibbes

John Davenport

Sermon One

1 Thessalonians 5:17
"Pray continually."

The Apostle here, in the latter end of this epistle, heaps up many precepts together, and, therefore, we shall not need to seek out the dependence of these words upon those that go before or those that follow after. "Rejoice evermore. Pray continually, in all things give thanks; for this is the will of God in Christ Jesus to you wards."

We are now fallen upon this text, where this duty of prayer is commended to us; and it is a command from God Himself delivered shortly, as laws are wont to be, without any great premises and reasons, and, indeed, having therefore the more authority in it.

In the handling of this command, "pray continually," we will do these three things:

First, we will show you what prayer is.

Second, why the Lord requires this at our hands. For a man might object, "The Lord knows my wants well enough. He knows my mind and how I am affected." Aye, but yet the Lord will have us to pray and to ask before He will bestow it upon us.

And, last, what it is to pray continually.

I. What prayer is. If we should define prayer in general to you, I would give you no more than this description of it. It is an expression of the mind to the

1

Lord. Sometimes it is by words, sometimes without words, but yet there must be an expression and some opening of the will to Him. This is the general.

But to know what a right prayer is—what such a prayer is as God accepts—you must have another definition, which must have more ingredients to it. And so prayer is nothing else but an expression or offering of those holy and good dispositions to God that arise from the spirit, or the regenerate part, in the name of Jesus Christ. Wherefore, you are to observe this: The prayers we make are divided into one of these two sorts.

① First, some are such prayers as are the expression of our own spirits, the voice of our own spirits, and there is nothing but flesh in them—such prayers as any natural man may make to the Lord. And the Lord does not regard these. He does not know the meaning of them, that is, He does not accept them.

② Second, there are prayers that are the voice of God's own Spirit, that is, such as arise from the regenerate part within us, which is quickened and enlarged to pray from the immediate help of the Holy Ghost. These prayers alone are accepted and, of these, it is said, "He knows the meaning of the Spirit." That is, He so knows it and sees it that He also accepts it. Therefore you shall see in Hosea 7:14 that when they prayed and prayed earnestly they set a day apart for prayer. They called a solemn assembly and kept a fast. Yet, says the Lord plainly, "Ye did not call upon Me when you howled upon your beds; for you assembled yourselves for corn and for wine, which any natural man may do." And therefore He says, it is but "a howling." It is the voice of beasts to seek for wine, oil, and corn; but, He says plainly, "You called not upon Me" when, notwithstanding, they spent a whole day in prayer. But the meaning is this: The Lord regards this as no prayer at all.

Therefore, to open this description a little unto you, there is one main business that we have to do in the handling of this text—to describe to you the meaning of this precept as to what the nature of prayer is so that you may know what kind of prayer it is that prevails with God. I say, it is an expression of holy and good dispositions. I use that expression "dispositions" rather than "desires" because there is some part of prayer that stands in thanksgiving, when you desire nothing at God's hand but give thanks for what you have received. Mark it, first they must be holy and good. The desires and the dispositions must be good, for that is a rule. All the affections and desires are good or evil, according as their objects are. Those that are fixed upon good things are good desires.

You will say, then, "What are the good things that make the desires and dispositions of the heart good?"

They are both temporal and spiritual things. A man may pray for temporal things in a spiritual manner, and the desire may be good. And again, he may pray for spiritual things in a carnal manner, and the desire may be naught. Therefore, it must be observed that it is not simply the object, but there is a certain manner of desiring too. For example, if a man prays for temporal things for outward comforts—such things as belong to the present state of his body here—if he prays for them so that he prays for that which is convenient for him, he prays for such a measure as God sees to be proper. Proverbs 31 says, "Feed me with convenient

food for me." This prayer is good, but (if as in 1
Timothy 6:9, "if any man will be rich") it is an inordinate desire when men will have an excess of these outward things and more than is fit for them. And again,
if you desire that which is convenient and spend it
upon your lusts, if you desire health and long life so
that you may live more pleasantly, if you desire wealth
that you may live more deliciously and not simply that
which the creature may desire, to the end that you may
be the more enabled to serve the Lord in these things,
your desire is not good. So I say, first, it is for that
which is convenient. Second, you must not spend it
upon your lusts but in God's service.

And, last, we must pray for them in a right
method—first the kingdom of God and then other
things. That is, set a price on them as you ought—not
too high a price, but value them rightly. We should so
pray for outward things as our prayers may be spiritual.
On the other side, a man may pray for spiritual things
in a carnal manner as he may pray for temporal things
in a spiritual manner.

A natural man may pray earnestly for faith, for
grace, and for repentance, not out of any beauty that
he sees in them, not out of any taste and relish that he
has of them but because he thinks them a bridge to
lead them to heaven, and that he cannot come there
without them. When he considers that he cannot be
saved without these things, then he may desire them,
and desire them earnestly. It was the case of Frances
Spira, who cried so earnestly for grace that he might
have but a drop of it because he could not be saved
without it. He gave the reason himself when he said
that he saw no excellency in it. He did not desire it for

himself and, therefore, he thought his prayers could not be heard. Thus you see that prayer is an expression of holy and good desires; it is an offering them up to the Lord.

I will not stand upon that (you are well-instructed enough in it), that whatsoever petition is made to the creature is not a prayer; they must be offered up to the Lord alone.

Then, I add, these prayers are such as must arise from the regenerate part; that is, look how much there is of the regenerate part in prayer. Look how much the Holy Spirit has to do in it. Look how much comes from that which is called "the inward man." As far as it is sanctified, so far that prayer is accepted and no further. But, that we may open this a little more fully, we will show you it by some other expressions of prayer that we find in the Scriptures.

It is called a lifting up of the heart to God, a "pouring forth of the soul to the Lord," 1 Samuel 1:15. Paul calls it "serving Him in spirit." Now, if we open these phrases unto you a little, you shall know more fully wherein the nature of right praying to God consists. That phrase the Apostle uses, "whom I serve in my spirit," Acts 13:21, in the original is used for fasting and prayer. Now, what is it to pray to God in the spirit? For a man may say, "A man cannot make a prayer, but there is an act of his mind in it, and every man, whatever service he performs, his spirit must have a hand in it, so it cannot be performed without the mind."

I take this to be the meaning of it. The Apostle's scope is to distinguish the true and holy services of God from those that are but shadows and counterfeit, that are but the body and carcass of right service.

Therefore, when he says "I serve the Lord in my spirit",
or "I pray in the spirit", the meaning is this: When the
prayer of a man is not only that which the understanding dictates to him, but when the whole soul, the will
and affections, goes together with his petition a man's
heart is affected accordingly.

For example, if a man comes to confess his sins,
and yet slights them inwardly in his heart, if a man
prays for reconciliation with God and yet has no longing and sighing in his heart after it, if he earnestly asks
for grace and the mortification of sinful lusts, when the
heart does not inwardly seek it, he is not now praying
in the spirit. To pray in the spirit is as we see in John
4:24, "He will be worshipped in spirit and in truth."
The meaning is, to pray so that the heart goes together
with the petition also. This is the meaning of that when
a man pours forth his soul before the Lord. So
Hannah said of herself, "I am a woman troubled", and
I "have poured out my soul before the Lord." That is,
when a man delivers to God that which the understanding and mind have devised (for prayer is not a
work of wit or of memory), when a man pours forth his
whole soul, that is, his will and affections, when they go
together, when there is no reservation in his mind, but
when all within him is opened and explicate, and is
exposed to the view of the Lord—not as Austin said of
himself when he came to pray for the mortifying of his
lusts. He said, "I had a secret, inward desire that it
should not be done." Therefore, when the soul is
poured forth, the meaning is that all is opened to him,
so that, when a man will make an acceptable prayer, he
must make this account; he must then call in all his
thoughts and affections, and recollect them together

as the lines in the center or as the sun beams in a burn-ing glass, and that makes prayer to be hot and fervent; whereas, otherwise, it is but a cold and dissipated thng that has no strength or efficacy in it.

Now, with all this, you must know that when we say the whole soul must go together with the petition, the meaning is that not only the will and affections must be employed (for in a natural man, in his desire of health when he is sick or lacks assistance and guidance in difficult cases, not only the understanding, but the will and affections are busy enough, it is likely), and therefore we add further that that which is called the spirit, which is diffused in the whole soul, is set to work in the performance of this holy duty to the Lord whenever we seek Him in prayer.

For this you know, there are two things in a regen-erate man (for you must take for granted, by the way, that no natural man is able to make an acceptable prayer to God, seeing there is no spirit in him, but there is in the regenerate man). There is flesh and spirit. Now, when we come to pour forth our hearts to the Lord, that which lies uppermost will be ready to be poured forth first; and that which is spiritual, it may be, lies in the bottom and is kept in. And so a man may make a carnal prayer, though he is a holy man, that is, when the flesh has gotten the upper hand. When the mind is filled with worldly sorrows, worldly rejoicing, and worldly desires, and these are expressed to the Lord, it is a prayer the Lord does not regard, though the man is holy from whom it comes. But right prayer is this: when the regenerate part is acted and stirred up and the flesh that hinders is removed.

You must know this, wherever there is a regenerate

part in any man, there is a regenerate aptness in that
man to call upon God, and it cannot be disengaged
from it, but that is not always in action. We see a fountain, and it always has an aptness to pour forth water. It
is ready to break into a current; but, if it is stopped
with stones and mud, and other impediments, it cannot break out. In the same way, he who is a regenerate
man, who has a holy part in him, has an aptness to
prayer. That is what our Savior said, Matthew 26:41,
"The spirit is willing," that is, there is always a willingness that follows the spirit, or the regenerate part in a
holy man; but, He says, the flesh is backward. That is, it
stops this fountain and, therefore, Romans 8:27, the
Spirit is said there to help our infirmities, and to make
requests for us. That is, even as a man removes stones
from a fountain with his hands and, when he has done
that, it breaks forth into a current, so the Holy Ghost
removes this flesh that stops up the current; the Spirit
takes away those carnal impediments that are in us.
And not only so, but it stirs up the regenerate part and,
when that is done, we are able to make spiritual
prayers to God in Christ Jesus.

So that is the thing that you are now to observe.
The Spirit must help our infirmities when we come to
call upon God, and our prayers are as acceptable as
they are the fruits of the regenerate part. Now, we want
but one thing to add in the definition.

They are such prayers as are offered to God in the
name of Jesus Christ. This is a thing you all know, that
those prayers that are not offered up in Christ are not
acceptable because the person is not regarded. It was
the sin of Uzziah, in 2 Chronicles 26, that he would go
to the temple, himself being a king on the throne, and

would offer incense without a priest. We do the very
same thing whenever we go to offer up any prayer to
God without Christ Jesus. In the old law men might
bring their sacrifices, but the priest must still be the
one to offer them up. So must we here; and the reason
is given in Revelation 8, because the prayers that come
from us savor of the flesh from which they come, and
the angel of the covenant mingles much incense with
them and makes them sweet and acceptable to God
with much incense. That is, as the flesh is more, so
there needs to be more incense so that they may be
made acceptable to God the Father.

So, then, we have a double intercessor. One is the
Spirit that helps our infirmities, who helps us to make
our petitions, who quickens and enlarges our hearts to
prayer. The other is the interecessor to make them acceptable to God, so that He may receive them and not
refuse and reject them. So much shall serve for the first
thing, to show you what the duty is, what a right, true,
and acceptable prayer is.

II. Why we must pray. Now, for the second, why we
must pray. A man may make this objection: "The Lord
knows my mind well enough, what need do I have to
express it by prayer?". The reasons briefly why the Lord
will have us to pray are taken partly from Himself and
partly from us.

1. From Himself. Though He is willing to bestow
mercies upon us, yet He will have us ask His leave before He does it. This, you know, fathers do with their
children. Though they intend to bestow such things
upon them as are needful, yet they will have their children to ask. It is a common thing among men, though

they are willing that a man should pass through their grounds, yet they will have permission asked because, by that means, the property is acknowledged. Otherwise it would be taken as a common highway. So the Lord will have His servants to come and ask so that they may acknowledge the property He has in those gifts He bestows upon them. Indeed, otherwise we would forget in what tenure we hold those blessings we enjoy, and what service we owe to the Lord. There is an homage due to the Lord so that the Lord might be acknowledged. So the Lord will have this duty of prayer performed so that we might acknowledge Him, so that we might remember the service we ought to do for Him, to rise and go at His command, that is, to do His service which we would be ready to forget if we were not accustomed to the duty of calling on Him.

Likewise, He will have it done for His honor's sake. He will have men call upon Him so that they might learn to reverence Him and, likewise, so that others might be stirred up to reverence Him, to honor Him, and to fear Him. The servants of a prince, doing honor and reverence to their Lord, stir up those who are looking on.

As the schoolmen say of glory, glory is properly this: not when a man has an excellency in him (for he may have and yet be without glory), but glory is an ostentation, a showing of that excellency. It is the phrase that is used in the Sacrament. You are to celebrate the Sacrament that you may show forth the Lord's death. So the Lord will have us come and call upon His name to show forth the duty of prayer, and that we may show forth His glory. This is for the Lord Himself.

2. For ourselves. We are to do it partly that the

graces of His Spirit may be increased in us, for prayer exercises our graces. Every grace is exercised in prayer, and these graces, being exercised, are increased. See an excellent place for this in Jude 20, "That you beloved edify yourselves in the holy faith, praying in the Holy Ghost." It is as if he should say, "The way to edify yourselves and build yourselves up is to pray in the Holy Ghost"—that is, spiritual prayer made through the power, assistance, and strength of the Holy Ghost. Every such prayer builds us up, it increases. Every grace in us—faith, repentance, love, obedience, and fear—are all increased by prayer. Partly because they are exercised and set to work in prayer—for the very exercises increases them—and partly, also, because prayer brings us to communion with God. Now, if good company increases grace, how much more will communion with the Lord Himself quicken and increase it?

Moreover, this duty is required that we may be acquainted with God, for there is a strangeness between the Lord and us when we do not call upon His name. It is the command which you shall find in Job 22:21, "Acquaint thyself with the Lord that thou mayest have peace with Him, and thou shalt have prosperity." Now, you know how acquaintance grows among men. It is by conversing together, by speaking to one another. On the other side, we say when that is broken off, when they do not salute, when they do not speak together, a strangeness grows. So it is in this.

When we come to the Lord and are frequent and fervent in this duty of calling upon Him, we grow acquainted with Him. Without it, we grow to be strangers and the Lord dwells far off. We are not able to behold

Him unless we are accustomed to it. And the more we come into His presence, the more we are acquainted with Him. Therefore, that is another reason why we should use this, that we may get acquainted with the Lord.

Likewise, we should pray that we may learn to be thankful to Him for those mercies we have received from Him. For if God should bestow mercies upon us unasked we would forget them. His hand would not be acknowledged in them, and we would not see His providence in disposing those blessings that we enjoy. But when we come to ask everything before Him, we are then ready to see His hand more, to prize it more, and we are more disposed to thankfulness. So this is a sure rule commonly: What we win with prayer, we wear with thankfulness. And what we get without prayer, we spend and use without any lifting up of the heart to God in praising Him, and acknowledging His hand in bestowing it upon us. So you see what this duty is, and why the Lord will have this duty performed.

III. What it is to pray continually. The word in the original signifies such a performance of this duty that you do not cease to do it at such times as God requires it at your hands. Compare this with that verse in 2 Timothy 1:3. The Apostle said there that he has him in continual remembrance, praying for him night and day. The same word is used here. Now we cannot think that the Apostle had Timothy in continual remembrance, that he was never out of his thoughts, but the meaning is that when he did call upon God from day to day, He still remembered him. So to pray continually is to pray very much, to pray at those times when

God requires us to pray.

Philosophers give this definition of idleness: A man is said to be idle when he does not do that which he ought in the time in which it is required of him. He is an idle man who does not work when he ought to work. So he is said not to pray continually who does not pray when he ought to pray. So I conceive this to be the meaning of the Apostle, "Rejoice evermore." But when he comes to this exhortation of prayer, he does not content himself to say "pray very often" but "pray continually." When we would have a thing done frequently, we would say that you are always to be doing it. So the Apostle's scope is to show that it should be done frequently and that it should be done much. Hence, we gather this, by the way, that we are bound to keep our constant course of calling upon God at least twice a day, whatever more we do.

But, you will say, what ground have you for that? Why do you say twice a day?

The ground of it is this: When the Apostle bids us to pray continually, to do it very often, the least we can do it is twice a day. We may do it more often, but this, I say, is the least. When we have such a command as this, when we have such a precept as this, to pray continually, and this rule is illuminated by such examples as we have in the Scriptures, why is it recorded if it is not true of every example in that kind that is said of the general example, 1 Corinthians 10, "they are written for our learning"? It is said that Daniel prayed often. Daniel expressly, in Daniel 6:3, is said to have prayed three times a day. That was his constant course.

I say, we may think we are bound to do it at least twice a day. Consider a little why we are bound to do it.

In the temple, you know, the Lord was worshipped twice a day. There was the morning and the evening sacrifice. What was the ground of that commandment? There was no reason for it but that the Lord might be worshipped, and that was the time that He would have it done, twice a day, morning and evening. But, besides that, it was not only that the Lord might be worshipped (wherein we should follow that example of worshipping Him morning and evening), but likewise our occasions are such that this is the least we can do to call upon Him constantly morning and evening.

There is no day where we do not use many of His blessings and take many of His comforts. Now we may not take any of them without His permission, so that you are bound to ask for them before you take them, and pray for a blessing upon them, or else you have no right to them. You have no lawful use of them, that place is plain, 1 Timothy 4, "Every creature of God is good, and ought not to be refused if it is received with thanksgiving; for it is sanctified by prayer." So that, if you take common blessings every day, and do not seek them at the Lord's hands before you take them, they are not sanctified unto you. You do not have a lawful use of them. You have no right unto them.

Besides, my beloved, it is that which the Lord commands in everything. "Make your requests known in everything." That is, whenever you need anything, make your requests known; so "in everything give thanks." And, therefore, the least we can do when we have received, and need, so many mercies, is to give thanks and to seek Him so often from day to day.

Moreover, do not our hearts need it? Are they not ready to go out of order? Are they not ready to contract hardness, are they not ready to go from the Lord and to be hardened from God's fear? Therefore, this duty is needful in that regard to compose them and bring them back again into order.

Moreover, do not the sins we commit daily put a necessity upon us of doing this so that they may be forgiven and done away with, so that we may be reconciled to God again? Therefore, do not think that it is an arbitrary thing to call upon God twice a day because there is no particular or expressed command. For, if you consider these places that I have named, and the reasons, we shall see there is a necessity that lies upon us to do it. So much shall serve for that. I now come to make some use of this that has been delivered.

USES

First, in that such prayers as the Lord accepts are an expression of holy duties, such desires as rise from the regenerate part of a man. Hence, then, we see that all natural men are in a miserable condition when times of extremity come, and when the day of death comes, when there is no help in the world but seeking the Lord, when all the creatures forsake them, and are not able to help them; and there is no way to go to the Lord but by prayer. If prayer is an effect and fruit of the regenerate part of a man, a carnal man is not able to help himself—he is in a miserable condition. Therefore, let men consider this that puts all off to times of extremity. Put the case, you have warning enough at such a time. Put the case, you have the use of your understanding, yet you are not able to do any good without this. For if there is not grace in the heart you are not able to make a spiritual prayer to the Lord that He accepts. Therefore, take heed of deferring and putting off. Labor to be regenerate, to have your hearts renewed, while you have time. And if you are not able to call upon God in the time of health, how will you do it when your wits and your spirit are spent and lost, and when you are in times of sickness and extremity? Therefore, let that be considered which we are only touching on briefly.

Second, if the Lord commands us to "pray continually," then take heed of neglecting this duty. Rather, be exhorted to be frequent and fervent in it, to continue therein, and watch thereto with all perseverance. It is a common fault among us that either we are ready to omit it, or to come to it unwillingly, or else we perform it in a careless and negligent manner, not considering what a command lies upon the sons of men to perform it constantly and conscionably.

I beseech you to consider that this is a privilege purchased by the blood of Jesus Christ. Christ died for this end, it cost Him the shedding of His blood, so that we, through Him, might have entrance to the throne of grace. And will you let such a privilege as this lie still? If you do, so far as is in you, you cause His blood to be shed in vain. For if you neglect the privileges gotten by that blood, so far you neglect the blood that procured them. But to neglect this duty is to neglect that. Besides, if we ask you the reason why you abstain from other sins, why you do not steal, why you do not commit adultery and murder, the reason you give is that the Lord has commanded you not to do those things. Has not the Lord commanded you to pray constantly, pray at all times?

If you make conscience of one commandment, why do you not of another? Consider Daniel in this case, Daniel 6. He would not omit a constant course of prayer. He did it three times a day, and that was his ordinary custom. If he would not omit it to spare his life, if he would not omit it in such a case of danger as that, why will you omit it for business, for a little advantage, for a little gain, for a little wealth, or pomp, or pleasure, or whatever may draw you from that duty? Do but consider what an unreasonable, and how unequal, a thing it is that when the Lord gives us meat, drink, and clothes from day to day, when He gives us sleep every night, when He provides for us such comforts as we have need of (as there is not the least creature that does us any service but as far as He sets it to work to do that service), for us to forget Him and not give Him thanks, and not to ask these things at His hands, not to seek him but to live as without God in the world, as we do when we neglect this duty, is a profession of living without God in the world. We are strangers to Him. It is open rebellion against Him. Therefore, take heed of omitting it.

Besides all this, we should do it for our own sakes, if we consider what use we have of this duty for ourselves. Is it not the key that opens all God's treasures? When heaven was shut up, was not this the key that opened it? When the wombs were shut up, was not this that opened it? You know, Elijah prayed for rain, so we may pray for every other blessing. All God's treasures are locked up to those that do not call upon His name. This opens the door to them all. Whatever they are that we have occasion to use, this is effectual. It does better than anything besides.

If a man is sick, I will be bold to say it, a faithful prayer is more able to heal his disease than the best medicine. "The prayer of faith shall heal the sick," James 5:5. You know, the woman that had the bloody issue, when she had spent all upon physicians and they could do no good, then she came to Christ and offered faithful prayer to Him. That did it when so many years of medicine could not do it. Beloved, if there is a prince or a great man whose mind we would have turned towards us, a faithful prayer will do it sooner than the best friends. So it was with Nehemiah. You know his request, that the Lord would give him favor in the sight of the man. If we are in any strait, as it was in Joseph's case, if we have any difficult matter to bring to pass, this prayer and seeking the Lord will expedite and set us at liberty sooner. It will find a way to bring it about more than all the wits in the world because it sets God to work. You have no power to do anything.

Certainly, a praying Christian who is prevalent and potent with God is able to do more than all the riches in the world. Riches set the devil to work, but prayer sets God to work. It sets Him to work to do us good and to heal us, to deliver us out of extremities. Therefore, I say, for our own sakes, even out of self-love and for common comforts, you need to do this. Certainly, if these things were believed (you hear them, you give us the hearing for the time, but if they were believed), many would be more frequent in this duty. They would not be so negligent in it or come to it in so careless a manner as this.

Besides, I beseech you to consider this. Every man desires joy and comfort, and one thing that commonly keeps us off from this duty is sports and pleasures, one thing or another that we take delight in which dampens and hinders us in these things, in spiritual performances. Prayer is the best way of all others to fill your heart with joy, as we see in John 16:24. He said there, "In my name you have asked nothing hitherto, but now ask that your joy may be full." This is one motive that Christ uses to exhort us to be frequent in this duty, that our joy may be full. That I take to be the meaning of James 5:13, "If any be sad, let him pray." Not only because prayer is suitable to such a disposition, but likewise it will cheer him up. It is the way to get comfort. So it is in Philippians 4:6, "In all things, make your requests known, and the peace of God shall keep you in the communion of Jesus Christ." That is it that brings peace and quietness, and, therefore, there is much reason why we should be constant in this duty. It is that which quickens us, it is that which fills us with peace and joy and comfort, and with that peace which is what everyone desires.

Moreover, consider it is your buckler. Prayer is the helmet that keeps you safe. When a man neglects it, when he ceases to go to God in prayer, when he once shows himself to be a stranger to the Lord by neglecting this duty, then he is out of the pales of his protection, like the moles that go out of their burrows. For so is the Lord to those who pray. The Lord is a protection to those who call upon His name. The very calling upon His name is a running under God's wings, as it were, putting our souls under His shadow; but when you neglect that, you wander abroad from Him.

Now, do we not need protection from outward dangers from day to day? Do we not need to be kept

from the inward danger of sin and temptation? Surely,
prayer is one part of the spiritual armor, as we see in
Ephesians 6. In the complete armor of God, prayer is
reckoned up the last, as that which buckles up all the
rest. The Apostle says, "Continue in prayer, and watch
with perseverance." And you have all the more reason
to do it, because it is not only a part of this armor, but
it enables you to use all the rest, to use the Word and
to use faith. For prayer stirs them all up.

What is it to have armor and not to have it ready?
Now prayer makes it ready. Therefore, you see Christ
prescribes the same rule in Matthew 26:41: "Pray that
ye enter not into temptation", as if that were the way to
secure and shelter us, and to keep us safe from falling
into temptation. It is a thing I would advise you to, to
pray and to seek the Lord continually. Therefore, if we
should use only this reason to you to be constant in
this duty, because it is for your safety, it would be sufficient.

When a man is as a city whose walls are broken
down, when he lies exposed to temptation, he is in a
dangerous case. So I may use this dilemma to you if
you have a good disposition, if you think thus: "I hope
I am well enough. I am not now exposed to any temptation; I fear nothing."

Make this argument against yourself, "Why do I neglect so good a gale? If my heart is so well disposed to
pray, why do I then omit it? Again, if there is an indisposition in me, why do I hazard myself?"

What if Satan should set upon you? What if the
world should set upon you? What suitable temptations,
agreeable to your lusts, are offered? Are you not in
danger? And, therefore, a constant course should be

kept in it. We should take heed of negligence in it.

And will a man now profess that he hopes he is the servant of God, and in a good estate, although he does not pray as much as others (we speak not of frequency simply, but of such a performance as is required), I say, to profess that you are a servant of Christ, and that you love Him, and that He is your husband, and that you are His servant, and yet you do not call upon Him from day to day. This is an idle thing. It is impossible.

If you loved Him, you would express yourself in calling upon His name. Shall a friend who is but an acquaintance to us, in whom we delight, come to us (we are willing to spend many hours with him), and shall we profess ourselves to be friends of God, and Him to be a friend to us, and that we delight in Him, and yet neglect this duty?

This is a common thing among you. When you see a man who meditates all his matters himself, or if he opens his mind and tells them to somebody else, it must be such a one as professes to be a friend to him. Now, if this friend should never hear from him, nor ever speak to him, or if he does it is in such a negligent manner as it may appear that he does not trust him, and he does it so shortly that he can scarcely tell what his business is, I say, in such a case, would you not reckon his profession of friendship to be an idle and empty profession?

Now, apply it to yourself. Those who say they have communion with God, and hope their estate is good enough, stand in good terms with Him. But yet, if they are in any necessity, for all the matters and occasions that fall out from day to day, either they think of them in themselves, or they are apt enough to declare them to man. Or, if they go to God, they do it negligently. They post over the matter so as they have scarcely any leisure to express themselves and their doings. Do you think He will take such for friends? And do you think that this is a true, sound, and hearty profession? Therefore, to end this, I beseech you to consider it, and take heed of being remiss and negligent in it. You see, it is a command from the Lord, "Pray continually."

And so much for this time.

Sermon Two

1 Thessalonians 5:17
"Pray continually."

Not to repeat what has been delivered, but to press this point on us a little further (for what is more necessary than that we should keep a constant course in this duty, since the very life of religion consists in it?), I add this to all I pressed in the morning, that if you neglect it, it exposes you to great disadvantage, both for the outward man, and for the inward man, and there are but these two that you need to care for.

For the outward man, it deprives you of the blessing. Put the case, you have never so good success in your enterprises. Put the case, you have outward comforts in abundance, yet still the blessing is lacking and, not only so, but it uncovers the roof, as it were, and the curse is rained down upon your tables, upon your meat and drink, upon all the endeavors and enterprises you take in hand. We do not consider what we do when we neglect this duty, what dangers we expose ourselves to from day to day. For it is one thing to have outward comforts, and another thing to have the blessing with them.

Besides, consider what loss you suffer in the inward man when you neglect this duty at any time, for the inward man is ready to be distempered and to go out of order. It is ready to contract hardness, to contract soil. Spiritual grace is ready to decay. It falls out with a man's heart as it does with a garden that is negelected. It will quickly be overcome with weeds if you do not look diligently to it, and the way to look to it is constancy in this duty.

That was a notable place in Job 15:4, when Eliphaz observed some distemper in Job's affections (as he apprehended it). He told him that the speech he used was not comely but vain and sinful. And what then? "Surely Job, thou restrainest prayer from the Lord." It is as if he should say, "It is impossible, Job, that you should fall into these distempers if you kept your course constantly in your duty. Therefore, you restrain prayer from the Lord."

So it is with us. Let us restrain prayer from God, and distempers will quickly arise in our spirits. Worldly mindedness will be ready to grow upon us. We shall be apt to be carnal. We shall forget God, forget ourselves, and forget the good purposes and desires we had. And, therefore, that you may keep your hearts in order, you must keep a constant course in this duty; for, if you do (though your peace is interrupted), this will repair it again. It will make up the breach again, though there are some distempered actions that grow upon us, yet prayer will compose all. As sleep composes drunkenness, so prayer will compose the affections. A man may pray himself sober again. Nothing does it sooner, nothing does it more effectually. And this you shall find as you either omit it or slight it over. So you shall find a proportionate weakness growing upon the inward man, as the body feels when it neglects either sleep, or diet, or exercise. Therefore, to end this exhortation, let us be constant in it.

Only remember this (when we exhort you thus to

keep a constant course, for which you hear so many reasons in the morning, I say, remember this caution), that if it is performed in a formal or customary and overly manner, you would be as good to omit it altogether; for the Lord takes our prayers not by number but by weight. When it is an outward picture, a dead carcass of prayer, when there is no life, no fervency in it, God does not regard it. Do not be deceived in this, it is a very common deception. It may be a man's conscience would be upon him, if he should omit it altogether. Therefore, when he does something, his heart is satisfied, and so he grows worse and worse. Therefore, consider that the very doing of the duty is not that which the Lord heeds, but He will have it so performed that the end may be obtained and that the thing for which you pray may be effected.

If a man sends his servant to go to such a place, it is not his going to and fro that he regards, but he would have him to dispatch the business. So it is in all other works. He does not care about the formality of performance, but he would have the thing so done that it may be of use to him. If you send a servant to make a fire for you, and he goes and lays some green wood together and puts a few coals underneath, this is not to make a fire for you. He must either get dry wood, or he must blow until it burns and is fit for use.

So when your hearts are unfit, when they are like green wood, when you come to warm them and to quicken them by prayer to God, it may be you post over this duty, and leave your hearts as cold and disptempered as they were before. My beloved, this is not to perform this duty. The duty is effectually performed when your hearts are wrought upon by it, and

when they are brought to a better tune and temper
than they were before.

If you find sinful lusts, your business there is to
work them out by prayer, to reason the matter, to ex-
postulate the thing before the Lord, and not to give
over until you have set all the wheels of your soul right,
until you have made your hearts perfect with God.
And, if you find your hearts cleaving too much to the
world, you must wean them and take them off. If you
find a deadness and unaptness, an indisposition in you,
you must lift up your souls to the Lord and not give
over until you are quickened. And this is to perform
the duty in such a manner as the Lord accepts, otherwise it is a hypocritical performance; for this is
hypocrisy, when a man is not willing to let the duty go
altogether, nor yet is willing to perform it fervently,
and in a quick and zealous manner.

He that omits it altogether is a profane person, and
he that performs it zealously, and to purpose, is a holy
man; but a hypocrite goes between both. He would do
something at it, but he will not do it thoroughly. And,
therefore, if you find you have carelessly performed
this duty from day to day, that you have performed it in
a negligent, perfunctory manner, know that it is a hypocritical performance. Therefore, when we spend so
much time exhorting you to a constant course in this
duty, remember still that you must perform it in such a
manner that it may have heat and life in it, that it may
be acceptable to God. Do good to your own hearts to
bring them to a more holy frame of grace, and to a
better tempter, than it may be you found them in
when you went about the duty.

You may object now, "Aye, but it will cost us much

time to do this."

Indeed, one common cause among the rest, that keeps us from the thorough performance of this duty is this: Remember that the time spent in calling upon God does not hinder you, and though it takes so much from the heap yet indeed it increases the heap. It is said of tithes and offerings, "Bring them in," and do not think that, because you lessen the heap, that you are poorer men. No, says the Lord, it will increase your store. "I will open the windows of heaven," and you shall have so much the more for it. So it is true in this case.

In other things you see it well enough. You know, the baiting of the horse does not hinder the journey, nor does the oiling of the wheel. The sharpening of the scythe is no hinder to the work, even though there is a stop in the work to do it. As our common saying is, "A whet is no let," and the doing of this is no impediment.

Second, put the case as it were, yet is it not the greater business? What is it that you get by all your labors and travails? If it is riches, it does not come into any comparison with grace and holiness, with those riches wherewith prayer makes you rich. But, say it is somewhat more noble than that, as learning and knowledge; yet, what is that to the renewing of God's image in us? Would it not be better to spend time to get grace to make us rich towards God, to make us to get strength in the inward man, to pass through all varieties of afflictions, in getting that which is the chief excellency of all others, for is not that the best excellency?

When Adam was in paradise, having God's image,

you know, excelled all other excellencies in the world, and it still does. And the more you pray, the more you get of this image; for a man of much prayer is always a man of much grace. It greatly increases those spiritual gifts, which are better than all the outward things you can get by your employment and diligence in them. Therefore, though it does cost you much time, yet know (as Christ said to Mary), he who prays much, though he is looser in other things, yet he has "chosen the better part."

Last of all, consider this: When you come to offer sacrifice to God, would you offer that which costs you nothing? If your continuing in prayer and spending much time in it should cost you some disadvantage in your affairs, and you should lose that which another gains so that you do not gain as much knowledge as another, so that you do not do as well in your business, so that you do not set things in order as you might have done, yet know this: It is great wisdom to make our service to God costly to us. You know David's choice, "Shall I offer to the Lord that which costs me nothing?" And, therefore, he needed to give the worth to Auranus the Jebusite for that which he bought; and, therefore, since it is to a good Master who sees what you do, who knows what it costs, and what loss you are at and, with all that, is willing and able to recompence it, why should you shorten this business, and post it over, because of other occasions and other business that you have to do?

OBJECTION. "O but," a man will say, "I am willing to do it, but I am unfit for it, and it may be that the longer I strive, the more unfit I grow."

ANSWER. To this I answer, first in general, if you do it as well as you can, though you do not do it as well as you would, in this case God accepts the will for the deed. When a man puts his strength to it, when there is no indiligence in him, when there is no laziness (for in that case He will not accept the will for the deed), when a man does his utmost, like those who would have given more and could not, their will was accepted for the deed, in 1 Corinthians 8:12. I say, when you do what you can, when you spare no labor to get your heart upon the wing, to raise and quicken it and to enlarge it in this duty, there God accepts it.

But again, I add further, there is an unskilfulness in going about this duty. Many times, when we are not fit, we think to make ourselves more fit by spending time in thoughts and meditations before, which I do not deny but that they may be profitable, but yet this I will propound to you. The best way to fit our selves to this duty when we find an indisposition to it is not to stay until we have prepared ourselves by meditation but to fall immediately upon the duty because though preparation is required for the performance of every spiritual duty, yet the remote preparation is that which is intended and meant when we say we must prepare. For, if we speak of that which is immediate, the very doing of the duty is the first preparation to it.

For example, if a man were to run a race, if he were to do any bodily exercise, there must be strength of body. He must be well fed that he may have ability, but the use of the very exercise itself, the very particular act that is of the same kind as the exercise, is the best to fit him for it. So it is in this duty of prayer. It is true that to be strong in the inward man, to have much knowl-

edge, to have much grace, makes a man able and fit for
the duty; but, if you speak of the immediate preparation for it, I say, the best way to prepare us is the very
duty itself. As all actions of the same kind increase the
habits, so prayer makes us fit for prayers. And this is a
rule: "The way to godliness is in the compass of godliness itself", that is, the way to grow in any grace is the
exercise of that grace.

It is a point that Luther pressed out of is own experience, and this is the reason he uses. In this case, he
said, when a man goes about to fit himself by working
on his own thoughts, he goes about to overcome himself by his own strength and to contend with Satan
alone. But when a man feels an indisposition, and goes
to God by prayer, and rests on God to fit him, he takes
God's strength to oppose the indisposition and deadness of his flesh and the temptations of Satan that
hinder and resist him.

Therefore, you shall find this to be the best way to
fit yourselves for prayer, namely, to perform the duty.
If you seek to expedite and devolve yourselves out of
your unfitness by the working of your own thoughts,
commonly you involve yourselves farther into those
labyrinths and are caught more and more. But this I
speak, by the way, concerning matters of unfitness. The
main objection is that which I gave you before, that if a
man does what he can, and does it faithfully and in
sincerity, that indisposition shall not hinder him; but
still remember, it must be done. It is not an excuse to
use at any time, nor ought to be, that we should omit
the duty wholly under pretence of an unfitness.

OBJECTION. A man is ready to say again, "But I

find many difficulties; what shall I do to remove them?"

ANSWER. The best way hereunto is the very naming of the difficulties to you, that you may know them and make account of them. Therefore, you must consider in general that, indeed, it is not an easy thing to call upon God constantly. Our misprision of the duty, our reckoning of it, that it is a more facile and easy thing than it is, makes us more to slight it, and causes us not to go about it with that intention which otherwise we would, but consider a little what it is. The duty is very spiritual and our hearts are carnal, and it is no easy thing to bring spiritual duties and carnal hearts together.

Besides, our natures are very backward to come into the Lord's presence, partly by reason of His great glory, by reason of His majesty, who dwells in light inaccessible, and our weak eyes are apt to be dazzled with it and partly out of an accustomedness. We are not used to it and, therefore, we are as ready to fly from Him as beasts who are wild and are not tamed to our hands are ready to fly from us, so backward is our nature to come into His presence.

Again, the variety of occasions hinders us—everything keeps us back. If a man's heart is cheerful, it is apt to delight in other things. If a man's heart is sad, on the other hand, if it is a slight sadness, men are ready to drive it away with company and sports, with doing other things. And if the sadness is great, we are swallowed up with an anguish of spirit, and then anything is easier than to pray, as you may see by the case of Judas. It was easier for him to dispatch himself than to go and call upon God. So it is with high men when they have excessive grief, when their anguish of heart is

exceeding great. Therefore, whether a man has a
cheerful disposition or a sad disposition, whether the
sadness is great or small, still you shall find a difficulty.
If we are idle and have nothing too, our hearts will be
possessed with vain thoughts, and, if we are full of
business, that distracts us also and indisposes us on the
other hand. So still there are impediments.

Impediments to Prayer

1. Worldly cares and worldly-mindedness. There is
one great and very common impediment among the
rest: worldly cares and worldly-mindedness. Worldly
cares hinder spiritual prayer, spiritual conference, and
the holy performance of nearly every duty. Therefore,
if you find a difficulty in it, look narrowly to see if that
is not the cause.

2. Ignorance of the nature of God. Another great
cause of this difficulty in prayer, of such backwardness
to it, of such indisposition to it, is because we do not
well consider the nature of God. We lack faith in His
power and in His providence. We do not consider that
He has that disposing hand which He has in everything
that belongs to us in health, in sickness, in poverty, in
riches, in good success, and ill success. For, if we saw
the providence of God and acknowledged it more, we
should be ready to call upon Him. But the lack of faith
in His providence, that the Lord is not seen in His
greatness and mighty power, causes men to be backward to seek Him but very forward to seek the creature.

When we have anything to do of any consequence,
we are ready to post from this man to that man and

from this means to that means but very backward and
negligent to go to God in prayer to have the thing
brought to pass that we desire. And this arises from
lack of faith and from ignorance of God, from not
considering Him.

Besides, Satan hinders us exceedingly in this duty,
for he knows of what importance it is, and of what consequence. And therefore he does as the Aramites did:
He "fights not against small nor great, but against the
King," 1 Kings 22:31. He knows that it is this duty
which quickens every grace. It is the greatest enemy he
has, and if he can keep us from prayer he has the
upper hand. He has wrested the weapon out of our
hands. He has disarmed us, as it were, and then he may
do what he will with us.

3. The sins we commit. The sins we commit, especially gross sins, are a great hindrance to this duty.
They keep us from the spiritual and cheerful
performance of it, for sin wounds the conscience. It
disjoins and dismembers the soul, and a disjointed
member, you know, is unfit to do any business. Yea,
when the sin is healed and forgiven, there is yet a
soreness left in the heart, though some assurance of
pardon should follow upon the commission of a great
sin. So that is another impediment. I must not stand to
reckon up many, we shall find enough by continual
experience.

But if the impediments are so many, and the difficulties that keep us from a constant course in prayer,
and from the performance of it to purpose, are so
great, then we must put on a resolution to break
through all and lay it as an inviolable law upon ourselves that we will not alter. Let us think to ourselves

that the thing is difficult and will cost all the care and all the intention that may be. Yes, when you have overcome the difficulties at one time, it may be, the next day you shall meet with new conflicts, new distempers, new affections, new strength of lust, and a new disposition of mind will be on them. And, therefore, he who will be constant in this duty must put on a strong resolution.

It was the saying of a holy man, one of the holiest men that these recent times had, that he never went to pray to God but he found so many impediments that, unless he bound himself by an unalterable resolution that he resolved not to break upon any occasion, he could never have kept a constant course in it—or, if he had, he should never had kept himself from a formal, customary performance of it. But I will add no more to press this upon you. Enough has been said. I beseech you to consider it.

OBJECTIONS REMOVED

Now that which I promised in the morning to do, that which exceedingly strengthens us to the performance of this duty of calling upon God, of praying continually (which we are here commanded to do), is to remove certain objections which are in the minds of men, that secretly weaken the estimation of this truth, and insensibly take them off when we do not mark them. For, beloved, when we are so negligent in it, surely there is something that is the cause of it. If we could find the cause and remove it, we could not spend an hour better.

The objections that are commonly in the hearts of men are many. I will name only these four to you briefly.

OBJECTION 1. First, a man is ready to say, "What need do I have to spend so much time, and be so large in the expression of my wants to God when He already knows them? I cannot make them better known to Him. He knows them well enough already, and, therefore, what need is there of it?"

ANSWER 1. To this I answer (in a word, because it is an objection that does not have much weight in it), it is true, the Lord knows your wants, but He will have *you* to know them. Otherwise, you will not seek Him. You will not set a price upon the things that He bestows on you. You will not be thankful to Him when He has granted them, and, therefore, you shall find our Savior Christ uses this very argument as a means to quicken us to prayer, saying, "Your heavenly Father knows what you have need of." What, then? Shall we not therefore pray? Yes, says He, therefore pray all the more earnestly and importunately to Him. Since He knows your wants, He will be more ready to hear your requests.

OBJECTION 2. Aye, but it is said again, "He does not only know them, but He also means and purposes to bestow them. For He has made a promise to us, and His promise is firm and sure. God is just and must keep His promise. So when He has fully purposed it, what need is there for so much praying to bring it to pass?"

ANSWER 2. I answer, the promises of God are to be understood with this secret condition annexed, "I will do such and such a thing for you if you pray," though it is not expressed. We see that when God promised a thing in particular, yet they still prayed and prayed earnestly. When He promised Elijah that it should rain, yet we see that he prayed and contended much in his prayer. When He made a promise to David that He would make him a house, yet you know David went to the house of the Lord and sat before Him, and made earnest prayer, as is recorded in 2 Samuel. So Daniel had particular promise, and yet he prayed, and prayed long. The example of our Savior Christ is without exception, who had all the promises sure to Him, yet He prayed, yes, He spent whole nights in prayer. And, therefore, you must so understand that, though you have a promise made, though the thing is never so sure to you; yet it is to be understood with that if you call upon God.

And why the Lord would have you do it I showed you in many reasons in the morning. We will add this to it. What, if the Lord will have you call upon Him, though He purposes to do the thing for this end: that you may worship Him? For what is it to worship the Lord? You shall find this normally in the Old Testament, "The people bowed themselves and worshipped", or, "they fell upon their faces and worshipped." The meaning is this: to worship God is nothing else but to acknowledge the worthiness that is in Him. For example, when you worship a man, you use so much outward demeanor and observance to him as may acknowedge the worth in him above another man. So you use an outward gesture, that is the outward worshipping of God. The inward worship is inwardly to acknowledge His attributes.

Now, you shall see that prayer gives an acknowledgment of His attributes more than anything; for He who prays to God, in so doing, acknowledges His omnipresence and His omniscience. They acknowledge that He hears that which the idols of the Gentiles could not do, and that He knows the secrets of men's hearts that neither men nor angels can do.

Again, it acknowledges His almighty power, that He is able to do anything. For that is presupposed when we come and seek Him.

Again, it acknowledges His mercy and His goodness, that He is not only able, but exceedingly willing to help.

Again, it acknowledges His truth, that as He has promised so He will perform it. When I go and seek Him, all the attributes of God are acknowledged in prayer. Therefore, therein you worship Him in a special manner when you go and seek Him, and pray to Him. In doing so, you acknowledge Him. Yea, you acknowledge Him to be a Lord and a Father. It is like when we see a child run to a man and ask him for a blessing. When we see him ask him for food and raiment, we say, "Surely such a man is his father." So this very praying to God is a worshipping of Him, because it acknowledges His attributes, and His relation to us and ours to Him.

OBJECTION 3. But it will be objected, "Aye, but alas, what can the endeavors or the prayers of a weak man do? Can they change the purpose of almighty God? If He does not intend to do this thing for me, shall I hope to alter Him?"

ANSWER 3. In answer to this, I say, briefly, that when you call upon God, He is not changed by your prayers, but the change is wrought in you, as we have said to you before. When a physician is sought by a patient, the patient desires earnestly to receive such a cordial, such restorative medicine, that is pleasing to him. The physician denies him for a long time, and yet, in the end, he yields to him. Why? Not because there was any change in the physician but because there is a change in the patient. He is fitted for this now, whereas he was not before. So then the physician yields now whereas, before, he refused; and yet the change is in the patient, not the physician.

Therefore, beloved, when you go about to strive with God in prayer, when you contend and wrestle with Him (for so we ought to do), when you use many reasons to persuade Him, you do not alter Him but yourselves. For those arguments you use are not so much to persuade Him to help you as to persuade your hearts to more faith, to more love, to more obedience, to more humility and thankfulness. And that, indeed, is the reason why prayer prevails with God—not that the very sending up is that which prevails with Him, but because a faithful, spiritual prayer puts the heart in a better disposition so that a man is now made more ready to receive a blessing at God's hand than he was before.

So, when you think you draw God to you with your arguments, in truth you draw yourselves nearer to Him. It is like this: when a man in a ship plucks a rock, it seems as if he plucked the rock nearer to the ship, when the ship is really plucked nearer to the rock. So, I say, we draw ourselves nearer to the Lord. And when we draw nearer to the Lord in prayer, and there is a spiritual disposition wrought in our hearts by the exercise of this duty, then indeed the Lord draws near to us, to send us help and to grant our requests that we put up to Him. Therefore, He does this so that we will mark by the way that any prayer, as it has a higher pitch of holiness in affection, and as it has stronger arguments in it, so it is a better prayer. This is not because this prayer shall prevail with God more, or that the excellency of this prayer should move Him, but because this pitch of holy affection and strength of argument works upon your hearts. For the strength of arguments moves your understanding, and the holiness of affection puts your will in a frame and so disposes your hearts and fits you, like the patient is fitted when the physician is willing to give the thing he desires.

OBJECTION 4. But the last objection, which indeed is more than all the rest, is this: A man is ready to say, "We see there are many men who do not call upon God, and yet enjoy many mercies. It may be that a man can say with himself, when he did not use to pray, that he had health, sleep, and protection."

Again, on the other hand, he has prayed for such and such things, and yet they have not been granted.

So this objection has two parts: that a man has obtained blessings without prayer and, again, he has prayed and yet has not obtained the blessings he sought for at the Lord's hands.

ANSWER 4. First, there are many young men, and old men too, who have health, wealth, peace, liberty, and an abundance of all things. Yet, either they do not seek God, or, if they do, they do not do so in a holy and spiritual manner. Therefore, this objection needs to be answered, and I will do so briefly.

Though they have these blessings, yet they have them uncertainly. They have no promise of them, they cannot build upon them, whereas they are sure mercies to the righteous man. He can build upon these blessings, for he has a father to go to whose love he knows, and he has sure promises to build on. The other, though he has them, yet he is in a slippery place when he enjoys them. It is an accidental thing. He has them from the hand of an enemy, and he does not know how long he shall enjoy them.

But I answer again (which is the chief answer to this objection) that there is a great deal of difference between having blessings through the providence of God and having them from the mercy of God, and by virtue of His promise and out of His love to us in Christ Jesus. A natural man may have many blessings of God. God made Jeroboam a king and gave him a kingdom. When men come unjustly to blessings, as Jereboam did to the kingdom, yet God did it—that is, it was by His providence, and yet the natural man does not have these blessings in mercy. For if you have these blessings—health, sleep, and success in your daily enterprises—and yet your heart tells you within that you have not sought them at the Lord's hands as you ought, I say to such a man that it would be better for him that he should lack them, for certainly, when he has them in this manner, he has them without a blessing. Yes, he has them with a curse, and so would be better off without them.

It would have been better for Ahab to have been without his vineyard, and it would have been better for Gebezie to have gone without his reward that he had

of Naaman the Assyrian (for you know he had the lep-
rosy with it). It would have been better for the children
of Israel to have gone without their quails, for you
know the curse that followed: Death went along with
them. So when a man shall have peace, prosperity, and
the abundance of all things, without seeking them at
the Lord's hand from day to day, I say, he would be
better to have lacked them, for death goes together
with them.

It is said plainly that "ease stayeth the foolish." This
very prosperity, this thriving while neglecting prayer
and other holy duties, carries death along with it as the
obtaining of a vineyard brought death to Ahab. Getting the kingdom was the destruction of Jeroboam.
And, therefore, men have little cause to comfort themselves with the fact that they may enjoy many blessings
and never pray for them.

But, to answer this point more fully, I say that many
blessings are bestowed upon men, not for their own
sakes but for the church's sake. A man may have
strength of body, he may have great gifts of mind, he
may have great success in using those gifts, he may
bring great enterprises to pass, so that you may truly
say the hand of God is with him. All this may be done
not for his sake but for the sake of the church and the
glory of God in some other way, so that he might do
some service. You see that it is plainly said of Cyrus,
Isaiah 45:4, where the Lord says, "For Jacob My
servant's sake, and for Israel, Mine elect sake, I have
called thee by name, and have given thee this great
power, and all this great success, although thou thyself
have not known Me." Mark it, Cyrus was a most
prosperous man. God's hand was mighty upon him.

Yet all this was not for his own sake but for the church's sake. So you may think it is when men prosper. Many times, it is not for their own sakes but to fulfill some other end of God's providence, and, therefore, mark this and keep it as a rule: If you prosper in your enterprises, if you enjoy wealth, peace, and the abundance of all things, and know that you do not see God from day to day, that you do not keep your heart right and straight and perfect before Him, you do not call upon Him in a holy and spiritual manner, certainly it is for one of those causes. You have it without a blessing and with a curse. You have it for other ends and not for good to yourself. Therefore, you have it very uncertainly. It may be taken from you, you do not know how soon.

Yes, and this you can be sure of, it shall be taken from you then when, of all other times, it will be most unfit for you. As a thief comes at a time when men least look for him, so destruction comes suddenly upon these men. God cuts them as a man, when he would have trees to die, lops them in that season that of all others is the most unfit, when the sap is in the tree, when the lopping will cause them to wither. So the Lord will strike them in such a season.

It is quite contrary with the saints. He cuts them in due season; He lops them in due time that they may grow the better for it. It is good for them.

But now, for the other part of the objection, it may be that many among you are now ready to say, "I have prayed for such and such things, and I have been earnest, and yet the Lord has denied me."

My beloved, if we can satisfy this objection, we shall then take this impediment away that we propound in this objection that has these two parts. Therefore to this I answer:

If you have not been heard in your prayers, consider if you have not prayed amiss. It is a common fault among us, when we have spent much time in prayer—and, it may be, we have spent time in fasting and praying—and the thing is not granted, we immediately lay it upon the Lord that He has not heard when, many times, the cause is our not praying as we ought. It may be that you have been very earnest and, therefore, you hope you have done very well.

I tell you, you may be very earnest and importunate with the Lord when it may be no more than a natural desire, for example, when a man needs to be directed in a difficult case that greatly concerns him, when he needs to be extricated and taken out of such a difficulty and strait wherein he is involved, when he needs success in such an enterprise or anything of that nature. I say, a man may be earnest with the Lord in such a case, and yet his prayer may be amiss. It may not be a spiritual prayer, it may not be an expression of holy desires to the Lord, for they only prevail with Him. Not that the natural are excluded (that is not my meaning), for they may add winds to the sails, though holiness may guide the rudder, keep the course, and make the steerage. Yet natural desires may make us more importunate, and may add much to it. Therefore, I say, consider your prayer.

Consider again, when you have sought God earnestly, whether it is not to bestow it upon your lusts, as the Apostle says in James 4:3. When you have a business to be performed it may be you are earnest with God. But do you not have an eye to your own glory, to

your own praise and credit in it? When you were
earnest for health, was it not that you might live more
deliciously? When you desire wealth and success in
your enterprises that tend to mend your state, is it not
out of some ambition? You know that desire is condemned, "if any man will be rich." Is it not a desire of
greatness? Would you not be somebody in your place,
and set up your house and family? Such things God bestows upon men, but to have our desires pitched upon
them and to pray in that sense for them, is amiss. And
my rule for it is in 1 Timothy 6:9, "If any man will be
rich." That is, when a man desires excessively, when he
desires more than food and raiment convenient for
him, now the natural affection is degenerate into a
lust. For when any affection exceeds, it ceases to be an
affection and begins to be a lust. Therefore, where it is
said, "if any man will be rich," it is later said that it is a
lust.

QUESTION. "But," you will say, "how shall a man
know when he prays for God to bestow that which he
prays for upon his lusts?"
ANSWER. I answer, if a man consults with his own
heart and deals impartially with himself, he may know
what his ends are. But, if you cannot find out that way,
you may know it by the effect, you may know it by the
bills you bring in. What is the expense of the things
God has bestowed on you when He has put a price into
your hands? Consider how you bestow it.
If a steward has a great sum of money which his
master has entrusted to him, and his bills are that he
has bestowed so much in fine apparel, so much in
riotous living and the like, but there has been so much

bestowed for his master's advantage, it is an argument
he has spent it poorly. So, when we see that there has
been so much health spent, so much time and strength
spent, in following our own plots and our own worldly
business without respect to God, not serving God and
men in our calling as we should do, and that there has
been little time bestowed in prayer, reading, making
our hearts perfect with God, and taking pains in them
from day to day; if we look upon this bill of expense
and consider how we have bestowed our time, our
health, our strength, and our wits from day to day, and
our speech (for that is one price that we have in our
hands by which we may do good, it is as a bucket by
which we may draw from others, and likewise it is a
spring and found with which we may feed others with
the waters of life), consider how we have laid out all
these things and, by that, we may know how we are disposed to use the blessings we seek for at God's hands,
whether we seek these blessings to bestow them upon
our lusts, or to spend those gifts to our Master's
advantage. And, if we find we do it for our own lusts, in
this case I say to you, go and amend your prayers, and
God will amend your spending.

We must do in this case like an angler does when
he has thrown the bait into the river. If it stays long
and catches nothing, he takes up the bait and amends
it. And, when he sees it is well, he then continues and
waits. So we must do in this case. If you pray, and pray
long, and have not obtained the thing you pray for,
look diligently to your prayers. See whether they are
right or not. If they are not, amend your prayers, and
God will amend His readiness to hear you. If you find
that they are sincere and hearty, mingled with holy de-

sires and not with carnal, corrupt affections, then let
the bait lie still. That is, continue to pray and to wait
and the Lord will come in due time.

But this is not all. When you are not heard,
consider that you may have prayed amiss. It is a
common fault among us, when we do not succeed in
anything, to attribute our failure to many other things,
but not to our "remissness" and carelessness in seeking
God. If a man lacks sleep, and if he finds sickness,
weakness, and distemper of body, he thinks that he has
eaten amiss. He does not consider whether or not he
has prayed amiss, however. If a man has miscarried in
his business, he begins to think whether or not he has
been improvident, whether he has not dealt foolishly,
whether he has not omitted such and such means as he
might have used. He never thinks whether he has
prayed amiss; and that, indeed, is the cause of our mis-
carrying, and not commonly the thing which we attribute it unto. Though God is not the immediate
cause, you know He is the great cause. There is no ill
that He has not done, and that which moves Him is always grace and sin. That which moves Him to do good
is our obedience to Him. That which moves Him on
the contrary is neglect on our part.

But, to answer further, suppose your prayers are
right. Still you must consider this: When you think you
are not heard, you are oftentimes deceived. Therefore,
you must rectify that misconception. For example,
sometimes, when we would have the thing in one fash-
ion, God bestows the same thing upon us in another—
and, therefore, you may be deceived in that.

It may be that a man prays earnestly that he may
have a strong body with which to do God service. But it

may be that sickness of body makes him do Him better service because it keeps him in more awe, it weans him from the world, and makes him more heavenly-minded.

You know the case of Paul. He would fain have had that lust taken away that is spoken of in 2 Corinthians 12:9. And why? Surely the thing he would have had was to have his heart in a holy and right frame of grace. Now, though Paul did not have it the way that he looked for, yet he had it another way. The Lord increased in him the grace of humility. He saw his own weakness and the power of Christ all the more. And when this was revealed unto him, he was content.

It is all one whether a man is preserved from the blow of an enemy or has a helmet given to him to keep it off. It may be a man prays for money and for estate. If God provides meat and drink and clothes immediately, instead of this, is it not all the same?

It may be that another would have a great deal of convenience for his dwelling house and many other things. If God gives him a body able to endure that which is more coarse, it is the same as if he were provided for more delicately. It is all the same whether a physician quenches the thirst of his patient by giving him beer and drink that is comfortable unto him or by giving him berries or something else that will do the thing as well.

It is all the same whether the Lord keeps an enemy from doing us hurt, or if He gives us a strong helmet, a buckler, to keep the injury from wounding us. I might give you more instances. Though the Lord does not give you the thing in the very manner that you would have it, yet He will do it in another manner.

Second, as we are deceived in the manner, so we are deceived in the means, oftentimes, in seeking God. When a man prays, he pitches upon such a particular means, and thinks verily that this is the way or there is none. It may be the Lord will find another way that you never dreamed of. Paul prayed to have a prosperous journey to Rome. He thought little that, when he was bound at Jerusalem, and posted up and down from one prison to another, God was now sending him to Rome. Yet He sent him, and sent him very safe with a great company attending him. He sent Him, it may be, in a better manner than he would have gone himself, and yet it was by such a means as he could never dream of.

Also, you know, Naaman the Assyrian pitched upon a particular means. He thought the prophet surely would have come forth and laid his hands upon him, but to go and wash in the Jordan? He thought that his labor was all lost, and the request he made to the prophet was to no purpose, for it was a thing that he never thought of. It was a weak and poor means that he made no account of, yet it was the means that God intended.

So, I say, we deceive ourselves. We pitch upon such a particular way and when these fail us, and when we have prayed that these means might be used and God does not use them, we immediately think we are deceived. Joseph thought verily that Pharaoh's steward should have been the means to bring the promise to pass, and after that Pharaoh's butler was used as a means. Joseph desired the butler to remember him, and yet all this was not the means but another which he never thought of: Pharaoh's dream.

The case of Mordecai was the same. Deliverance
came in a strange way, a way that Mordecai never imag-
ined. Abraham thought that Ishmael was the son of the
promise, but God told him he was deceived. Isaac was
the son in whom He would make good the promise. So
the Israelites thought that Moses should have delivered
them, that it should have been immediately true. But
we see that God went another way to work. He sent
Moses away into a far country, and the bondage was
exceedingly increased upon them. So they thought
they were further off now than ever they were before.
But in truth they were nearer, for the increase of the
bondage increased Pharaoh's sin and made him ripe
for destruction.

Again, it increased the people's humility. It made
them pray harder and cry more fervently to God for
deliverance, and so it made them more fit for it. And,
at last, Moses was more fitted to be a deliverer after he
was trained so long and was so much more humbled.
So that, when God seems to go a completely contrary
way, yet it is the next way to bring it to pass.

Beloved, it is a common thing with us. We pitch
upon a certain particular means. We think such a man
must do it, or such a course must do it, when the Lord
intends nothing less. And the reason often is because,
if we should have deliverance many times by such
means, by such men, and by such ways, we would attribute too much to the means. Therefore, we see that,
when Gideon had a great army, the Lord would not do
it. It was too great for Him, and, therefore, we see to
what a small number He brought it.

Oftentimes men think, "Oh, if I had such a man's
help, or if I had such a means, it would do the thing. It

would bring the enterprise to pass."

When we make too much account of it, the Lord, it may be, casts that away which seemed most probable and (even as He does most of His works, as He builds His own kingdom by the most foolish and improbable means of all others) often He does our business by such means that we least dream of. Therefore, do not be discouraged.

Suppose we pray that such a great prince should raise the churches, that such a war, such an enterprise and project may do it. Put the case to the Lord. If He does not do it that way, are we then immediately undone? And is there no help because such a king did not succeed, because such a general did not have success, according to our expectations? It may be that this is not the way the Lord will help. He may help the church in another manner that we do not even dream of. And so, for a man's self, he has business to be done, or he is in distress and would have deliverance, and he thinks, "It must be done this way or not at all." And therefore, he is earnest to have it done. Now it is good, in this case, to leave it to the Lord, to make our requests known to Him and, when we have done that, to be no further careful, but leave it to the Lord to do it His own way. He is skillfull.

If you take a skillfull workman, and say no more to him but this, "Sir, I pray you, do me such a thing." If it was the bringing of water, or the setting up of a building, it may be that he will go away to work. You do not know what he is doing, but you will trust him. Why, then, will you not trust God, and allow Him to go His own way? And, when you are crossed in that thing, wherein, it may be, of all others you would not be

crossed, it may be that it is the best way of all others to
bring the thing to pass that you desire.

Again, as we are deceived in the manner and the
means, so likewise we mistake the time. It may be the
Lord is willing to do the thing, but not in that time that
you would have Him do it. When a man prays to be delivered from such a trouble, and such a distress, and
such an affliction, he thinks the time is very long and
says, "I have not been heard, because I have not been
delivered immediately!" We would have all the painful
plaster immediately taken off, but the Lord is wiser
than we (as the physician knows what is good for the
patient better than the patient does). Though He does
not do it immediately, He will do it.

Therefore, do not say that you are not heard. You
must take heed of taking delays for denials. The Lord
will defer to do the thing, yet He will do it in the best
season. For this is a general rule: God's time is the best
time.

When you come to pray for a thing, you would have
it done immediately, and you think it is the best time.
All the controversy between God and you is over which
is the fittest time to have it done. You think it is immediately. God, it may be, will do it a year from now.
Surely He is the best one to choose, and we shall find it
so. Therefore, be content to wait for His leisure. He
has many ends in deferring it. One may be to try your
faith (as He did the faith of the Canaanite) and, therefore, He will not hear. It may be to increase your holiness, to put your heart into a better temper and, therefore, He defers longer.

He meant to do that for Jacob which He did, yet He
allowed Jacob to wrestle all night; but He did not do it

until the instant the morning appeared. So it was with
Daniel. The answer went forth when he began to pray,
yet he would have him instant and continue in prayers.
So, I say, the Lord has many ends why He defers; let us
be content to take His own time.

Last of all, consider this: When you seek the Lord
to have anything done, it is possible that it may cross
some other passage of His providence. In this case, you
should be content to be denied.

QUESTION. "But," you will say, "why may not both
be accomodated?"

ANSWER. I answer, so they shall, though you do
not see how. It is not with God as it is with man. If a
man does a good turn to one, if two become petitioners, he needs to do an ill turn to another, but God
composes all for the best. For example, David greatly
desired to build a temple; the Lord had another end.
He had resolved in His providence to make Solomon
the builder of it. Indeed, this was much better for
David, for what more would David have gotten if he
had done it? He tells him that, for the purpose of
building him a house, He would build him a house. So
David had his end to the full, though it was Solomon
who built the temple. So it was for Israel. The Lord
kept the Canaanites among them, but it was for their
profit.

There are some passages of God's providence that,
if we knew, we would yield to, so that it would be better
that it should be so than otherwise. Therefore, it is
better in some cases that we should be denied.

Sermon Three

---

1 Thessalonians 5:17
"Pray continually."

Now we proceed to that which remains, something we might and for the answering of this, for the time of God's granting our petitions, and for the measure, we touched it the last day a little.

For the time, we are deceived in that we think when God defers, He denies. Many times God defers for special reasons, and yet He grants the request in the fittest time for us, as the physician knows the fittest time to give the patient medicine of one kind or another, and in this we must yield to God. As he does all His works in the fittest time, so He grants our petitions in the fittest time. There is an appointed time for any deliverance to be granted, for any blessing, for any comfort that we need and have at His hands. Now, if we were judges, we would have things done for us in the most convenient time. We would have the hurting plaster pulled off before the wound was healed, whereas it is best for us to have kept it on.

Beloved, you shall find that God divides between Satan and us in this case, as we see in Revelation 2:10, "Satan shall cast some of you into prison, and you shall be there for ten days." It was not as long as Satan would have had it. It may be that he would have had it for ten days and ten days more. Nor again, it was not as short as they would have had it, but God sets down the time between them both. And, therefore, we must rest upon Him and think that, many times, there is a great reason why we should be deferred when we ask things at His hands. You shall find He defers for one of these causes, for the most part:

Sometimes, for the trial of our faith. We see that He deferred to grant to the woman of Canaan. Although He meant to grant her request, yet He deferred long that He might put her to the trial. And, you see, she was no loser by it, but when she held out in her prayers, she had her request granted to the full.

Sometimes He defers to grant it that we may be more humbled. As you know, Paul prayed earnestly, but God told him that He would defer him because he needed more humility. In the same way, He deferred to grant the request that the men of Benjamin put up to Him, when the cause was just and God intended to help them, yet they fell before their enemies twice. Though they fasted and prayed, His end was, as we see in the text, that they might be more humbled, that their hearts might be more broken, that they might be more fitted to receive it.

Again, sometimes God defers that we might be more able to use those blessings that He means to bestow upon us. So He deferred to raise Joseph to preferment. So He deferred to bring David to the kingdom, that those afflictions that they endured might the better fit them to enjoy so great prosperity as He had provided for them afterwards.

And, last, He defers that He might set a higher price upon His blessings, that He might enhance the price of them. As the fisherman draws away the bait that the fish might follow it all the more, so God withholds blessings so that we might have a greater edge set upon our desires, that we might pray harder for them, that we might prize them more when we have obtained them.

Now, as He does this for the time and, as we are often deceived in the time— taking delays for denials— so likewise we are often deceived in the measure. Many times God grants the things that we would have, but because we do not have as large a measure as we expected, therefore we think we do not have it at all. We think the Lord has denied our prayers, when indeed He has not. A lesser measure, many times, may serve as well as a greater. As God said to Paul, "My grace is sufficient for thee." Though the temptation abides upon us, if there is sufficient grace to keep us in a continual conflict and war against it, if there is sufficient grace to obtain pardon, to uphold and to comfort us in it, it is sufficient. It may bring us to heaven. We have a deliverance from it even when we do not seem to be delivered. Though we do not have as full a victory as we would like to have, yet that grace may be sufficient.

You shall see this almost in all the things we have occasion to request at God's hands, that a lesser measure may serve as well as a greater. Take it first in outward things.

A little may serve as well as great revenues, as in Psalm 38:16, "A little that the righteous hath is as much as great revenues to the wicked." This is because a little, when God fills it with His blessings, shall serve the turn as well. But if a man has great revenues, and God blows upon them and leaves an emptiness in them; if a man has great revenues, if he has great outward comforts, yet, if there is an emptiness, if there is a vanity in them, if they are as the husk without the grain, as the shell without the kernel, as they often are (though there is a great bulk, and they seem very fit to comfort us), yet they will do us little good; whereas a little, on the other hand, will do much good.

In this case, it is as it was with manna. Those who had little still had enough, and those who gathered too much had never a whit more for their use and comfort. You know, the little that Daniel had nourished and strengthened him as much as the great portion of the king's meat that others had. And, therefore, a little, in this kind, may serve as well as much.

And so, likewise, a little grace may be so used and improved that it may enable you to do much. It may preserve you from sinning against God as well as a great measure. For the confirmation of this, look to Revelation 3:8, which is a notable place for this purpose. It is said there, to the church of Philadelphia, "thou hast a little strength." They had but a little strength, and yet you see there what that little strength did, "thou hast but a little strength, and yet thou hast kept My word, and hast not denied My name."

There were but two things for them to do: to keep His word and to be kept from running out to the denial of His name. Now the little strength they had was sufficient for those ends, so that we see He finds no fault with that church. Other churches that had more strength, it may be, fell into greater sins, but this is a rule which is true. You will find it true in all observation, throughout the Scriptures, that sometimes those who have great grace may still fall into great sins, that they may be subject to some strong prevailing lust. David, you know, had great grace, and yet we see that he was subject to great sins along with it.

And again, a man may have but a little grace, and yet that little grace may be so ordered, and husbanded, and improved, that the little grace may keep him from sin more than the other. This must be warily understood. Not that great grace enables a man to do greater works than the other. It enables a man, in the ordinary sense, to resist greater temptations more than less grace. But (I say for our comfort) though a man has but a little strength, yet it is said there in the same place in Revelation 3, in that little strength, "I have set a door open to thee." It opened the door of heaven wide enough so that no man could shut it.

And, as we say for grace, so likewise for gifts. Smaller gifts, lower gifts, may serve the turn, many times, as well as greater gifts. You know, a little finger, a small hand, may serve to thread a needle as well as a greater. It may be that it will do better. In the church, there are varieties of operations and varieties of functions. Meaner gifts may serve for the discharge of some operations, of some services, for the church as well as greater ones. And, therefore, as there is a variety of functions, so there is a variety of members: some stronger, some weaker. And the weaker may serve, in some cases, as well as the stronger.

A little boat may do better in a small river than a great ship. So a man who has but mean gifts may serve mean capacities as well as greater and better. Therefore, do not think that things are denied when the thing is granted, but not in the measure that you would like.

And, last, to be faithful in a little gift will bring as great a reward as to be faithful in greater. "Thou hast been faithful in little" may make a man ruler over much, and may bring a great increase of the talents afterwards. Therefore, do not let a man be discouraged if he does not have as great a measure as others have.

So, likewise, if a man desires patience and strength to go through all varieties of conditions, through all the troubles he meets with, sometimes the Lord lays a great burden upon a man's shoulders and gives him great strength to bear it. Sometimes again He gives but a little strength, but then He proportions the burden to it. And is it not all the same, whether the burden is great and the strength answerable, or the burden is less and the strength little?

Sometimes He takes away calamity, sometimes He lays it upon a man and gives him as much strength as will bear it. And that is as good as if it were removed. Else what is the meaning of that phrase, "you shall have an hundredfold with persecution," but that you shall have so much joy and strength in persecution that it shall be the same as if you lacked the persecution altogether? So we see in Hebrews 5:7, when Christ prayed for deliverance in that great hour of trial, the text says, "He was heard in the things He feared." And yet, we see that the cup did not pass from Him because He was strengthened to bear it. And so it is this case. This shall serve for a full answer to that, so that we are not mistaken in judging our prayers not to be heard when they are heard.

And now, beloved, what remains but that we set ourselves to the duty, to do that which we are exhorted unto here—namely, to pray continually. That is, to pray very much, to keep at least a constant course in it. For, if we neglect it, we rob God of His mercies. We take them without His permission.

Again, we are guilty of the sin of unthankfulness, for we ought to give thanks in all things. Again, we neglect His worship, for you know prayer is a part of His worship, and the neglect of it from day to day, or at any time, when we omit it, is a neglect of that worship and service we owe to Him.

Again, we allow sin to lie unforgiven, which is very dangerous. We deprive ourselves of blessings and bring a curse upon ourselves, and we allow our hearts to grow hard and to be distempered. For from our neglect of prayer comes that deadness of spirit, that worldly-mindedness and unaptness to pray, to hear the Word, and to keep the Sabbath. What else is the reason for it why those who have been forward and zealous professors in former times have lost their light and are fallen from their places. I say, what is the reason for it when they are sometimes fervent in spirit serving the Lord? That fire was not kept alive with the fuel of prayer, and when they declined from that pitch, from that degree of faith, which they had obtained, you shall find it commonly to arise from remissness in this duty. Therefore, we say to such, repent and amend, and do your first works. That is, use your former diligence; renew that, and that will renew grace and strength again.

Therefore, take heed of being negligent and remiss in this duty. We have great cause to be encouraged in it, for there is not a faithful prayer that we make which shall be lost, but they come up into your remembrance. And, therefore, you must consider with yourselves not only who you do for the present, but what stock of prayers you have layed up.

You know, a man may have much in bills and

bonds, as well as in present money. So there is a certain stock of prayer, a certain treasure, layed up that shall not be forgotten. The husbandman looks not only upon the grain that he has in his garner, but he looks upon that which is sown, though it is out of his hands. Yes, he reckons that the better of the two. So those prayers that have been sowed, it may be, many years ago are such as will bring in a sure increase. Therefore, let us be exhorted to be constant in this duty, to be frequent therein, to continue in it, watching thereto with perseverance.

SOME CASES OF CONSCIENCE

Now that we have dispatched this, we will come to answer some of the many cases of conscience that fall out in the performance of this duty.

CASE 1. What shall a man judge of his prayers when they are accompanied with wandering thoughts? Does God wholly refuse such prayers? What is he to do in such a case when he is subject to wandering thoughts, to vanity of mind and distemper in the performance of that duty?

ANSWER 1. To this I answer that we must distinguish the cause from whence these wandering thoughts arise.

Sometimes they arise not so much from our own neglect as from weakness, from temptation. In such a case, God does not lay them to our charge. For example, one who aims at a mark and does his best to hit the mark, yet, if he has a hand or an arm that is palsied, or if someone jogs him while is about to shoot, the fault is not so much in him. It was not a lack of good will to do it, nor lack of diligence, but it is either his weakness or it is an impediment cast in by another.

So it is in this case. This wandering of mind proceeds from a natural infirmity and imbecility that hangs upon the nature of man, which is not so able to keep itself close to such a spiritual business. And your God considers this, for He is wise, and knows that we are but flesh. When a weak servant goes about a business, though he does not do it as well as a stronger man, yet a man is wise to consider that the servant is but weak. The Lord considers that natural weakness that we are subject unto, and He deals mercifully with us in such a case. For herein a man is as one who has a bow in his hand, but he has a palsied arm and, therefore, he cannot keep it steady, though he has a mind to do so.

But the other case is when he is jogged in his shooting by another. That is, when Satan interrupts him, when he is diligent to hinder him in such a duty. In this case, God does not charge it upon him, and does not cast us off nor reject our prayers because of that. But on the other hand, when this wandering of mind shall rise from mere negligence on our part, from profaneness, from lack of reverence, because we do not intend holy duties as we ought, we do not come to them with that conscionableness, with that carefulness as we should—in this case, it is a great sin. This moves the Lord to anger when we perform the duty in that manner, when we do not so much as set ourselves about it with our strength, but allow our minds to wander without any resistance.

Second, when we ourselves are the cause of it by

admitting loose thoughts, by allowing ourselves to be
worldly-minded, by allowing an indisposition to grow
upon us, and not laboring to resist it and cast it off
again. You know, when an instrument is out of tune, if
the lesson that is played upon it is unpleasant be it
never so good. And whose fault is that? So, when you
come to God and allow your heart to be distempered,
and do not look to keep it in order, that is your sin as
well as your profaneness and neglect in the very time
of the performance. By this, you may learn how to
judge wandering thoughts in the performance of this
duty; and, likewise, you may see how to prevent them.

The way to prevent them is to keep our hearts in
tune before, to have them ready, as "the wise man has
his heart at his right hand." That is, he has it ready
when he has it to use. When a man is to use his horse,
he does not allow him to run up and down in the pas-
ture wildly. So we should keep our hearts in frame so
that they may be ready to do us service in such a holy
duty when we have need of them.

Second, we must be diligent when we come to perform the duty that, though our minds wander, we may
be ready to recall them immediately, to set ourselves to
it with all diligence. So much for answering this first
case.

CASE 2. The second case is what a man is to do
when he finds a great disposition to prayer, such a
dullness and deadness in him that he does not know
how to go about the duty. And, he thinks, if he does
pray, it might as well not be done.

ANSWER 2. To this I answer, briefly, that in all such
cases a man is bound, notwithstanding, to perform it.

Let his heart be never so much out of temper, let there
be never so great a dullness and deadness of spirit
upon him, yet he is still bound to do it.

"But," you will say, "why, I am altogether unfit."

I answer that a man, by setting himself upon the
work, shall gather a fitness though he was unfit at first.
If you use members that are numb, they get life and
heat and come in the end to be nimble enough. So it is
with the heart, in this case, when it is numb. The very
using of it makes it fit for the duty.

You know that if wood that is green is blown on
long enough, at length it will be dry and take fire. So it
is with the heart. A man may be long about getting it
on the wing. Yet, with much ado, he may do it; and,
therefore, he ought to do this duty in such a case.
There is never more need of calling upon God than at
such a time, for then a man lies most exposed to temptation. Then if any sin comes, he is ready to be over-
taken with it. He is unfit for anything and, therefore, if
ever he has a need to call upon God, it is at that time.

"But," you will say, "it may be that God will not accept it."

I answer briefly, if a man's heart is so indisposed
that, when he has done all he can, he can still get no
life, he can get no heat in the performance of such a
duty, yet God may accept that prayer as well as that
which is most fervent. And that you may understand
rightly, you must take it with this distinction.

This dullness and deadness in prayer comes from
one of these two causes. One is when God withdraws
His own Spirit, that is, not when He withdraws His
Spirit altogether (for there may be a help when we do
not perceive it), but when He withdraws the liveliness

and quickness of His Spirit. In this case, if we do our
duty, if we do the best we can, the Lord accepts it.
Though He has not promised such enlargement of our
hearts, though He has not poured out His Spirit upon
us in the performance of the duty as at other times, He
gives a secret help that perhaps we do not feel, nor
perhaps is as great as at other times. Yet, I say, when it
arises from His own withdrawing of that fitness, and we
are not negligent but do our best, in this case God accepts the will for the deed, as we have often said to you.
That rule always holds good. When the impediment is
such as we cannot remove, when the dullness of spirit
is such as it is not in our power to remove, when we
have used our utmost diligence, in that case it is no
hindrance. Therefore, it is a great comfort unto us that
we have used our dilgence in this duty, when we have
used our best to quicken our hearts, though it is not
done, yet God accepts our prayers as well as if they had
been performed in a more lively and fervent manner.

CASE 3. The next case is what a man is to do after
he has committed some great sin, after he has
wounded his conscience, whether then, notwithstanding, he must come and keep his constant course in
prayer morning and evening; in other words, whether
he shall be so bold as to come into God's presence after he has so exceedingly offended Him.

ANSWER 3. To this I answer that a man is bound
(notwith-standing any sin that he has committed, be it
what it will be) to keep his course constantly in prayer,
and not to omit it, not to keep off, not to defer it. And
my ground for it is because this is a duty. It is a charge
that God has layed upon all to pray continually, that is,

at least twice a day, as we showed before, to keep a constant course in it. Now, it is certain, our failing in one thing must not excuse us in another. When the duty lies on us, we have no dispensation to be negligent in it. Therefore, we are bound to do it.

Again, consider this. A particular offence does not offend as much as if we grow strangers to God, as if we grow to a general rebellion against Him. Put the case, a child commits a great offence against his father, yet, if he runs away from his father's house and becomes a stranger to him, that is more than the particular offence, for a general rebellion must be more than the particular. To give over calling on God, to break off that course, to grow a stranger to Him, to run away from His house, and (as it were) to be ready to give over all His ordinances and a constant course of obedience to Him, is a general rebellion, and is worse than the particular. Yes, such carriage, after sin committed, moves God to anger more than the sin itself. Many times, the contemptuous, negligent, rebellious carriage, after an offence, moves a master, a husband, or a parent more than the particular failing, though it is exceedingly great.

Besides, consider when a man commits a great sin, he makes a great gap in his conscience. He makes a great breach there, and will you have that breach lie open? Is not that very dangerous? Is not that the way to bring in more sin and allow those good things that are in the heart to steal out? I will give you but one instance for this. When St. Peter had committed a great sin in denying his Master, and forswearing Him too, yet, because he came in immediately and repented, and sought pardon (as you know he did), he was preserved from running into further problems. For he made up the gap, he made up the breach.

We see, on the other hand, when David had committed that sin with Bathsheba, and did not come to God as he should have done, to keep his constant course in sacrificing to Him, in repenting and renewing his repentance, and praying to Him, you know how many sins he fell into. And, likewise, that was the case of Solomon. You know to what a height he grew by not coming to God at his first failing. And, therefore, I say there is a reason that we should do it. Though the sin is great, we ought to come in and keep our course constantly.

"But may I not stay until I am more fitted, until my heart is more softened and more humbled?"

Beloved, to stay in this case is dangerous, for the heart commonly grows more hard in continuance. The conscience is more tender immediately after the sin is committed than it is afterwards. When you stay for more humility, you find less. And, therefore, while the wound is green, and when the fire has newly taken hold, it is then best to quench it before the wound is festered, before it has continued long. For the heart will grow worse and worse, as it is in Hebrews 3:12, "Take heed that you be not hardened through the deceitfulness of sin." The meaning is this: When you commit a sin, you think that if you stay a week, or a fortnight, or a month, you shall come in as well as at the first. No, says the Apostle, "while it is today." Come in, that is, do it immediately, for sin will deceive you. It will harden your heart before you are aware. It will make a distance between God and you, it will take you from Him, it will lead you further on. And, therefore,

take heed that your hearts are not hardened through
the deceitfulness of sin, that sin does not deceive you.
And it will do it before you think of it.

Therefore, in this case, you should do as you do
with waters. When waters break out a little, it is best to
stop them immediately. If you allow them, they will
make the breach greater until, at length, you are unable to stop them. So in this case, when you have
committed a great sin, come in speedily.

"But," you will say, "what, shall a man come into
God's presence, who is most holy, after he has defiled
himself with some great sin? Is not this an irreverent
thing?"

I answer briefly, it is very true. If you are bold to
come into God's presence with the same disposition
wherewith the sin was committed, with a mind so fash-
ioned, and so framed, in that case you exceedingly
provoke Him. This is a very high degree of profaneness. Therefore, when we say you must come in and
keep a constant course in prayer notwithstanding, the
meaning is that you must come in with a dispostion
turned aside from your sins and brought home to God,
with a mind to abhor that which is evil and cleave to
that which is good. There must be this conversation of
the mind to Him. You must not come in with the same
disposition; that must be altered. So much shall serve
for the answer to this case.

CASE 4. Another case is whether we may use a set
form of prayer, and, likewise, whether it shall be sufficient?

I need not say much to you, for I think there is
none here that doubts but that a set form of prayer

may be used. You know, Christ prescribed a form. You know there were certain Psalms that were prayers that were used constantly. Therefore, there is no doubt but that a set form may be used. We have that example for it.

And in the church at all times, in the primitive times of the church and all along to the beginning of the Reformed times, to Luther and Calvin's time, the church had set forms they used. And I know of no objection of weight against it.

One main objection is this: in stinted prayer, the spirit is straitened. When a man is tied to a form, then he shall have his spirit, as it were, bound and limited. He cannot go beyond that which is prescribed. And, therefore, some say it is a reason that a man should be left to more liberty (as he is in conceived prayers) and not tied to a strict form.

To this I answer, even those men who are against this, and who use this reason, do the same thing daily in the congregation. For when another prays, that is a set form to him that hears it. I say, it is a form to him, for put the case. He that is a hearer, who hears another pray, suppose that his spirit is more enlarged; it is a straitening to him. He has no liberty to go out. He is bound to keep his mind intent upon it. And, therefore, if that were a sufficient reason that a man might not use a set form, because the spirit is straitened, a man should not hear another pray (though it is a conceived prayer), because, in that case, his spirit is limited. It may be that the hearer has a larger heart, a great deal, than he who speaks and prays. So there is a bounding, a straitening, and a limiting of the spirit. And, therefore, that reason cannot be good.

Again, I answer, though the spirit is limited at that time, yet he has a liberty at other times, to pray as freely as he will in private. And, therefore, he is not so tied but, though at that time he is, yet it is no general tie. At another time, or immediately after, he may be as free as he will in secret.

Again, I answer, it is not a tie and a restraint of the spirit, because there is a tie of words. For the largeness of the heart does not stand so much in the multitude and variety of expressions as in the extent of the affection. Now, then, the heart may be very large for all that. Though he is tied in words, yet there is not a tie upon the affection. That may be extended more in putting up the same petition when another man's is more straitened. Therefore, there is no tie and limit upon that. And this is enough to satisfy us that a set form of prayer may be used.

But now, suppose you ask whether that is sufficient, whether a man may think that, because he has been present at a public prayer, this is sufficient.

My beloved, it is a matter of some importance to consider what we ought to do in this case; for we may be deceived in it. And I answer plainly: It is not sufficient! A man who is diligent in public prayers, who keeps them morning and evening and thinks that he has now discharged his duty, is in a very great error, This is the reason—they are not sufficient. Indeed, they are to be used for God is worshipped in them, and it is a more public worship when God is honored before many. When a man is honored before many spectators, more honor is done to him. So it is when men join in this worship. And there are many other reasons, but that is not the thing I am now to commend to you.

Although it ought to be done, it is insufficient because there are many particular sins which cannot be confessed in public prayer. There are many particular wants which in public prayer you cannot unfold, open, and express to the Lord.

Again, the end of a set form of prayer is to be a help for the private (for the public is another case), a help that one may use who is exceedingly weak. A child who cannot go may have such a prop, but we must not always be children. We must not always use that help.

Besides, we must consider this: There is no man who has any work of grace in his heart but he is enabled in some measure to pray without a set form of prayer. He is able to express his desires to God in private, one way or another. There was never any man, in any extreme want, who did not know how to express himself where he had liberty to speak. So it is in this case.

Besides, the spirit of a man has greater liberty in private. There a man may "pour forth his soul to the Lord," as Hanna said, 1 Samuel 1, which in public he cannot do freely. There are many particular mercies which he has cause to be thankful to God for.

Besides, there are particular pains a man is to take with his heart from day to day which, in the public common petitions, he is not able to do. Beloved, know this: The prayer that is required from day to day is not so much the performance of the duty, the doing of the task. But the purpose is to keep the heart in order. For if sinful lusts grow upon it, and distempers, and wordly-mindedness, the end of this duty is to work them out again, to renew repentance again. And when there is a forgetfulness of the covenant, when grace grows weak, when good desires begin to languish, the work of prayer is to renew and recover them, to put fuel to them—and this is not done by the performance of the public prayer only. Therefore, I say, though you perform it in your families, and meet in the congregation, you must not think that this is enough. You are bound to a private performance of this duty.

CASE 5. What is a man to do in the private performance of this duty? He is always bound to use his voice? Is he always bound to use such a kind of gesture?

I answer this briefly (for there is no great difficulty in these things and, therefore, I pass them over), for the gesture in public, there is more heed to be taken of that, because it is a public and open worship of God. Therefore, in public, the gesture is always to be reverent. You kow how often it is repeated (in the Old Testament especially), that they bowed down and worshipped. Christ looked up to heaven, Paul kneeled down, and the rest with him, and prayed. And you have many similar expressions mentioned in the Scriptures. Where you have prayer mentioned in public, you shall find an expression of some reverent gesture, and when we appear before the Lord in the public performance of this duty, special care must be taken.

In private, the case is different. A variety of gestures may be used. I do not see but all variety of gestures may be used. There are many examples of walking, lying, and sitting. Only take heed that, even in private, as far as may be, the gesture is such that may both express the inward reverence of the heart as well as the outer man. But there is liberty even in that.

I think this is the best rule in private, that the gesture be used that most quickens and helps the duty. Some gesture may bring a dullness and indisposition, while another may quicken the body and make it more fit for prayer. Sometimes lying is inconvenient, and sometimes more convenient; and, therefore, in this case, the best rule is to use that gesture which quickens most, which most helps the duty. Some gesture may breed a weariness in the body; some may breed a dullness; some are painful to the body. All this is a hindrance to the duty, when the change of it may quicken and help.

Now for the voice. I say, for that (as for the gesture), it is not simply required. For God is a Spirit, and He will be worshipped in spirit, John 4:24. Men who have ears and bodies must have men speak to them. But God, who is a Spirit, delights in that which is like Himself. Therefore, all His eye is upon the inward behavior of the spirit. Besides, the spirit may speak to God when the voice does not. You know, the angels speak to God, and they speak to one another. The scholars have great disputes about the speech of angels, but in this they agree, that one angel speaks to another after this manner.

When anyone has a conceit in his mind of anything, with a will that another should understand it, and that God should understand it, that is enough for the expression of it. So it is with the spirit of a man when he has such a petition in his heart, in his mind, and there is a desire in his will that God should understand that petition. That is offering it up to the Lord. It is as true a speaking to the Lord as when you deliver it by an outward voice, for the spirit agrees with the angels, as it is a speech. As they speak one to another, and to the Lord, so does the spirit of man—though, indeed, the tongue is to be used, as it is in James 3:9, "therewith bless we God"; and therewith we should pray among others and before others, and speak before others. But, when there is any cause to use the voice in private, it is this: as far as it may quicken the heart (as I said of gestures), and as far as thereby we may keep our thoughts from wandering.

If the voice were not used, perhaps, thoughts would be subject to more wandering, and we should not be ready to take notice of them. But they would slip before we are aware. And therefore, when the voice is used, it must be to keep in the thoughts. In some cases, to omit the voice is more convenient when it may draw any other inconvenience, but that is left to every man's particular case, as he shall find the use of it to hinder or further him. And so much shall serve for this case.

Sermon Four

1 Thessalonians 5:17
"Pray continually."

CASE 5. Another case of conscience (in the business of prayer) is what a man is to do when he does not have time by reason of some weighty business that requires a quick and sudden dispatch and does not give him the leisure and liberty that otherwise he might have had.

ANSWER 5. To this I answer, you shall find that in Scripture the prayers of saints have been sometimes larger and sometimes shorter. Our Savior Christ, you know, sometimes spent a whole night in prayer. Surely He did not take so much time always, and, no doubt, we have liberty sometimes to be larger, sometimes shorter, according as our occasions will permit. But yet, you must remember this: though the business is great, yet that business that concerns the salvation of our souls and the worship of God is greater. And therefore, unless it is a true strait, this is still to be preferred, for it is a business of greater importance. And, therefore, you must give a just weight to your business and not to allow every small business that comes in to thrust out this duty. For here you do not keep the due proportion, but neglect the greater and take the lesser.

Besides, you not say, when you have great business in hand, that a man must have a dining time and a sleeping time? Why may we not say as well? A man

74

must have a praying time—is it not as necessary? You
know what Job said, you know the course that he kept
in reading the Word (for that is clearly meant in that
place). It was more precious to him than his appointed
food. That is, he would rather omit his usual meals (for
that he means by his appointed food) than to omit a
constant course in performing those holy duties.
Therefore, I say, we ought to take careful heed that we
do not omit it, unless it is a great strait. If it is, we may
be short in it. God does not tie us so exactly.

You see therein that there are not rules set down in
the Scriptures wherein we are tied precisely to such an
hour, to such a time. But God, in mercy and in wisdom, has left it to our liberty. Only, you see, this is the
command: "pray continually." Do it exceedingly much.
At the least, keep a constant course in it, as we heard
before, but you may be shorter in it.

Four Cautions to Observe Regarding Prayer

Now, let these four cautions be observed.
1. Take heed that this straitening does not come
from your ill husbandry, that is, from your ill husbanding of time. For if a man were careful to redeem time
before, it may be that he does not need to be put to
such a strait as he is at that time when he is to perform
this duty. Suppose you have a journey to go on that requires so much time, and you must be gone early. You
may so husband your time before that you may get
time for your journey. And, for the performance of this
duty, and so for other business, as I said in the morning, when you should sequester yourselves to perform
this duty of prayer, take heed that you be good stew-

ards of your time, that you husband it well.

And, likewise, this is another part of husbanding your time, that you do not let that which is very precious go for things of small importance, for that is ill husbandry. You should redeem the time, and buy it with the loss of something. You have time to bestow in the weighty business of your calling, in things that belong to the good of man, much more should you in this that belongs to the worship of God. And, therefore, it may be, redeem it with some loss. In this way you ought to husband it, otherwise you do not redeem the time as you ought. This is the first caution that ought to be observed, to husband and redeem the time well.

2. If we are straitened at any time, recompence it another time. For it is not a feigned excuse and pretense if you are straitened, to be careful to spend more time in prayer when you have liberty. By that you shall know your sincerity in it, that it is true, and that it is not an excuse and a putting off.

3. Another caution to be observed is that you do not take too much business upon you. If you are straitened with business, and therefore cannot be so large in the performance of this duty, as otherwise you would, if you do not take too much upon you, you yourselves are the cause of it. Therefore, he who takes less, who spends more time in the things that belong to salvation, has made the better choice, just as Mary made a better choice than Martha though her employment was good.

Likewise, as you must not pester yourselves with too much business, so likewise you must take care that your minds are not too much intent upon worldly cares. For too much intention of mind upon business causes distraction in prayer as well as too much business. When a man's mind is too much occupied about business, when it is too intent, when the soul cleaves too fast upon the worldly duties and cannot loose itself to the performance of spiritual duties, which require freedom.

4. The last caution is that the strait does not rise from diffidence in God and confidence in the use of the means; for it falls out oftentimes when we have business of importance in hand. There is a turning and posting from one creature to another, from the use of one means to another, so that we cannot get time in prayer; not so much for lack of time simply, but because we mind the means too much. We intend them too much, we do not trust God enough with the business. If we did, we might spend less time in them and more time in seeking Him. So much for that case.

CASE 6. Another case of conscience in this business of calling upon God is, what is a man to do for the use of the means, for when we are bid to pray and seek God, that is the ordinary question. But may we not use the means too?

ANSWER 6. To this I answer, prayer is so far from excluding the means that it includes them. If the desire is fervent, when we desire anything at God's hands, it will make us diligent in the use of means, as it will make you earnest in seeking God and in putting up your request to Him. For if a man shall pray and be negligent in the use of the means, I will be bold to say it, it is but like the desire of the sluggard. It is a languishing, fainting desire. He desires, but his soul has nothing. He desires, but he puts his hand into his bosom. The desires which you express when you pray are not fervent, they are not earnest, if you are remiss in the use of the means. He who desires grace, desires strength against sinful lusts and temptations, and yet is remiss in the use of the means by which grace should be increased and strength gained to resist those temptations and corruptions, certainly reveals that those desires are but vain desires.

Besides, it is an argument that we do not trust in God, that we do not make account of our own prayers unless we are diligent in the use of the means. Therefore, we are far from excluding them. For if you seek God and trust your prayers, and think they will prevail with Him, it will work this effect: You will be careful to use such means as God has ordained to bring a thing to pass.

It is like this. If a man seeks a physician, such a physician that he trusts, into whose hands he would put his life, when this physician prescribes such a course, such a diet, and such a thing to be taken at such a time, the more he trusts the physician the more careful he will be to observe his prescriptions and rules. And so, in this case, the more you rest on God, the more careful you will be to use such means as He has appointed when He has said these and these means are to be used. In this case, I say, it is a sign that your prayers are more to purpose when you are diligent in the use of them, when you dare not slight or neglect them.

Again, you must consider this, that when we pray at any time, we do not pray to have anything done without means, but we pray to have a blessing upon the means; and, if we pray for a blessing upon the means, our mind is not that they should be omitted. You see, God does all things by second causes. He does not save us without ourselves. That is, He uses us as instruments. He does everything by men and by creatures, and by means. And the end of our prayers is not to have them done without means, but to have a blessing upon them. But that which is chiefly to be observed to clear this point to you is this: Prayer is not the only means; it is but part of the means to bring anything to pass.

There are two things to effect a business, that is, prayer and means both. We do not say prayer is the only means; indeed, then the other would be excluded. But since it is but a part, and the other makes up the total means of bringing anything to pass, it does not exclude them, but they may both be joined together, prayer and the use of means. This is enough to show that we may use means. We may pray and lay our hand on the plow. We may see God and be diligent, and as diligent as anybody else. But now these three cautions are to be observed.

1. The first is that if we do use means, we use those that are right. For if you trust God and depend upon Him, you will not step out to any inordinate means, nor use lawful means in an inordinate manner. If you do so, it is an argument that your prayers are of no value in your own esteem. You do not rest on God, for if you did you would not use other means than He has appointed.

2. Though you use the means and pray too, yet you must so use the means that your confidence is in your prayers. For it is one thing to use the means, and it is

another thing to have confidence in them. And, therefore, we say to you in this case that you must do as he that uses the light of the sun. He so uses that light that he has an eye upon the sun from whom that light comes. For he knows that if the sun were set, the light would be gone.

Or it is like he who takes water in a cistern or river. He so takes it as that he has an eye to the fountain. He knows if the fountain is stopped, the river will quickly dry up. So you should think with yourselves. If I use any means, any creature, any instrument, to bring things to pass, my eye must be upon God. For all the help that we have from the creature is but a beam to the help that comes from God Himself. And, therefore, you must do, in this case, as physicians are wont to do. They put many ingredients into a thing, but it is one principal ingredient among the rest that he makes account will cure the disease.

So, in this case, make use both of the prayer and of the means. Yet you must know that prayer is the principal effector of the thing, and the principal means is that wherein your confidence is to be. For indeed, it is God that brings everything to pass. There is no good or evil in the city but He does it. You know He takes all to Himself.

All the means by which good and evil is conveyed to you do not do the thing. They are only the vehicles, they are only the instruments. Beer and wine, wherein medicine is taken, are only the instruments by which the medicine is taken. But it is the medicine that cures. So all the means cannot do it. It is the help, and the power of God, the efficacy that comes from Him that brings things to pass. Therefore, we must remember to use the means that you use with dependence upon God, with an eye upon Him, so that your hearts do not rest upon them. For if they do, it is an inordinate use of them.

Last, you must take heed of sticking in any particular means. For if you do, it is a sign that you do not trust God as you ought to do. It is a common fault that we pitch upon such a particular way, and we think that must do it or nothing will. Now, if God is trusted, He has more ways to the wood than one. He has more means to bring a thing to pass than one. And, therefore, we must leave it to Him, who often does it best by another means than we dreamed of.

For example, David had a promise of the kingdom. When he had the kingdom of Judah, yet you know that the kingdom of Israel stood out. For Ishbosheth had the kingdom and Abner was his chief captain. Besides, in his coming into the kingdom of Judah, we see how God wrought the business without device by a means that he never thought of. In that battle, when Saul was killed, and so many of his sons, there was so much way made for him, when he himself used no means to bring it to pass. Afterward, when the kingdom of Israel was kept from him, and he had only Judah, we see that God caused a division between Ishbosheth and Abner, his chief captain. Upon that, Abner came and offered David the whole kingdom, yet he was only a reconciled enemy, and what Abner might have done, he did not know.

Therefore God, by His providence, though Joab sinned, caused Abner to be taken away by Joab. When this was done, Ishbosheth was still alive. Then there were two men set by the providence of God (though it

was a great sin in them) to take away his head, and so
the kingdom came wholly to David, for there were only
two sons—Mephibosheth, who was lame in his feet,
and Ishbosheth, who was lame in his mind, a weak man
who was unable to manage so great and weighty a
business. So God brought the business to pass by a way
that David did not think of.

Therefore, though we may use means, yet, after we
use them, we must depend upon God, and leave it to
God to take one means or another. We must do, in this
case, as we do when we go to a man who is very skilled
to do work for us. If we go to a carpenter and tell him
we have such a thing to be done, or if we go to those
we call "aquarioli," who bring water from place to
place, we tell him that this is our desire. But how he
will work, and which way he will bring it to pass, we do
not know; yet we trust such a one. We say that he is an
honest man, a man of his word, and if he has under-
taken it, it is enough.

Why will you not trust God, who goes so much beyond us, who has infinite wisdom and infinite power?
And, therefore, we should so use the means that we
deepen our dependence upon Him, that we leave it to
Him to use this or that means as it pleases Him. For
sometimes, it may be, He takes away that which we are
about. Sometimes, He leaves us partly destitute, and
finds a way of His own, that we might trust Him and
consider His power and wisdom, what He is able to do.
So much, likewise, shall serve for this case.

CASE 7. Another case is this: What is it to pray in
faith? You know that is required. Now, there is a common error in this point, for a man may say, "If I pray

for the salvation of another, I have no promise. How can I pray in faith?"

When a man prays to be guided in such a business, to have such an enterprise be brought to pass, to have deliverance from such a trouble, such a sickness, from such a calamity that he lies under, he finds no particular promise. For all he knows, it shall never be granted. How can he be said to pray in faith if to pray in faith is to believe that the thing shall be done?

ANSWER 7. I answer, to pray in faith is to go as far as the promise goes. Now, no particular man has any particular promise that he shall have such a deliverance, that he shall have such a particular mercy granted him. And, therefore, it is not required to believe that this particular thing should be done.

"But," you will say, "what faith is it, then, that is required?"

I say, it is enough to believe that God is a Father, that he is ready to hear, and not only that He is ready to hear, but that He is ready to do that which is best for me in such a particular. Both are required: that you believe Him to be well-affected towards you as a Father, as one who tenders your good, and not only so, but that He will do that in that particular that shall be most for His own glory and for your good. If you do so, you pray in faith though, for the particular, you do not know whether it shall be granted or not.

Indeed, if we had a particular promise, as Elijah had that it should not rain, we would be bound to believe in particular. But, not having that, we are not tied to it, for the promise is the object of faith, and the habit is not to work beyond the object. The object is the rule and the limit of the habit. Therefore, you may pray in faith when yet you have no ground to believe and think that the particular thing should be granted.

For example, if a father prays that his son may have grace wrought in his heart, that his soul may be saved, it may be that the Lord will never do it. Or, if one friend prays for another to the same purpose, though the thing is not done, yet the prayer returns to his bosom. He is no loser by it, there is a reward that belongs to him for seeking God in sincerity. It is his duty that he should do so. The same I may say for every particular case.

And this encouragement you may have, that there is never any particular prayer put up wherein you seek things that are not granted but you err in it. For, if you believe this far, as I said to you, be sure that your prayers are accepted. God will do that which is best for you, and your prayers shall not be lost. So much also for that.

CASE 8. The last case is, how shall a man know whether his prayer is heard or not?

ANSWER 8. For an answer to this, I will give you this one rule (and that is as far as I can go), it is certain that those prayers which are made by the assistance of God's Holy Spirit are always heard. If you find that, at any time, you need make not question, but that God hears and will do the thing. But observe the caution that we have given you heretofore, that is, for the means, the manner, the time, and the measure, for it cannot be but that when the heart is enlarged by God's own Spirit the prayer is an expression of holy desires, and the Lord always hears.

That place is clear for this in Romans 8:27. He

knows the meaning of the Spirit, that is, He so knows it that He hearkens to it, He always accepts it. Therefore, when you come in such a case that your hearts are enlarged in a special manner and with holy desires, certainly God means to grant our requests then. He would not send His Spirit to be an Intercessor in your hearts if He did not mean to do it. In that case, He withholds His Spirit. He does not give us that enlargement of heart.

Only this distinction must be carefully remembered. You may be very earnest sometimes. The parent may be very earnest for his child, as David was for his. Moses, for all we know, was earnest to have gone into the land of Canaan. These were things they desired, Yet that may be an expression of natural desires.

In that case, a man may be very earnest, yet he cannot build upon it to say, "My heart is much enlarged in prayer, and, therefore, I shall be heard." But take in this: When the heart is enlarged with holy desires, and that in a special manner, somewhat more than ordinary, it is the work of the Spirit of God, quickening your heart, opening it wide, strengthening and enlarging it, sharpening grace and holiness in you in those requests you put up to God. In this case, build upon it. Your prayers are heard from that ground we have given you, "He knows the meaning of the Spirit." So much shall serve for those cases of conscience in this spiritual duty of calling upon God.

Now the last thing I propounded was this, what the qualification is that is required in our prayers. For now I have said so much of prayer. It is a necessary thing, that we know.

WHAT MAKES OUR PRAYERS ACCEPTABLE?

What conditions are required that it may be acceptable?

1. *The first (I will commend to you that which is the ground and first in order before all the rest) is that the person is right.* "The prayer of the righteous availeth much," James 5:16.

The ground of it is this. A man must first have Christ before he can have anything else. "He hath given us all things else with Christ." If we have all things else, and if we do not have Him, it is nothing. All the promises, you know, are yea and amen, but it is in Him. So we must first have Him.

Besides, the general covenant must go before the particular. For the ground of all prayer is this or that particular promise, but you must first be within the covenant. You must first have the general covenant belonging to you before you can have the particular branches. Therefore, a man must be within the covenant. His person must first be righteous and accepted. Therefore, let none deceive themselves in this case. He hopes his heart is sincere, and his prayer is right, and his ends are good. For although all this is true, if his person is not right God does not regard it.

You know, the blood of a sheep and the blood of a swine are both alike. It may be that the blood of the swine is better than the other, yet the blood of the swine was not to be offered because it was the blood of a swine. So, in this case, the prayer of an unregenerate man may be as well-framed, for the petitions, for everything that is required immediately to a prayer, but the heart from which it comes, the person from which it proceeds, is that which makes the difference, and, therefore, that must be observed.

See that the person is right. Therefore you find in Psalm 4:3 that David makes that the ground why his prayer should be heard. He says, "be ye sure that God hath chosen for Himself the godly man." And when I call upon Him, I shall be heard. For that is the ground that he takes to himself why he shall be heard, that God has chosen to Himself the godly man. It is as if he should say, "I am of the number. And, therefore, you who are my enemies, and think to prevail against me, I do not fear you. I pray to a God who will defend me. I am a godly man and, upon that ground, I believe that my prayer is heard."

Beloved, otherwise, though we pray and pray hard, yet our sins cry louder than our prayers. They drown our prayers. They make a greater noise than they. The noise our sins make is like the noise of a thunder while the noise of our prayers is only like the cracking of thorns. And the noise of our prayer cannot be heard for the noise that sin makes in the ears of the Lord. Thus it is, in this case, when we come before God in our sins, when a man comes into His presence in his unregenerate state.

But this is not all. Likewise, a man who is within the covenant may have a particular sin (as you heard before) that may intercept his prayers and may hinder the blessing. So that the sin must be removed before his prayers can be heard. It is true, the son abides in the house forever, but the son may commit such an offence that his father may use him as a servant. He may deny his requests and refuse them when he comes to seek anything at his hands. Therefore, there must be a particular reconciliation, a particular repentance. That sin must be removed and done away that stands in the way.

Therefore, the saints have kept this method in calling upon God. See it in David and Ezra, all of them. We see, for the most part, when they make any complete prayers, they still begin with humiliation and confession of sins. And the reason is that their person might be clear and innocent, that those sins might be removed which would stand in their way. Likewise, that is a ground of that in 1 Timothy 1:8. The Apostle says there, "I will that prayers be made in all places, that you lift up pure hands without wrath and doubting." The meaning is this. Not only that a man is within the covenant, but that he is cleansed from all particular sins that cleave to him and hang upon him.

For example, when you would be accepted of God, if there is any particular sin hanging on you, it must be removed by renewing your repentance. Besides that, see what the Scripture takes notice of when a man comes to pray. His heart must be cleansed from pride (for God resists the proud). His heart must be brought to a humble disposition. Likewise, it must be cleansed from wrath, for he must lift up pure hands without wrath. This is often required. Matthew 5:23-24, "Leave thine offering, and go and make peace with thy brother." Also, the heart must be cleansed from unthankfulness. Our prayers are not accepted unless we are thankful for mercies received. The same may be said of every particular case. We must be careful to cleanse ourselves from all sinful lusts and corrupt affections so that they do not have dominion in our hearts. But we must lift up pure hearts and innocent hands. And that is the first thing that is required: that the person be right. Not only must he be within the covenant, but, likewise, those particular sins must be removed that may be an impediment to his prayers.

2. *The second thing required is faith.* Lift up pure hands without wrath and doubting. You know what it says in James. Let him ask of God, let him ask in faith and waver not. Though prayer is the key to open God's treasures, yet faith is the hand that turns the key, without which it will do no good.

Now the Lord requires faith, partly for His own sake. He would not otherwise be acknowledged if you did not trust Him when you come to seek Him, if you did not rest on Him. Besides, He would lose His glory, for in this we glorify Him, when we trust Him; and we dishonor Him when we distrust Him. When we come and seek Him, and do not rest upon Him, we dishonor Him.

Besides, in regard of us, He requires faith, and will not hear us without it. In James 1:6, in the same place where faith is required, there is good reason why it is required. For the Apostle says there, "He that believes not, or he that wavers, he is like the wave of the sea." That is, sometimes in prayer he is very earnest like a wave that swells high; sometimes again, he will be nothing at all. Yes, says the Apostle, he is not only uneven in the business of prayer, sometimes earnest and forward, and sometimes giving over again, off and on, but such a man is unstable in all his ways; for he who trusts in God will be careful not only in prayer, but to keep all his ways right. But he who does not trust Him wavers in everything.

He is, it may be, diligent in prayer. He will look to his ways for a time, but he does not rest upon God. He rests upon other things. He is like a wave; he is not constant, and, therefore, faith is required. Now, when I say that faith is required, know this: There is a double faith required in our prayers to God. The one is a faith in the providence of God; the other is a faith in His promise.

First, I say, faith in the providence, which is a thing of such importance. And we are apt to forget it. We see it clearly in Psalm 146:5-6, "Blessed is he that trusts in the God of Jacob, &c. who made heaven, and earth, and the sea, who keeps covenant, and mercy forever." You see, faith is there required in the providence, "He made heaven and earth and the sea." Is He such a God, who is able to bring anything to pass, for He made heaven and earth, and is He not able to do anything besides?

Second, there must be a faith in the promises, as is expressed in the other words, "He keepeth covenant forever." So, likewise, to express the defect of it. You see, when Martha and Mary came to Christ to raise Lazarus, they believe he was ready enough to do it (there was faith in His willingness), but they lacked faith in His providence. For Martha comes to Him and tells Him, "Lord, he hath been in the grave four days." It is as if she had said, "Surely, now, it cannot be done. If You had come sooner, it might have been brought to pass." So she believed Him to be willing, but she lacked faith in the providence.

Again, as faith in the providence was lacking, in this case, so we see in the leper, there was faith in the providence (it may be that the other was lacking, but that is not expressed; it is more probable he had both), "Lord, if Thou wilt, Thou canst make me whole." Here was an evidence of faith in the providence. He acknowledges His power, "If Thou wilt, Thou canst make me whole." But, because Christ answered him, it is likely he had faith in the promise, too. So, I say, there must be a faith, first, in the providence.

Second, there must be a faith also in the promise of God. You have ground enough for that, you have His sure word for it. He has said, "Ask and ye shall have, seek and ye shall find; knock and it shall be opened to you; and whatsoever you ask, if it be according to His will, it shall be done for you." So that is the thing we are chiefly to look unto, to consider this faith in God's promise; for men are ready to say, "I do not doubt but that God is able, but all the question is whether He is willing or not."

And, therefore, if we would have our prayers strong and prevalent, we must be careful to strengthen our faith in His promise. For, as that is strong, so our prayers prevail more with God. It is a matter of such importance. And, therefore, I will show briefly how your faith may be strengthened and, likewise, how you may know it.

First, you shall strengthen your faith if you consider that nature of God. Beloved, this is a great cause why we do not believe the promise of God, and His readiness to help us in difficult cases, because we are ignorant of the nature of God, of the attributes of God, or at least we do not consider them. For example (that I may open it to you a little, and show you the way of making use of the attributes of God in calling upon Him and strengthening our faith from them), consider, first, the justice of God (I will give you examples how the saints have strengthened their faith from God's attributes). David used this argument, "Lord, Thou art just, I am innocent." When he tells God of His justice, and withall expresses his own innocence, it is a strong argument. David, you see, uses it often (I need not name particulars. "Lord, reward me according to mine innocence"), Thou knowest I am righteous, and mine enemies have done me thus and thus much wrong, and Thou art just. God cannot deny this, for it is a strong argument that is taken from such an attribute.

So again, the goodness of God, "Lord, Thou art full of mercy." On the other side, "I am full of misery." And, when these are put together, it is a great means to strengthen our faith. Therefore, we see David often expressed his own calamity, his disease, how he was oppressed by enemies and slandered, and God's mercy. That is the ground of it, God is full of compassion. It is as if he should say, "Thou art full of goodness, and I am in calamity and misery at this time." And that was an argument whereby he strengthened his faith.

So again, another attribute of God is His glory. We make the argument thus, "Lord, Thou hast an eye to Thy glory, and I am aiming at Thy glory." In such a request, it is a strong prevailing argument with Him. You know, Moses prevailed with Him, when he sought the saving of the whole people of Israel. He said, "Lord, Thy name will be polluted, what will the heathen say? And since I aim at Thy glory in it, do not deny me."

Likewise, Ezekias and David used the same argument with God. "Shall the dust praise Thee? Shall any glory be given Thee in the grave? Shall we be able to do anything for Thy honor when we are dead?" So that the arguments that are taken from God's glory, and our aim at His glory, are another means to strengthen our faith.

Moreover, the power of God is another attribute whereby we may conceive the same argument as before, when we go to God and express our weakness and His power. Lord, we are weak and are able to do nothing. Lord, Thou art almighty, Thou made heaven and earth. It is a strong argument to prevail with Him.

So we see that Asa prevailed with God, 2 Chronicles 14:11: "Oh Lord, it is all one with Thee to help with many or few," and we rest upon Thee. It is as if he should say, "We are exceedingly few; we are exceedingly weak. We are able to do nothing, but Thou art able to do it with a few as well as with a great multitude." There he puts them together.

And the like we have of Jehoshaphat, "Lord, we have not strength to stand before our enemies, but our eyes are to Thee," 2 Chronicles 10:12. It is as if he should say, "Thou hast strength and power enough; Thou art able to do it, thou we are unable." This is another argument taken from the power of God.

Also, the unchangeableness of God. When one comes to the Lord and says to Him, "Lord, Thou hast done this and this in former times for Thy servants. Lord, Thou hast done this and this for me in another case, and Thou art unchangeable. Thou art the same God," this is a great means to strengthen our faith. As you know, it is in your lawsuits. When you have a precedent, it adds strength to the cause. When we have precedents for this, it will add strength to us, and that strength is taken from God's unchangeableness. If we put them together, "Lord, Thou art unchangeable; and Lord, Thou hast done it to other men in the same case, Thou hast done it to me also in the same case," it is a strong argument that David uses.

You see how he is stayed by it, Psalm 22:4, "Lord, our fathers trusted in Thee and they were delivered, they trusted in Thee and were not confounded." It is as if he should say, "Lord, Thou art unchangeable. Thou heard them in the same case when they trusted in Thee. Now it is my case, and therefore I beseech Thee to help me in my distress."

Also, the faithfulness of God, the fidelity of God, is another of His attributes. And when we make our argument thus, "Lord, Thou art faithful, and I trust in Thee," it is a strong argument. You know, it is an argument that prevails much with men. A man is ready to say, "He trusts me, I must not deceive him."

Now, the Lord keeps covenant and mercy forever. When we come and use this with Him, "Lord, Thou art faithful. Thou hast said Thou wilt keep covenant and mercy forever, Thou can not do otherwise. It is Thy nature. Thou can not deny Thyself, and I rest on Thee. I depend on Thee in such a case." It cannot be that the Lord should fail us. If a man will not fail one who trusts in him, certainly the Lord will not, and that is an argument that is used often. God never fails those who trust Him.

Then, besides the absolute attributes of God, consider His relative attributes. He is a Father and a Master. It is a strong argument that is taken from these. If we go to the Lord and say, "Lord, Thou art a Father, Thou art a Master, Thou art a Husband. Where

should the children go but to their Father? Where
should the wife go but to her Husband? Where should
the servants go but to their Master, to their Lord?
Lord, Thou hast commanded us to provide for our
own, and he is worse than an infidel that provides not
for his own. Lord, we belong to Thee, we are Thine."

We see that David used this argument, that God
had made him. You have it often in the Psalms, that
God had made him, not only His creature, but had
made him again. He was His servant. He often used
this relation, "I am Thy servant." God was his God, and
he was God's servant, one who belonged to him, one
who depended upon Him. And surely, my beloved,
dependence upon God and seeking God are great
means to win Him to us.

When we see another depend upon us, one who is
ours, that is an effectual motive with men. The same is
as prevalent with God, and therefore may strengthen
our faith. Now, when I say these arguments prevail with
God, the meaning is that they prevail with us, they
strengthen our faith, they enable us to believe that
God is ready to help us. And when we believe it and
trust Him, then indeed God is ready to second it, because then we are prepared. We can then put up our
desires in the prayer of faith. Otherwise, they are put
up with doubting, and that makes them unacceptable
to God and ineffectual.

And now, as I have showed you the way, so likewise,
in a word, I will show you that, when we pray in faith
(for that is a thing that is very useful), you shall know it
by this (I add that because I see the Scripture requires
it as such a main condition, without which a man cannot be accepted: "Be it done to thee according to thy

faith." It is everywhere calculated): the quietness of your mind and your security. When a man calls upon God and his mind is quiet in it, it is a sign that he believes and trusts in Him. It is a prayer of faith.

Hannah, you know, in that case, "looked no more sad" because she trusted in God. She believed the thing should be done. Therefore, if you find solicitude and perplexity in your minds, it is a sign that your prayers lack so much faith. For if you rested upon God, you would be quiet and secure in Him.

Second, if you believe, you will continue in prayer. You know it was an argument of the faith of the woman of Canaan that she continued, that she would take no denial. Though the Lord denied her and put her off, yet she held out. And what was the reason for it? Because she believed that he was the son of David, that He was merciful, and that He would hear in the end. So that continuance in prayer is an argument that we believe the Lord. If we believe, we will be content to wait. "He that believeth will not make haste" because he trusts in God and depends upon Him.

Likewise, an argument of faith is a diligent use of those means that God has prescribed and no other. And so, I have shown you two things that are required in prayer. The person must be righteous and within the covenant. Second, faith is required. And, likewise, how this faith is wrought, both in His providence and in His promises. Likewise, how we shall know whether our prayers are the prayers of faith or not.

Sermon Five

1 Thessalonians 5:17
"Pray continually."

3. *The next condition required in prayer is fervency.* You know the place in James 5:16. The prayer of the righteous prevails much if it is fervent. The Lord requires this qualification in prayer because it puts the heart into a holy and spiritual disposition. For it is not simply the making of the request that God looks for at our hands, but such a working upon our hearts by prayer, such a bringing of them to a good frame of grace by that duty that thereby we are more fitted to receive the mercy that before we were not. When a man is fervent in prayer, it sets all the wheels of the soul the right way. It puts the heart into a holy and spiritual disposition and temper. So that the Lord sees it now fit to bestow mercy upon such a man who before was unfit by reason of his untowardness and stubbornness of heart, by reason of that unclean and holy disposition that He saw in him.

Therefore, He will have prayer fervent, not so much because the very fervency of prayer itself is respected, but because, by virtue of that fervency, the heart is made better when a man comes to God with a request, like the request of the patient to the physician. It may be the physician denies a long time when the patient asks for things that are pleasant and agreeable to him—not because he is unwilling to give them, but

97

because his body must be brought into another temper. He must vomit or purge that which is grievous to
him, but this must be done before he is fit to receive
such medicines.

So the Lord does with His servants. Though He is
willing to bestow such mercies on them, yet, because
they are not fitted, He requires continuance and fervency in prayer. Therefore, we say, in prayer all the
graces of God's Spirit are set on work and, the more
they are intended, the more they are acted, the more
they are increased. And, therefore, the Lord is moved
by this fervency to bestow a mercy on us that otherwise
He would not do.

But now, the question is what this fervency is?

You shall find it usually expressed in the Scriptures
by such metaphors as these: "crying to the Lord,"
"wrestling with the Lord," "striving with Him," and
"giving Him no rest," wherein these two things are to
be marked.

First, a man is said to be fervent when he puts all
his strength to prayer, when he is very earnest and importunate with the Lord, when he strives and contends
with Him. Though he finds many difficulties and impediments, yet he breaks through all. This is to be fervent in prayer, to be importunate with the Lord.

For example, when a man comes to pray and finds
many discouragements and finds himself guilty of
many sins and finds little holiness, he has but feeble
faith to his own sense. He finds much deadness of
spirit, yet he continues, notwithstanding. And when,
likewise, he does, he not only finds these impediments
in himself, but he finds the Lord exceeding backward
to the thing, either giving no answer, turning the deaf

ear to him, or, it may be, giving a contrary answer, as to the woman of Canaan.

Consider, for example, a man coming to pray for health. It may be that his sickness increases upon him more. When he prays to overcome such a lust or temptation, it may be that it is doubled upon him. When he prays for such a deliverance, it may be that the oppression grows more and more, as it was upon the Israelite. When they fought for deliverance, the oppression grew greater. Now to hold out, notwithstanding this, and to continue in prayer, and to outwrestle God in it, though He seems backward to the request, is to be fervent in prayer.

Second, fervency is not only loud praying but continual knocking—when a man is not only importunate with the Lord but he continues long. He will not give over until he has got the blessing. You know, Jacob's fervency was seen in that he continued all night long in wrestling with the Lord. What was the reason that he wrestled? He would not let go till he had the blessing, till he had obtained the thing he sought for. So, I say, this earnestness and continuance in prayer, this breaking through all difficulties, is to wrestle with the Lord. For all wrestling and striving, you know, supposes some opposition on the other person's part. Indeed, if there were no opposition, it would be a small thing. But when the Lord is most backward, when the thing is most improbable, when there is much difficulty, so that you do not know how it should be brought to pass, yet you continue in striving and give the Lord no rest. You will not give over. This is fervency in prayer, and this is a condition that the Lord requires.

Only these two cautions must be remembered, so

that we do not make a mistake in this fervency. First, remember that fervency, if it is right, must be a fruit of faith. For there is a fervency that does not come from faith but from a natural fear of lack. A man can be indeed like a swine that is pinched, which will cry exceedingly loud—not because it looks for help but because it is pinched. So any creature or man naturally will use any importunity when he lacks anything. He will be earnest in his requests. Such fervency the Lord does not regard, because this is nothing more than a mere expression of natural desires. There is no holiness in it, there is no fire of the spirit. But when this is added to it, there is not only a sense of the thing we want, but also a hope of mercy, a ground to believe that I shall have the thing granted. And, out of this ground, I am earnest and importunate. So earnestness is a fruit of faith.

When Jesus Christ lived upon earth, when men came and cried earnestly to Him, and were exceedingly importunate, some to be healed of their diseases, some to have devils cast out, we see that His answer to them was that it would be to them not according to their importunity and fervency, but according to their faith. It is as if He should say, "I do not heed, I do not regard all this clamor and earnestness if they are only expressions of such wants, if they are only in the sense of such need and no more. But if they proceed from faith, and that faith sets you to work to call upon Me, then "be it unto thee according to thy faith." For, indeed, these two things make up fervency in prayer: sense of need and hope of mercy, when a man has faith and hopes to increase his fervency. And it arises from that ground as well as the other (not that I ex-

clude the other, for it is a very great help, and that
which puts sticks on the fire, as it were, to make our
fervency all the more), I say, from a sense of our need,
when we consider seriously what lack we have, and
then add this: hope and faith. When these two shall set
you to work, this fervency is a fruit of faith. This is one
caution that must be remembered.

Another caution is this, that your fervency is joined
with sincerity. For a man may be fervent to obtain such
and such blessings as he may beg at God's hand. Very
earnestly, he may ask credit. He may ask to have guidance in such a business. He may ask wisdom to bring
such an enterprise to pass. He may ask health and continuance of life, but to what end? If it is that he may
bestow it upon his lusts, if it is that he may live more
deliciously, that he may be somebody in the world, that
he may have outward conveniences such as his flesh
desires, if this is all, here this fervency is not regarded.
Not that these things are excluded, for the Lord gives
us leave to seek our own comforts, and you may be
earnest and importunate, even for the comfort itself;
but yet all these, if they are not capable of a further
use, if that is not intended, but rather the abuse of
them, and in intent to use them another way, the Lord
does not heed it. It is no true fervency; and, therefore,
in Romans 12:11, it is the exhortation of the Apostle,
"be fervent in spirit, serving the Lord." When we, many
times, are fervent in serving ourselves, we are fervent to
ask such and such requests out of ends of our own, as
when a man desires able gifts, high gifts, to get glory
and wealth for himself, and not to serve his Master.
This is to ask the talent, not for the Master's use, but
for his own use.

Do you think the Lord will hear such prayers? Can you expect it at His hands? You shall see the contrary disposition in the saints. When they were earnest with the Lord for anything, they still expressed that to Him and said, "Lord, we do not desire this for ourselves, but for Thy glory, that we may use it for some good purpose."

When David was earnest for his life, when he was in sickness, and doubted his recovery, what argument did he use? "Lord," he said, "shalt Thou have glory from the grave?" It is as if he should say, "If Thou give me life, I will give it to Thee again. I will improve it and husband it to Thy advantage and not to my own."

And so Hannah, when she was earnest for a son, made this promise to the Lord: that he shall be for Him and His advantage. She dedicated him to His use and consecrated him to His service. So Jacob, when he was earnest with the Lord to give him meat, drink, and clothes, said, "Lord, if Thou do, I will give the tenth part to Thee again." I say, our fervency is rightly ordered when the heart is thus disposed in our fervency, in our importunity, when we we ask anything at the Lord's hands that our conscience tells us that, if we had it, we would bestow it upon the Lord. We would not abuse it, we would not spend it on our lusts. It should not be to serve ourselves but to serve the Lord. Then our fervency is rightly ordered.

4. *The next condition required is humility.* James 4:6, "The Lord gives grace to the humble;" and in 2 Chronicles 7:14, "If My people humble themselves, and call upon My name, then will I hear in heaven and grant their requests." And throughout the Scriptures,

you see that this is a condition that the Lord puts in everywhere. "He hath respect to the low estate," Isaiah 66:2. The Lord said, "All these things have My hands made," looking upon all the creatures, the whole frame of them. They are good, and I have respect unto them. But, said He, I do not regard all these in comparison of a humble heart. "To him will I look, that is of a humble and contrite spirit." When the Lord looks upon our prayers, if they do not come from a broken heart, they lack that condition that He looks for. He gives grace to the humble because such a man is little in his own eyes and fit to be exalted, fit to receive a mercy at God's hands.

You know, it is a rule that the Lord keeps for those who are humble and low. Such He exalts. Those who exalt themselves, He puts down. Now, when a man is little in His own eyes, that sense of his own unworthiness is a prevailing argument with Him. And, therefore, Genesis 3:2, Jacob uses that argument when he came to put up that petition to be delivered from Esau, "Lord, I am less than all Thy mercies." That is, take any of Thy mercies and put them in one end of the balance and me in the other, and I am less than it, and lighter than it. Take all the worth that is in me, it is not heavy enough for the least mercy.

Now, when he was thus humbled, and little, and vile in his own eyes, the Lord bestowed that mercy on him. He was now fit to receive it. When the Lord sent word by Nathan to David that he would build him a house forever (you see how he expressed himself), "he went into the house of the Lord and sat before Him and said, Lord, what am I, and what is my father's house?" It was as if he had said, "I was taken out of the dust. I was one of the lowest men of Israel, and a man of no account, of no worth, and yet Thou hast had respect unto me thus far, not only to make me King over Thy people, but to build my kingdom and my house, to make me a constant house forever."

I say, this sense of our own unworthiness makes us more fit to receive the mercy, to be exalted by receiving such a request as we put up to the Lord. And therefore He regards the prayer of the humble.

Moreover, God gives grace to the humble. That is, He shows favor to them when they come and ask anything at His hands, because a humble man will be ready to do whatever He wills. It is an expression used of David, in Acts 2:22, "he will do whatsoever I will." That may be said of every humble man. He is exceedingly pliable to the Lord's will. He is ready to do whatever he knows to be His pleasure. He resists Him in nothing. Now, when a man will do whatever God wills, the Lord will be ready to do whatever the man wills. He will be ready to say to him, as He said to the Canaanite woman, "be it to thee as thou wilt."

When a man, on the other hand, resists the Lord (as every proud man does, the text says), the Lord resists him. "The Lord resists the proud and gives grace to the humble." A resisting spirit causes the Lord to resist our prayers. And therefore it is that the Lord is ready to the humble man because he yields to the Lord in all things. When a man yields to the Lord (take that for a rule) in obeying God's commandments, God will yield to us in granting our petitions.

Besides, when the heart is humbled, broken, and contrite, it is an acceptable sacrifice to the Lord which wins it at His hands. He smells a sweet savor from such a sacrifice above all others. Yea, it is that which sets a high price upon every sacrifice that we offer. The best prayers, the best works, that do not proceed from a humble heart are not regarded by Him. He says, in Psalm 51, "Lord, if I offer sacrifice, Thou wilt not regard it, but the sacrifices of a contrite and humble spirit, those Thou will regard, and those sacrifices that proceed from it."

When we come to make a petition to the Lord (it was the manner in the old law not to come empty-handed), a proud person comes empty-handed. But a humble person comes with a sacrifice, and the best sacrifice, because he sacrifices himself and his own will. That is, he empties himself of himself. He opens a door to the Lord to come in and dwell with him, while a proud man bars Him out. Such a sacrifice the Lord is well-pleased with, and such a sacrifice speaks for one. It makes way for his requests, and therefore the Lord hearkens to it.

Last, the Lord is ready to hear those who are humble because, whatever they receive, they take it as grace and not as debt. Whereas a proud man, a man who has a good conceit of himself, a man who is lifted up in his own opinion, thinks it his due. He thinks there is some correlation between his works and the wages. You know what is said of the Pharisee in Luke 18, that the publican went away justified rather than he. Why so? Because the publican thought himself worthy of nothing. Therefore, in Ezekiel 36:31, when the Lord promises those great mercies to His people, He requires this condition of them, that they should acknowledge themselves worthy to be destroyed.

When a man has a sense of his own unworthiness,

and so comes to the Lord and asks it as of mere grace
and mercy, that is a great motive to prevail with Him,
for He is very careful of that. You know, in
Deuteronomy 8:11, how wary the Lord was in giving
this rule to them, "Take heed when thou comest into
the good land, think not to say with thyself, The Lord
hath done this for my own righteousness." He said,
"No, I have not done it for that, but for My covenant
which I made with Abraham, Isaac, and Jacob." That is,
for My own name's sake, for My mercy's sake, for the
covenant that I confirmed with them, that is the
covenant in Jesus Christ. It is for that reason I have
done it, and not for your own righteousness.

So you see that this is a condition the Lord will
have observed in our calling upon Him, that our hearts
are humbled, that a man be little and vile in his own
eyes, that he come with a broken and contrite heart,
pliable to Him in all things, ready to obey Him. When
the heart is disposed, He gives grace—that is, He shows
favor. He is ready to grant our requests.

5. *The next condition required in prayer is that we sanc-*
tify the Lord in our hearts. You know, when Nadab and
Abihu drew near unto Him with a common fire (when
they should have brought such fire as came from
heaven, holy fire), the Lord destroyed them, giving this
reason: "for I will be sanctified in those that draw near
to Me." When we come to call upon the Lord, we know
that we draw near to Him and, in such drawing near,
we must sanctify Him in our hearts. That is, we must
conceive Him to be as He is, most holy. Now, if the
Lord is most holy, if He who is unclean, impure, and
unholy shall come near Him, he does not sanctify the

Lord God. That is, he does not come to Him as a most holy God, but he looks upon Him as if He were a common person.

Therefore, whenever they came to offer a sacrifice in the old law, they were first purified. If any man was unclean and should offer a sacrifice, he was to be cut off from his people. Therefore, to sanctify the Lord in our hearts is to come with holy hearts, as in 1 Timothy 2:8. It is the charge that the Apostle gives there, "lift up pure hands without wrath or doubting." Lift up pure hearts and innocent hands, without wrath or doubting.

You will say unto me, "What is this holiness?"

Beloved, it is nothing but a sequestering or separating of anything from a common use, and appropriating it to God alone. That is holiness. You know, whatever was holy to the Lord in the temple, or otherwise, whether it was holy vessels or holy men, as the priests, it was separated from all other uses and made particular to Him and to His service.

Now, the heart of a man is holy, then, when it is withdrawn from all other things and made particular to the Lord alone. As a chaste wife is to her husband, whose affections are bestowed upon him and no other person, so when the heart is to the Lord alone, when all the affections are intent upon Him, and bestowed upon Him and no one else, this is to have the heart holy to Him. So that, he who will have an eye upon credit, upon vain glory, upon wealth, upon his lusts, upon anything besides the Lord, so that his heart is wedded to it, so that he bestows any part of that conjugal affection upon it that should be wholly the Lord's, this man is an unholy man. His heart is not holy, for it is not sequestered from other things and consecrated to Him alone. That is what it is to be holy.

And as the heart must be holy, so must the prayer be holy. When a man prays to the Lord with respect unto Him, and has an eye upon Him, and nothing else comes in to take away part of this prayer. If worldly and carnal thoughts come in and set you on work to pray, now these have a portion and interest in your prayers. They make your prayers profane and common; they are not peculiar to the Lord. They are unholy.

So that is the holiness, then, in seeking the Lord— when we are knit and wedded to Him; when one takes this resolution to himself: "I am the Lord's servant, and Him will I serve. I am not the servant of man, nor of any creature. I am married to the Lord, and His will I be alone. I will withdraw my heart from all other things."

So, likewise, when a man prays so that his soul is intent upon the Lord, and upon nothing else besides, when the whole stream of his affections are carried to Him, this is to seek Him in holiness. This is to sanctify the Lord in our hearts.

Last, if there is any conscience of sin (that phrase I find used in Hebrews 10), that is, if there is an evil conscience, if a man is conscious to himself of any sin that is unrepented of, such a man cannot pray. That makes him unholy. If there is any sinful lust yet living in him that is unmortified in him, which is not washed away, such a man is unholy. Yea, my beloved, the saints themselves, when they sin against God, as you heard heretofore, are suspended from the covenant. Though they are within the covenant, yet they are suspended from receiving the benefit by it that they might otherwise have. Until that sin is washed away, they are not holy.

If a priest, or one who was holy, touched any un-clean thing, he remained unholy until he was washed, though otherwise he was holy habitually, wholly dedi-cated to God's service. So it may be with those who are within the covenant. Though you are a holy man, yet if you touch pitch, that is, if your heart is polluted with any sin of one kind or another, as long as that remains, you are unholy. If you come now and seek the Lord, you know what the judgment was in the old law, such a man was to be cut off from his people. And, therefore, you shall find, this was the constant practice of the saints. When they sought the Lord for any special mercy, they began with taking pains with their own hearts, with humbling themselves for their own sins and the sins of the people. This is what Daniel, Ezra, and David did in their prayers (I do not need to give you specific instances). And, indeed, so should we al-ways when we come with any request and petition to the Lord.

First, let a man examine his heart and life dili-gently. Look back to all your former ways. Consider, and go through all the particulars. See if there is any-thing amiss, if there is any tincture of uncleanness yet lying upon you that is not yet washed away; if there is any pollution or defilement of flesh or spirit, and know that it is but labor lost. It is but a provoking of the Lord to come as a man unprepared, to come near to Him unless you are cleansed.

QUESTION. "But," you will say, "how shall we be cleansed?"

ANSWER. I answer, you are cleansed by renewing your repentance and sprinkling the blood of Christ. It is when a man humbles himself for his sin and enters into covenant with God not to return unto it, when he makes his heart perfect and sincere with the Lord in that particular.

And second, it is when he shall believe that it is for-given through Christ, when he is sprinkled in His blood to wash it away. Though your sin is great, yet this will make you pure. Now you are washed, as we have it in 1 Corinthians 6:9, "Now you are washed, now you are sanctified, now you are justified." Therefore, let a man not be discouraged in this case. For, I confess, there is nothing that gives such a check to our prayers, that gives so many stabs to them (as it were), that hin-ders us in our duty, as the conscience of sin, when a man remembers such and such a sin he has commit-ted. Yet do not be discouraged, for the blood of Jesus Christ is able to wash them away.

Though a man's face is very foul, you know that a basin of clear water will wash it clean, and all the filth is gone. Now the blood of Christ is more effectual to wrench your conscience, and to cleanse it from dead works, to take away both the guilt of sin and the power and stain of it. And, therefore, if you have any sin, la-bor to be washed from it that you may then come to the Lord having your heart sprinkled from an evil con-science and your body washed in pure water, as we read in Hebrews 10:22: "Let us draw near in assurance of faith." But how? "Having our hearts sprinkled from an evil conscience." It is as if he should say, "Otherwise, your drawing near will be to no purpose. You shall only provoke the Lord in drawing near unless you are thus sprinkled, and thus washed, and thus purified."

OBJECTION. Aye, but you will say to me, if this is required, who shall be heard in his prayers? For who can say that his heart is pure and his hands are innocent? And, if this is required that we must lift up holy and pure hearts or else we shall not be accepted, what comfort shall we have in calling upon the Lord at any time?

ANSWER. To this I answer, to have a pure heart is not to be free from sin and daily failings (for, indeed, none would have a pure heart), but pureness of heart, holiness of heart, is to have our hearts sprinkled from an evil conscience and to have our bodies washed with pure water. That is, to be purified before the Lord is nothing else but to have such a habitual disposition which makes a man ready to wash himself, though he is still spotted with sin. So that this is the disposition of a holy man: If a man draws near to the Lord with a pure heart, though he is still spotted, polluted, and defiled, yet he has a habitual disposition. He has a principle within; he has a new nature within that is still working out that impurity and washing it away. Though he is still opposed, assaulted, tempted, and sometimes foiled, yet he still resists and fights against it, as the Israelites had a charge never to make peace with Amalek. Such a disposition is in such a man, he never makes peace with any sin. Though he is led captive by it sometimes, yet he does not yield to that captivity. This is to have a pure heart. Though his heart is defiled sometimes, as a vessel will be foul, yet he washes and rinses his heart. He never allows it to be muddy, unclean, and in a filthy disposition, but he has a fountain, a spring of grace within that will work out all impurity like a spring works out mud.

He who thus purifies himself, though the fountain
is muddy, though there are many injections, many
temptations, many lusts and sins, yet, if he is purified
himself, so that he will allow no sin to mingle with his
heart—to rest, abide, dwell, lie and continue there—
such a man has a pure heart. We say that is pure that is
full of itself and will have no other thing mingled with
it. Such a thing is pure, as pure oil is nothing else but
oil. Now he who has a pure heart is not he who has
simply nothing else, who has no sin mingled, who has
no dross mingled with his wine, but he who does not
allow it to rest there. But, as oil and water, when you
jumble them together (as you know, when they are
shaken together, they mingle), yet the oil works out
and purifies itself. It will not allow itself to abide with
the water.

In the same way, a man who is regenerate, a man
who is born of God, has a seed remaining in him.
Though he sins, yet he cannot sin, says the Apostle—
that is, he does not agree, he does not mingle with that
sin. It has no rest in his heart, but he works it out in a
passion. When he is shaken, when he is transported,
when he is not himself, there may be a mixture, and
the fountain and the spring may be muddy, yet let him
come to himself and he will work it out. That is to have
a pure heart.

So that a man who is thus affected may come to the
throne of grace with boldness and not be discouraged.
What, though your sins are many, and very great and
often repeated, yet, if you find in yourself such a disposition of purity and holiness to still cleanse yourself,
though you are still polluted and defiled, I can assure
you that your heart is pure. You may go with confi-

dence to the throne of grace.

QUESTION. But now you will say this to me. Why, may not any carnal man say as much? He sins against God, and comes and asks mercy. He comes and cries for forgiveness and faith. He will sin no more, and yet he sins again the next day and adds drunkenness to thirst. That is, his sins and his repentance run in a circle, like drunkenness and thirst. How shall we distinguish between these two, that purifying disposition in saints, and those vanishing purposes that carnal men may have who never had any experience of the work of grace, of that purity of heart that we have been speaking of?

ANSWER. To this I answer, briefly, you shall know the difference by this: When a godly man falls into sin and is defiled with it, he washes himself from day to day. You shall always find this, that he gets ground of the sin, of the lust that manifests itself in any actual transgression. It does not gather strength, it loses strength.

In a carnal man, it is quite the contrary. His sin still increases and intends the habit. The lust grows stronger and stronger. It gets ground of him, and those good things that he has are more and more worn out. And so they grow worse and worse from day to day. That is the property of an evil man, of unregeneracy wherever. It is apt to grow worse and worse. And the more falls they have, the more sin gets ground and the more they lose. But it is not so with the holy man. The more he falls, the more strength he gathers. He is the more holy for it. The more wary and watchful, and the more emptied he is of himself, the more he draws nearer to the Lord, and the more he is enflamed with love to Him. He is strengthened in faith, in repentance, and in every grace. So that here the rule now does not hold true, that acts increase habits, but rather the contrary. Acts lessen the habits, which is a paradox in philosophy, but here it is so.

If you ask, "How can it be?" I answer, in its own nature, every act intends the habit as well in a godly man as another man, but it comes to pass by accident. As we say, because the grace in him is stirred up by those foils, slips, falls, and infirmities, to which he is subject. I say, grace is stirred up in him more and me, and receives more vigor and strength. As we say of true valor, it is increased more by opposition. So it comes to pass that the more the child of God falls into sin, the more grace is intended.

Satan gets less ground, like Hezekiah, when he fell into pride. The pride of his heart was lessened more by it than when he showed his treasure to the ambassador of the King of Babel. He did not know before this the pride of his heart, that sin, that fall manifested his corruption which he did not see before.

So that, when the heart is sincere, when it is pure, when there is a right principle within, grace is set more to work to resist sin. When David had numbered the people, that made him more humble. And, therefore, the Lord showed him more mercy afterwards than ever He did before. He showed him where the temple should be built and used him in that work, and never showed him much mercy and kindness before. So it is with the saints. Their hearts are never better, nor in a more holy temper, nor more fearful to offend and in a more gracious disposition than after their falls.

Therefore, consider that, so that you are not deceived, so that you may distinguish between this falling into sin and washing yourselves, and that relapse to which evil men are subject. Keep that for a rule, that wherever there is true grace, it stirs itself still more and more as it finds more resistance, even as the wind and the water and the fire does.

You know that, when water finds a stop, it becomes more violent, and so does the wind. Grace is of the same nature. Where it finds a stop, where it finds resistance, it grows more stronger and intent. The heathens had a little glimpse of this truth when they said of virtue that it grows more fresh and vigorous by being wounded. That is true of grace and holiness. True virtue, the more it is opposed, the more it grows. Even as you see in opposition in the disputes of scholars, and all kind of contention in law, or anything else. The stronger the objection is, where there is ability in the party, it produces new motions and new answers, and puts them more to it. So these assaults and temptations, when there is truth of heart within, it draws out more holiness to God, and more strength. It multiplies the graces of God within. So, then, the graces receive increase the more they are exercised and intended, and sinful lusts decrease the more the mind is emptied forth.

That chaff and the dross that is in us is more winnowed out; and the heart is more cleansed from it. So much shall I serve for this, that whoever will come to the Lord in prayer must sanctify Him in his heart. That is, he must come with a holy and a pure heart. We have showed what this holiness and purity is, wherein it consists, and likewise how the objection is answered that might deceive us. So much for that property.

I must add another. You shall find it in Philippians 4:6. Whenever you come to make your requests to the Lord, this is another condition that He requires: to be thankful for the mercies you have already received. He says, "In all things, let your requests be made known to the Lord with thanksgiving." It is as if He should say, "Take heed of this that, whenever you come to put up any petition to the Lord, you do not forget the duty of thankfulness; but still, when you come to ask anything that you want, remember that you give thanks for what you have."

Beloved, this condition must not be omitted. You see that the Lord Himself puts it in very carefully, "Let your requests be made known with prayer, and supplication, and thanksgiving." There are many reasons why our petitions and requests should be accompanied with thanksgiving to the Lord. For is it not a reason when you come to ask something for yourselves, that you should do that also which is acceptable to God? Will a man serve himself altogether, to come merely to ask the thing He wants? This a man may do out of love to himself, out of respect to himself. But you must remember to do something that is pleasing and acceptable to the Lord.

Therefore, you shall find in the old law that they were commanded still to come with peace offerings, that is, offerings that expressed thankfulness, whenever they had any special request for the Lord. You shall find that to be the manner in Leviticus and other places, that such a man as came to request anything at the Lord's hands might not come empty-handed. And what should he bring with him? A peace offering. What was that? Thankfulness for the peace he had enjoyed. That was a peace offering, for peace is a general word comprehending all kinds of mercies. For what is our heath, but peace of our humors within? What is our cheerfulness and joy, but the peace of conscience within? All the comfort we have in our name and estate is peace in the particular. So, I say, whenever you come with a petition, do not forget to come with a peace offering. That is, do not forget to come with thanksgiving to the Lord for that which you have received.

Do something that is acceptable to Him, as well as seek for that which is useful for yourself. Beloved, there is great reason for it; because, if a man is pouring over his wants still, if it is in his mind, when he comes to call upon God, it will indispose him for spiritual performance. It will beget murmuring, sourness, and discontent. It will embitter his spirit.

When a man remembers many mercies he has received, when he makes a catalogue of them, and ennumerates them, it sweetens his spirit. It makes him more gracious. It acts those graces that are in him. It draws him nearer to the Lord. It quickens him; it makes him more contented with the condition he is in. Whereas, on the other side, forgetfulness of mercies, when a man is only intent upon his portion to have the thing done, he breaks in many times into that dullness of disposition that we find in children who, when they cannot have all that they would, throw away what they have.

So that is our fault, many times. When we come and seek the Lord for anything that we need, we are so intent upon that that we forget all the mercies we have received, as if they were nothing. The Lord would not have it so, but will have us remember what we receive, that we may be content to want, that our hearts may be brought to patience and contentment under the cross, and to want what it shall please Him, for a time, to deny us. This is just as Job reasoned, "I have received good from the Lord's hands, and shall I not receive ill?" This was his answer to his wife.

So, if a good man is thankful for mercies, it will make him ready to do so. It will make him content with the present want, for he looks to that which he has in his hand. When a man says this to himself: "Thus and thus much good I have received at the Lord's hands. So what if I lack such a thing? So what if I am pressed with such an affliction and calamity? I will be content to bear it."

The Lord looks for this. Expostulating with Him and murmuring against Him is not a meek manner of asking things at His hands. But, when a man asks that way, he is content to be denied if God's good pleasure is such. Now, thankfulness for mercy makes us ready to be so affected, to be willing to be denied, to be content to resign ourselves to the Lord. And therefore, He will have thankfulness to go with it whenever we come to ask anything at His hands. Observe that whenever you come to seek the Lord, you are thankful for the mercies you have had. Remember them, for it is a great means to prevail in our requests. Thankfulness, as it were, is the incense that perfumes your petitions, that makes them acceptable and prevalent with the Lord, so much the sooner. Prayer goes up without incense when we offer up our petitions without thankfulness because that is a sacrifice. As you know, it is called the "salves of our lips," and ever, when you join thankful-

ness with your petitions, it is like a sacrifice mingled
with it that helps to prevail for you.

The next condition is, and it must not be forgotten
of all the rest, that we come to the Lord in the name of
Jesus Christ. "This is a thing commonly known," you
will say. "Who does not know that, unless we come in
the name of Christ, no petition can be acceptable?"

Beloved, I say to you in that case, as the Apostle
James speaks in James 4, where he gives this rule that
we should say "if the Lord wills, we will do such and
such a thing tomorrow," and when the answer would
be ready, who does not know this? He says, "If you
know the will of the Lord and do not do it, your judgment will be greater." This is a thing we are exceedingly ready to forget, or we are ready to do it in a formal and customary manner, but to do it in good
earnest, as we ought to do it, therein commonly we
come short. You know how great a sin it was in the old
law to offer without a priest. In Leviticus 17, it is said
that if any man brought his sacrifice, though it was the
best sacrifice, and the most choice, yet if he did not
bring it to the priest and to the altar, but slew his sacrifice elsewhere without a priest, such a man was guilty
of blood and was to be cut off from his people. That is,
he was to be cut off by the priest, by excommunication,
and later by the civil magistrate.

You know, it was Uzziah's fault to offer incense
when it was proper for the priest to do it. We commit
the same sin when we come to the Lord and think that,
because we have repented and prayed fervently, because we think that our hearts and spirits are in a good
disposition, because we know no sin of which we are
conscious, for this cause we think that we shall be

heard. It is true, the Lord requires these qualifications in the party when he prays, but take heed of thinking to be heard for this. This is to offer without a priest.

You must come to the Lord and say to Him, "Lord, I confess, notwithstanding all this, I am unworthy. I have nothing in me that should make Thou regard me. It cannot be that either I or my prayer should be acceptable, but I beseech Thee, take them at the hands of Christ, our High Priest. He who is entered into the veil; He who takes the prayers of the saints and mingles them with sweet odors." When a man can really do this with dependence upon Christ, and come boldly in His name, that is to offer a sacrifice to Him. And this we must carefully remember.

Therefore, we see an excellent expression of this in Leviticus 5:12, where this is made clear to you that it is not any excellency in the person, nor any fervency in the prayer, nor any purity or holiness that is found in him. Nothing that comes from man causes his prayer to be acceptable, but it is the priest! In that text, from verses 8-11, you shall find there that the law was that he who came to sacrifice must bring a sheep or a she-goat. But, if he were not so rich as to do so, he was able to bring two turtle doves. If he was not able to do even that, the text says that "he shall bring the tenth part of an epha of fine flour," a very small thing. He says, "Let him give this to the priest, and he shall make an atonement for him, and his sin shall be forgiven."

From this I observe that it is not the goodness of the sacrifice, the price, nor the choiceness, nor the excellency of that, when they came with a thousand rams, and so many sheep and bullocks (as you read of many great sacrifices that were offered by the kings), yet the

tenth part of an epha of fine flour, which was exceedingly little. This prevailed fully as much. It shows evidently that it is not in the sacrifice. But the poorest,
and the smallest and meanest sacrifice that will prevail
with God as well as the richest and the greatest. What is
the reason? So, he says, it is the priest that must offer
it. He makes it acceptable. So, in this case, let the sacrifice be never so mean. Yet, if it is Christ that offers the
sacrifice, if it is commended to the priest and he offers
it, the Lord will accept it.

You shall find that rule in Leviticus 5:11, "He that
brings a sacrifice (this caution was given) he must put
no incense to it, neither oil." But, should the sacrifice
be offered without incense? No, you shall find in
Leviticus 16 that always the priest, when he entered
into the holy of holies, burned incense, "that the cloud
of that incense might cover the mercy seat." The meaning is this, when any man comes to offer a prayer to the
Lord, he can put no incense to it. The priest only may
put in incense—that is, Jesus Christ only may offer the
sacrifice wherein the Lord smells a savor of rest. For
the Lord expresses Himself in this manner, as if He
were disquieted for sin and can take no rest. Now,
when Jesus Christ offers a sacrifice He smells a savor of
rest, because it comes from Him in whom he is well-
pleased. So, I say, we must be careful that we remember to come in the name of Christ.

"But," you will say, "every man does so, and how
shall we know it?"

You shall know it by this: If you have boldness and
confidence, this is an argument that you do not look
upon yourselves, but upon Christ. When a man is so
exceedingly timorous, doubting, and fearful that he

dares not come to the throne of grace—or, if he does, yet he makes a great question whether he shall be heard or not—this is too much looking at himself. Here, the High Priest is forgotten.

If you come in His name, there is enough to carry you out. It will breed boldness in you, it will breed confidence. If you come in the name of Christ, and offer up your prayers through Him, it will cause you, in every petition you put up, to think of yourself as being so beholding to Christ that you will be ready to say in your heart, whenever any petition is granted to you, "I may thank Jesus Christ for this."

When a man shall be so much put upon his score, it will make him so indebted to the Lord Jesus for his remitted sin and this petition that He has granted that his heart shall be more enlarged to thankfulness. When he is able to consider the benefit of redemption, he will be ready to say to himself, "If Jesus Christ had not died, if I did not have such a High Priest who has entered into the very heavens." This is what the Apostle said in Hebrews 9:10: If Christ had not made intercession for me, I would have lost this benefit. I would never have come to put up a prayer to the Lord—or, if I had, it would not have been heard."

QUESTION. "But," you will say to me, "if we are heard for Christ, then, though a man is sinful, and though he has none of the precedent conditions, though he does not have that holiness that is required, if the Priest makes him acceptable, why may he not hope as well as the most holy man?"

ANSWER. I answer briefly, though the Priest gives all acceptance to the sacrifice and our prayers are ac-

cepted through Him, yet that is not all. There are two
things required besides. One is that the person who
brings the sacrifice be clean. No impure person was to
bring a sacrifice. Second, that the sacrifice be without
blemish. He who has a male and brings a female is
cursed.

So this is required: The person must be righteous
and the prayer must be fervent. Such as is indicted by
the help of God's Spirit, that it may be a sacrifice fit for
the Lord. But now, what we have from Christ is this:
though the person is so, and the prayer thus qualified,
and has those forenoted conditions in it, yet it is not
acceptable without the Priest.

Therefore, this should encourage you when you
consider the glorious God—His holiness, that great
distance between Him and you. Then, on the other
side, think of yourselves, how vile and sinful you are,
how unfit to come and put up your requests to Him.
Now, when you think of a Mediator, of a High Priest
who is entered into heaven, who is gone there and sits
at the right hand of Majesty making intercession for
you, when you consider there is one High Priest who is
able to prevail, not like the priests in the law but one
who is over the house of God, one who is the very Son,
who is not entered in through the blood of bulls and
goats, but with His own blood—when out of this you
shall receive confidence, and come near Him with
boldness, this is to make use of Christ and to offer sacrifice in Him.

There is no more remaining now but that, when
you have considered all the conditions mentioned and
fitted your prayers according to them, you be confident and expect much. When you have prayed, you

may say, "Lord, I expect now the granting of them. Thou cannot deny them now, Lord. I will wait." And this is our fault. When we have prayed and the thing does not come immediately, we are ready to give over. We are not willing to wait. Beloved, that is one thing especially to be remembered. We must so far magnify our prayers, we must set a price upon them so far, and so esteem and think them of that worth, that they will bring the thing to pass.

If a man takes a drug, a medicine, or an herb, and uses it to a wound or a disease, once, twice, or three times and sees it does no good, he will lay it aside and take another medicine. He says, "I have tried it, and it will do me no good." So a man does with his prayers. He says, "I have sought the Lord. I have prayed for this thing twice or three times, and it is not granted to me." And, therefore, he is ready to lay it aside as if it were not effectual, and to take another means. This neglect of prayer is not to know the force of the medicine.

You must know, therefore, of what efficacy prayer is and trust it. Do not give over (for it is effectual to bring the thing to pass) and make no haste, but stay and wait. It was Sarah's fault when Abraham and she sought the Lord for a son that she made too much haste to give Hagar to Abraham. They should have waited until the Lord had done it His own way.

So it was with Rebecca. There was a promise and, no doubt, Jacob and she prayed for the fulfilling of that promise. But she made too much haste. She took a wrong way to get the blessing by lying. This was not waiting, but a stepping out to another means because they thought prayer and dependence upon God would not do it.

In the same way, Saul would not wait upon God but offered sacrifice. This was to make haste. And so it is, when a man is discouraged. David was ready to give up when the thing was not immediately granted. He fell to a desperate complaint, saying, "One day I shall fall by the hands of Saul. "

Take heed of this, and when we offer our prayers thusly, learn to know what they are. Learn to trust them and to depend and wait upon God. Say certainly, "I shall not be denied. The thing shall surely be granted."

So much for this time and this text.

FINIS

The
Spirit
of
Prayer

or

*A Discourse wherein the Nature of Prayer
is opened; the kinds of Prayer are handled;
and the right manner of Praying discovered.
Several cases about this duty are resolved
from Ephesians 6:18.*

by

Nathanael Vincent
Minister of the Gospel

Introduction

"Praying always with all prayer and supplication in the Spirit, and watching thereunto with all perseverance and supplication for all saints." (Ephesians 6:18)

The Apostle, looking upon the Ephesians as militant saints, and fighting not against flesh and blood but against the principalities and powers of darkness, instructs them, towards the latter end of this chapter, how they might become more than conquerors. To this end he tells them, first of all, where their strength lies. They must "be strong in the Lord and in the power of His might," verse 10, and then he gives them a complete armor which, being put on and the several pieces of it skillfully used, will frustrate the wiles of Satan and enable them to withstand in the evil day and, having done all, to stand.

They must be girded about with the girdle of truth. By error, Satan has great advantage. How many, like children, are tossed to and fro by every wind of doctrine? But a judgment rightly informed and well-settled, that buys the truth and will by no means sell it, has a great influence upon a Christian's steadfastness and growth in grace.

They must have on the breastplate of righteousness. They must be righteous in heart, righteous in sincerity. A conscience purged from dead works is a better defense than a wall of brass. Satan cannot so easily disquiet them that are sincere, neither is he able to corrupt them. Their holiness being true, sin is hated, the allurements unto sin are condemned, and God is followed hard after.

Their feet must be shod with the preparation of the gospel of peace. They must be encouraged, by that peace which the gospel publishes, to run the way of God's commandments. And though those ways are never so difficult and unpleasant to flesh and blood, they must hold fast the profession of their faith, depart from evil, and go in the path that is called holy—even though, by thus doing, they never-so-much expose and make themselves a prey.

Above all, they must take the shield of faith whereby they may quench the fiery darts of the wicked. Satan's temptations are darts. He designs our wounding, our pain, our death, in shooting them. And these darts may well be called fiery. They are shot from hell, and a hell in the conscience they make if they are not quenched. But faith is a shield to repel and beat them back. Faith makes application of the righteousness and strength of Christ and, by this means, not only former wounds are assuaged and healed but the soul is more secured for the future.

The helmet of salvation must cover their heads in this day of battle with evil angels. A lively hope of salvation is very encouraging both unto patient continuance in well-doing, and also unto suffering for the sake of righteousness.

The Apostle tells them that the sword of the Spirit, which is the Word of God, must be made use of. If this Word is understood, believed, thought on, loved, and stood in awe of, and if it thus abides in us, we shall be strong and overcome the evil one.

These are the pieces of the armor of God. But in this combat with the devil, is there not need of auxiliary forces? Certainly there is a necessity of succour from heaven. The Captain, therefore, of our salvation must be looked unto, and divine aid continually implored and begged for. By prayer, we have power with God and power against our spiritual enemies. No wonder that the Apostle enjoins "praying always with all prayer and supplication in the Spirit."

The text may be divided into these parts:

A duty commanded, in the performance of which lies safety, and that duty is praying.

The extent of this duty—it must be always, and it must be with all prayer.

The due qualifications of this duty, which are these following:

First, it must be in the Spirit.

Second, it must be with watching.

Third, it must be with all perseverance.

Fourth, it must be with a public spirit. We must pray for all saints, as well as for ourselves, since they are engaged in the same war.

That these words may be better understood, I shall answer these several questions:

QUESTION. First, is there any difference between prayer and supplication?

ANSWER. I answer, the word which is translated prayer intimates that we have to do with God in prayer. To Him we are to direct our petitions as a Hearer and as a Helper. The word which is translated supplication intimates that there must be an acknowledgment of

our own indigency and wants and a looking to the all-
sufficient Lord for supply.

QUESTION. What is meant by praying always?

ANSWER. I answer, the Greek phrase which the
Holy Ghost uses signifies to pray every opportunity that
is offered. This text gives no encouragement unto the
fond sect of the Euchites, who thought that prayer was
to be their whole business: No, no! There are other
duties that God calls for which this duty of prayer must
not jostle out. But all those opportunities that are af-
forded for prayer must be heedfully observed, joyfully
laid hold on, and diligently improved. This is to pray
always. It is said of Mephibosheth that he ate always or
continually at the king's table, 2 Samuel 9:13. What?
Shall we from hence infer that he spent day and night
in nothing but eating? No such matter. But when the
season of mealtime came he was present. So to pray
always is to pray whenever prayer is seasonable.

QUESTION. What is meant by "all prayer"?

ANSWER. Bullinger refers this to the intention of
the mind, saying that, in this duty, there must be all
possible devotion, intentness, and fervency of heart.
But Musculus understands prayer of every sort; and
indeed all kinds of prayer which God has appointed
are needful, and the Lord is ready, by the communications of His grace, to encourage to the practice
of this duty in the full extent and latitude of it.

QUESTION. What are we to understand by prayer
in the Spirit?

ANSWER. Some refer this clause to the thing

asked, as if we should slight all worldly enjoyments and ask only for those blessings that are spiritual. It is confessed that spiritual blessings are to be most prized and are to be begged with the greatest importunity. Yet temporal mercies may also with submission be desired. Daily bread we are allowed to ask for. And that bread is sweetest and most blessed that is the fruit of prayer. Others observe rightly that this passage, praying in the spirit, may have relation both to the Spirit of God and the spirit of him who prays.

It may have relating unto the Spirit of God. The Holy Ghost makes intercession for believers according to the will of God; He helps their infirmities who, of themselves, know not what to pray for as they ought, Romans 8:26-27.

It may have relation unto the spirit of him that prays. Prayer must be the offspring of the heart or else it will not be of any value or efficacy. The spirit of a man must understand what, and the worth of what is prayed for, and the affections must be stirred in order to the attainment of it.

QUESTION. What are we to understand by watching unto prayer with all perseverance?

ANSWER. We must watch over our hearts, and watch for God, and this must be with continuance. Unless we continue to watch and pray, we may quickly enter and fall into temptation. And since all militant saints are in danger as well as awe, and stand in so near relation to Christ and to us, we should be much concerned for them, so as to desire their safety and welfare as our own.

There are six doctrines these words afford us:
1. A Christian's security lies very much in praying always.
2. All prayer is of concernment to be used.
3. Prayer, when rightly performed, is supplication in the spirit.
4. In prayer watching is a necessary ingredient.
5. We must persevere if we would speed in prayer.
6. Our spirits must be so public as to supplicate for all the saints as well as for ourselves.

Doctrine 1

Praying Always

I begin with the first of these doctrines, that a Christian's security lies very much in praying always. Although he is armed from head to foot with the armor of God, yet if any in the world is armor-proof he is not safe without prayer. Saints in Scripture have looked upon the throne of grace as their asylum and sanctuary and have come there for refuge and strength in their troubles and temptations. When David perceived the deceit and hatred of his adversaries who fought against him without cause, he said it was his course, and truly it was a wise one, to give himself to prayer, Psalm 109:4. When his soul was among lions, and he dwelt among those that were set on fire, he then cried unto God who performed all things for him, Psalm 57:2. When the Apostle Paul was buffeted by the messenger of Satan, he sought the Lord three times that it might depart from him, and received this answer, "My grace is sufficient for thee," 2 Corinthians 7:7-9. Nay, the very Captain of our Salvation, Christ Himself, not only used the Word of God in temptation, and overcame the devil by Scripture weapons, but also was wonderfully fervent in prayer. "In the days of his flesh he offered up prayers and supplications with strong crying and tears, unto Him that was able to save Him from death, and was heard in that He feared," Hebrews 5:7.

I shall speak unto this doctrine in the following order: first, give you a definition of prayer that you may know what it is; second, inform you what it is to pray always; third, show you why a Christian's security lies in prayer; fourth, give you some reasons why he should be always praying. And last, make application.

I. A definition of prayer. An old author gives this description, "Prayer is an ascension of the mind unto God, and asking those things which are convenient from Him." The mind must ascend as well as the voice, and both must be directed unto God alone. And those things only must be desired which the wise and gracious God sees convenient. Aquinus defines prayer as "an act of the practical understanding, explaining the desire of the will, and requesting something from another," which, being applied unto God, amounts to this much, that both the mind and will act in prayer. The mind makes known what the will desires. "Lord, all my desire is before Thee, and my groaning is not hid from Thee," Psalm 38:9. And then, likewise, there is an earnest craving to have this desire satisfied. "O satisfy us early with Thy mercy, that we may rejoice and be glad all our days," Psalm 90:14.

But a more full definition of prayer is this: Prayer is a duty performed unto God by sensible and believing souls in which they ask for things according to His will in the name of Christ, with thanksgiving for what has already been received. This definition I shall take in pieces, and explain the parts of it.

1. *Prayer is a duty.* It is part of that homage and worship which we owe to God. This is evident by the light of nature (The heathen mariners "cried unto the

Lord" for preservation in a storm, Jonah 1), but it is more evident by Scripture light that commands to pray are frequent. And he "that does restrain prayer, casts off the fear of God, and says unto the Almighty, Depart from me," Job 21:14-15. Prayer is a duty, for we are obliged to it by a precept, and that precept is for our profit. We need help from heaven, and our wants that are of greatest concernment to be supplied can be supplied by none but by Him who is all-sufficient. And when we cry to Him we give Him glory, for it argues that we believe His power and mercy which prove Him abler and ready to succour and relieve us.

2. *Prayer is to be performed unto God, and to Him only.* "Thou shalt worship the Lord thy God, and Him only shalt thou serve," Matthew 4:19. "Unto Thee, my God and my King, will I pray. I will direct my prayer unto Thee, and will look up," Psalm 5:2-3. God's hand is not shortened that it cannot save, neither is His ear heavy that it cannot hear. He is able to do not only to the uttermost of our desires, but "exceeding abundantly above all that we can either ask or think," Ephesians 3:20. The Papists dangerously corrupt holy worship by their sinful prayers to angels and saints, and especially to the Virgin Mary. Cardinal Bonaventure has blotted out the name of "Lord" in the book of the Psalms and put in the name of "Lady," and teaches Christians to ask the same things of the Virgin Mary which David asked for at the hands of God Himself. Under the Old Testament, we find that believers directed their supplications to God Himself and found Him ready to hear and save. Under the gospel, where the manifestation and communication of His grace are more full and

plenteous, is there need to go to any other? No, no, our God can supply our needs according to his riches in glory by Christ Jesus, Philippians 4:19.

3. *Those who pray must be sensible.* Ignorance, unbelief, and hardness of heart make the words of prayer a mockery and abomination. They who pray, therefore, must be sensible of their sins, of their needs, of their unworthiness to have those needs supplied. Finally, they must be sensible that none can help them but the God they are praying to.

1.) They must be sensible of their sins. "I acknowledge my iniquities," says David, and my sins testify against us. For "our transgressions are with us, and as for our iniquities we know them," Isaiah 59:12. Sin must be acknowledged with shame and sorrow, else it will separate between God and us and prove to be a cloud through which our prayers will never pass. There must be such a sense of sin as implies a hatred and weariness of it. For if the heart, out of love and liking of it, has a regard to sin, God's ear will be deaf and His mercies restrained. "If I regard iniquity in my heart, the Lord will not hear my prayer," Psalm 71:18.

2.) They who pray must be sensible of their needs. All the posterity of Adam are needy, however rich and full they imagine themselves to be. The first man, being a public person, had the whole stock in his own hand and, having lost it, has beggared his whole progeny. We are all come short of the glory of God, as descended from Adam. We are flesh, and in our flesh "dwelleth no good thing." This must be understood and believed. Poverty of spirit Christ commends, and pronounces those that are thus poor "blessed,"

Matthew 5:3. For they who perceive that they are wretched, miserable, empty, and naked will cry the louder to the Lord for gold tried in the fire to enrich them, and white raiment that they may be clothed. The poor man who is ready to starve for hunger, how he cries out "Bread, for the Lord's sake, bread," for he sees his need of it. The condemned malefactor roars out for a pardon because he sees his life must quickly go without it. And were we but better acquainted with our wants, oh, what strong cries would come from us that sin might be forgiven, that grace might be wrought, that peace might be spoken, that spiritual maladies might be healed! We all need these things as much, and more, than the hungry stand need of bread.

    3.) They who pray must be sensible of their unworthiness to have their need supplied. Paul cried out that he was less than the least of all saints. Jacob cried out that he was less than the least of mercies. Job says, "Behold I am vile, and I abhor myself." We cannot lay claim to anything as our due but wrath and the curse. Whatever God bestows, it must be reckoned as given, not of debt but of pure and free grace, Romans 4. Daniel in prayer disclaims all merit in his righteousness, acknowledges that confusion of face belonged to him and to Israel because of their rebellions and says expressly, "We do not present or supplications to Thee for our righteousness, but for Thy great mercies," Daniel 9:18. We may beg indeed for the greatest mercies, and the greater, the surer we are to speed—for God is most liberal of the greatest—but at the same time we must be sensible that the least mercy is too good for such evil ones as we are.

4.) They that pray must be sensible that none can help them but the God they are praying to. "Truly in vain is salvation hoped for from the hills and multitude of mountains, (the firmest things on earth will fail and deceive our hopes) truly in the Lord our God is the salvation of Israel," Jeremiah 3:23. Therefore, David lays this charge upon his soul—to wait only upon God, and to have all its expectation from Him. God will be seriously sought when we are under the power of this conviction, that no other helper can be found.

5.) It follows in the definition that those who pray must be believing souls. Faith is a grace that is required in all their duties. If this is wanting, God will not be honored by our duties, nor ourselves advantaged. Though we hear never so often, if the Word is not mixed with faith, it will not profit us, Hebrews 4:2. Unless our prayers are prayers in faith, they will not be effectual. Those who pray indeed must be believers.

They must believe "that God is, and that He is a rewarder of them that diligently seek Him," Hebrews 6:6. They must have right apprehensions of His gracious nature and of His good will towards men. He is willing to be reconciled and has Himself, without being sought unto, contrived a way how sinners' peace may be made. He sends ambassadors to them to treat about it, and entreats those who have offended Him that they would be no longer enemies by wicked works. He has declared that fury is not in Him towards those that are desirous of mercy, that He delights in nothing more than in compassion, and that if any understand and seek Him He is more willing to be found than they can be eager to find Him. These things, being rightly conceived, encourage prayer. And Satan, by suggesting the contrary, draws off many from this duty.

They who pray aright must, by believing, be interested in Christ the Mediator. Christ is the way, and no man comes unto the Father but by Him, John 14:6. Christ must be by faith received as the gospel offers Him, that is, as a "Prince and a Saviour." By this faith, being united to Him, God looks upon believers as the brethren of Christ, as the spouse of Christ, nay, which is nearer, as Christ's members, and will deny them nothing. Those who belong to Christ, God is a God to them, and a Father to them as He is to Christ Himself, and loves them as He loved Christ, John 20:17 and 17:23. Surely, He will then grant them their requests.

They who pray must, by faith, rely upon the promises that God has made of hearing. He has said that they who ask shall receive, that they who seek shall find, and to them who knock it shall be opened, Matthew 7:7. And, for further encouragement, because the Spirit teaches what to ask and how to ask, Christ assures us that God will more readily give His Spirit to those who ask Him than earthly parents bread unto their hungry children. Luke 11:13. "If ye then, being evil, know how to give good gifts to your children, how much more shall your heavenly Father give the Holy Spirit unto them that ask Him?" How comprehensive a promise is the promise of the Spirit? His work is to apply that salvation which Christ has purchased, and is sent on purpose that He may endite such petitions for the saints as will find audience.

How plainly has the Lord said that "His eye is upon the righteous and His ear open to their prayers?" Psalm 34:15. Such words should be rested on when we engage in this duty.

The more confidently they who pray conclude the performance of God's promises, the more certainly will they be accomplished. Therefore, we are commanded to ask in faith, nothing wavering, James 1:16. and we are encouraged to draw near with a true heart in full assurance of faith, Hebrews 10:22, and hearken to our Lord himself, "Therefore I say unto you, whatever things ye desire when ye pray, believe that ye receive them, and ye shall have them," Mark 11:24. If we more firmly believed that God, according to His covenant for His Son's sake, has pardoned sin and will heal our souls of their distempers and will give grace sufficient and make us to grow and increase with the increases of God, verily His promises would appear to be real, and according to our faith it would be to us. Thus you see how those who pray must be believers.

In prayer, things must be asked for according to the will of God. "And this is the confidence that we have in Him, that if we ask any thing according to His will, He heareth us," 1 John 5:14. Christ tells His disciples, "if ye abide in Me, and My words abide in you, ye shall ask what ye will, and it shall be done to you," John 15:7. The Word abiding in us declares the will of God and regulates our wills. And then what we will we shall have. Luther said, "Let my will be done, because my will, O Lord, is the same with Thine."

I do not wonder that many of the heathens reasoned against prayer. They, being unacquainted with the mind of God, knew not what to ask for. But in the Scripture God has declared His mind to us, and that is our directory.

The Three-fold Will of God in Prayer

There is a threefold will of God which we are to regard in prayer: His will of purpose, of precept, and of promise.

1. His will of purpose. God's purpose concerning His people is wise and gracious, therefore it is called "the good pleasure of His goodness" by the Apostle, 2 Thessalonians 1:11. And it is but reasonable that this purpose should be submitted to. We may ask, sometimes, for that which it may not be fit for us to receive. In temporals, especially, we are at a loss, and are unable to determine what measures of such kind of mercies are most meet for us. When, therefore, we beg for the continuance of life, the prolonging or restoring of health, it is for the enjoyment of outward comforts. All must be done with this proviso, that the will and purpose of God may stand and be accomplished; for we may conclude that when the Lord denies outward mercies, which we with submission beg for, He intends kindness in that very denial.

2. In prayer, God's will of precept is to be regarded. Whatever He commands us to do, we may with boldness go to Him for strength, which may enable us for the performance. The Lord calls and commands Israel to turn. "Turn ye, turn ye from your evil ways, for why will ye die, O house of Israel?" Ephraim turns this into prayer, "turn Thou me, and I shall be turned, for Thou art the Lord my God," Jeremiah 32:18. God commanded David to keep His precepts diligently. David takes hold of this and cries out, "O that my ways were directed, that I might keep Thy statutes!" Psalm 119: 4-5. He requires that we should love and fear Him; we

may without presumption beg that He would circumcise our hearts and love Him, and put His fear into our hearts that we may not depart from Him.

3. In prayer, God's will of promise is also to be eyed. And though the promises of the life that now is belong to believers, yet especially they prize and plead the promises of spiritual and everlasting blessings. These we are to look upon as "exceeding great and precious," and sure promises, and to beg that by them "we may be partakers of the divine nature, and escape the corruption that in the world through lust," 2 Peter 1:4. What can the Lord promise more than he does? "The Lord God is a sun and shield, the Lord will give grace and glory, no good thing will He withhold from them that walk uprightly," Psalm 84:11. When we entreat Him to make good His promises, we in effect entreat Him to glorify His power and love, His truth and faithfulness.

4. *Prayer must be in the name of Christ.* What name is more prevalent? "Verily, verily, I say unto you, whatsoever ye shall ask the Father in My name, He will give it to you." When we make use of the mediation of Christ, we go the way to speed. The Papists make use of the mediation of angels and saints departed, but the apostle tells us, as of "one God," so of "one Mediator between God and man, the man Christ Jesus." Saints indeed on earth may pray one for another because God has commanded it. It maintains love among them, and the strongest need the prayers of the weaker. How earnestly does the apostle Paul beseech the believing Romans that they would strive together with him in their prayers to God for him (Romans 15:30)? But

there is not a word of prayer directed to any saint in Scripture. And when Jacob was in distress, and the angels of God met him, he said, "this is God's host." But he begged nothing of them, but wrestled with God Himself and, as a prince, prevailed.

Four Things to Have an Eye to in Prayer

We must pray in the name of Christ, and there are four things which we are to have an eye to:

1. The satisfaction of Christ. He has been wounded for transgressions, He bare the curse so that we may beg with confidence to be delivered from it. He has made peace by the blood of His cross. We have encouragement to beseech the Lord to be reconciled, and that He would no longer be a foe but a Father to us.

2. We are to eye the purchase of Christ. He has purchased all the blessings of the new covenant. Heaven itself is called "a purchased possession," Ephesians 1:14. Christ paid a price for it that it might be ours. It is not only an act of grace but an act of righteousness in God, considering what Christ has paid to forgive sin and to give salvation.

3. We are to eye the intercession of Christ. "He is able to save them to the uttermost, that come unto God by Him, seeing He ever lives to make intercession for them," Hebrews 7:25. Our great High Priest is passed into the heavens, and His work is there, to pray for believers, and His Father hears Him always. How can prayers miscarry that are backed with the intercession of such a one?

4. We are to eye the strength of Christ, and His assistance. To pray rightly is a matter of difficulty. Christ,

by His Spirit, is ready to help the infirmities of believers so that, notwithstanding all discouragement and opposition from within and from beneath, they shall make something of this duty of prayer and obtain the blessing.

5. *In prayer, there must be thanksgiving for what has been already received.* Praise is the sublimest part of prayer. Praise is a debt, and how vast is the debt if we consider the multitude, greatness, freeness, and continuance of mercies? Praise sweetens prayer. Nothing is more pleasing to God, nothing more pleasant to ourselves. And to give thanks for benefits received is as effectual a way to prevail for more mercy as the most vehement and strongest cries. O, therefore, that all who pray would also "praise the Lord for His goodness, and for His wonderful works to the children of men," Psalm 107:8. Thus have I explained the definition, and opened the nature of prayer to you.

II. What it is to pray always. This I have touched upon already, but shall more fully speak of in these particulars.

1. To pray always implies being always in a disposition and frame to pray when God requires it. The heart must be reconciled to this duty and fall in love with it and go to the throne of grace with alacrity. Much may be gotten at the mercy-seat. The unsearchable riches of Christ are unlocked, and we may take as much as the hand of faith can grasp without being checked or upbraided. The God with whom we have to do gives liberally and like Himself, James 1:5. The heart should be forward to pray, and be weary of, and

through grace subdue more and more of that evil which, alas, is "present when good is about to be performed," Romans 7:21.

2. To pray always implies laying hold of all opportunities to pray that are graciously vouchsafed to us. Whenever there is a meet season and a motion to pray, we should catch such an occasion by the forelock; for when once it is past, it is past recalling. Stated times of prayer, ordinarily, should in no way be neglected. And, when there are extraordinary calls to this duty, they should by all means be heeded.

3. To pray always implies praying in every state and condition. In sickness, in health, in prosperity, in adversity, prayer is to be used. Without prayer, sickness will be unsanctified and an uncomfortable load. And if it is taken off, it will be in anger. Without prayer, health will be a judgment and will only serve to encourage a neglect of the soul and another world. Without prayer, adversity will be intolerable and prosperity will be a snare, an occasion of forgetfulness of God, and a daring to rebel against Him. No condition should cause a cessation of prayer, for the Apostle says, "pray without ceasing," 1 Thessalonians 5:17.

4. To pray always implies not to let fall any suit till it be granted. We must not faint in prayer, nor give over, though we do not presently speed. Luke 18:1, "He spake a parable to them to this end, that men ought always to pray, and not to faint." Importunity prevailed with an unrighteous judge; surely, then, it will be prevalent with the Father of mercies. God does not presently grant, sometimes, to try whether we duly esteem mercies. And, if we do, we shall think them worth our while to pray still for them, and wait till they are

given.

5. To pray always implies not to give over praying while we are on earth. This ordinance we must never be above, for we always need to engage in it. Our life is a continual warfare; we need to pray for defense and victory. Our knowledge and grace is imperfect. We need to pray for the increase of both, and that we may be helped to press toward the mark for the prize of the high calling of God.

III. Why a Christian's security lies in prayer.

1. Prayer engages God on a Christian's side. He promises to hear the cry of the righteous one. And hearing their cry implies the engaging of His power and goodness for their supply and safety. In prayer, there is an acting of holy desires unto which satisfaction is assured and there is an acting of trust and faith. And God will show Himself strong in the behalf of those who fly unto His name as to a tower of defense and rely upon His everlasting arms. He who believes and has his expectation from the Lord shall not be ashamed. The Apostle does not hesitate to say, "whosoever calleth on the name of the Lord, shall be saved," Romans 10:12—that is, whosoever calls with faith and fervency. Such calling engages God for us, and if He is for us, who can be against us? Romans 8:31. Our iniquities, though never so strong, He can easily subdue. The world, and the god of the world, are weak compared with the Almighty. He can deliver from the evil world, from the evil one, from every evil work, and preserve us to His heavenly kingdom.

2. Prayer weakens the flesh, with the affections and lusts of it. Our great danger is from these home-bred

enemies. Our lusts war against our souls, 1 Peter 2:11.
And the apostle threatens believers, "if ye live after the
flesh, ye shall die," Romans 8:13. What course does
David take to obtain the victory over his corruptions?
He prays against them. "Cleanse me from secret faults.
Keep back Thy servant from presumptuous sins. Let no
iniquity have the dominion over me. Create in me a
clean heart and uphold me with Thy free Spirit."
These and such like were his cries. Prayer pleads that it
is for God's honor to kill corruption, that it is His declared will, even man's sanctification; that it is His work
to sanctify; that He has promised to sanctify throughout, in body, soul, and spirit; and He is faithful and,
therefore, will do it, 1 Thessalonians 23-24. He pleads
that Christ died that He might redeem and purify from
iniquity—that He might cleanse His church, and present it unto Himself a glorious church, not having spot
or wrinkle, or any such thing, but that it might be holy,
and without blemish, Ephesians 5:27. And such pleas
are effectual to the obtaining of grace and mortifying
the deeds of the body.

3. A Christian's security lies in prayer, for prayer obtains better things than the world can boast of. Let the
world allure by the strongest baits, and present unto
the Christian the greatest gains, the sweetest pleasures,
yet blessings more valuable are to be gotten at the
throne of grace. The heart in prayer is taken up with
the thoughts of, and eager desires after, the privilege
of reconciliation and adoption, communion with God,
and the communications of His grace and spirit, an
eternal weight of glory, a crown of life, an enduring
substance, fullness of joy, and pleasures for evermore,
Psalm 16. These are the things above that, in prayer,

are sought. And what things below in comparison? The heart that is placed on these is the better armed against the world. As long as spiritual and eternal blessings are secured, the world is neither desired nor dreaded by it.

4. Prayer is an undermining of Satan. The powers of hell have felt the force of this duty. Christ commanded His disciples to pray when He perceived the devil about to winnow them, "pray that ye enter not into temptation," Luke 22:40. If as often as we are assaulted by the tempter, we did but look unto Christ, the temptation would be very unsuccessful. Two things are done in prayer against Satan. By our confession of sins this accuser is silenced; by petition, grace is obtained to withstand him.

1.) By confession of sin, this accuser is silenced. Satan is called "the accuser of the brethren," and to show how malicious and eager he is in his accusations, he is said to "accuse them day and night before God," Revelation 12:10. But in prayer, believers bring bills of indictment against themselves. All that Satan can truly lay to their charge, they also lay to their own charge. All that God has against them they acknowledge. They do not cover their sins but confess and aggravate them; they blame and judge themselves. And how earnest are they that sin confessed may be pardoned and urged away by the blood of Christ! Now Satan's mouth is stopped. His charge signifies nothing; for, thus confessing sin and looking unto Jesus for cleansing as well as atonement, God is faithful and just to forgive them their sins, and to cleanse them from all unrighteousness, 1 John 1:9

2.) By petition, grace is obtained to withstand

Satan. The apostle Paul, when buffeted by the devil, falls to prayer, and what answer has he? The Lord said unto him, "My grace is sufficient for thee, for my strength is made perfect in weakness." And the Apostle is satisfied that the power of Christ rested on him. Prayer brings us to the God of Peace, who promises to tread Satan under our feet shortly, Romans 16:20. By prayer, wisdom is derived from God. And the more wise the Father of lights makes us, the better we understand the devil's wiles. His design is seen through, which is to deceive, to defile, and at last to murder souls. As wisdom is increased, so faith, love, fear, and other graces are increased by praye. And the more we believe God, the less credit we shall give the evil one. The more we love God, the more we shall hate that evil which we are tempted to. The more we fear the Lord, the more will our hearts by united to Him, and it will be a matter of great difficulty to persuade us into departing from Him.

5. A Christian's security lies in prayer, for prayer is a great means to make every other ordinance effectual for our safety and spiritual advantage. The Word of God and prayer are coupled together. "But we will give ourselves continually to prayer, and to the ministry of the Word," Acts 6:4. Our sermons which we preach unto you should be begged from heaven, they should be begun, ended, and followed after with prayer; and if you who are hearers would but help us herein by prayer, it would be in effect to help yourselves. If there were but more praying before you come to the sanctuary, that you might be taught to profit, so many sermons would not be lost. So much seed would not be sown in vain. Prayer sets an edge upon the Word, and

makes it quick and powerful to kill sin and keep off
Satan. Prayer works the Word into the heart and, being
hid there, it is a mighty preservative against iniquity.
There is a spiritual instinct in believers to join prayer
with every ordinance of God, because they know that
ordinances cannot secure or benefit them unless the
Lord concurs and works along with them. I have
proved that a Christian's security lies in prayer.

IV. Some reasons why we ought to pray always.

1. We should pray always because God is always
ready to hear. "The Lord's ear is not heavy, that it cannot hear," Isaiah 59:1. He hearkens after prayer, and
"looks down from heaven upon the children of men,
to see if there be any that understand and seek God,"
Psalm 14:2. The Father is said to seek for right worship-
pers, namely, these that worship Him in spirit and in
truth, John 4:23. We have, therefore, encouragement
at all times to trust in Him, and at all times to pour out
our souls before Him. "God is a refuge for us," Selah,
Psalm 62:8. Verily, seeking God in sincerity never was
yet in vain and never will be. God has heard sinners
then, when they perhaps have little thought He
minded them. When Ephraim bemoaned himself, was
as a bullock unaccustomed to the yoke, was ashamed
and confounded because of his evil ways, he cried,
"Turn Thou me, and I shall be turned; God says, I have
heard him, I have surely heard Ephraim," Jeremiah
31:18-19. God gave him to understand that he was a
dear son, a pleasant child, and that He would surely
have mercy on him. There is not a tear but God has a
bottle to put it in, nor a sigh but God observes it, nor a
true desire but He is ready to satisfy.

2. We should pray always because Christ always intercedes. "He is able to save them to the uttermost that come unto God by Him, seeing He ever lives to make intercession for them," Hebrews 7:25. The prayers of believers will be well-seconded. This Angel of the covenant has incense sufficient to perfume, and to make the prayers of all the saints at all times acceptable. Christ in heaven is always presenting to his Father His sufferings and, by His sufferings, all that we pray for has been purchased. His blood, therefore, is said to speak in Scripture, and "it speaks better things than that of Abel," Hebrews 12:24. The curse that Christ has borne may be removed from them that the sins for which Christ was wounded may be forgiven them; and that out of the fullness of Christ they may receive, and grace for grace.

3. We should pray always because the Spirit is always ready to help our infirmities. This Spirit Christ promised and, according to His promise, sent Him. And this Spirit is called the "Spirit of grace and supplications," Zechariah 12:10; for He gives grace and ability to make supplications acceptable. His spirit abides with believers always. "I will pray the Father, and He shall give you another Comforter, which shall bide with you forever, even the Spirit of Truth, whom the world cannot receive, because it seeth Him not, neither knoweth Him; but ye know Him, for He dwelleth with you, and shall be in you," John 14:16-17. The Spirit is ready to instruct us what to pray for, to remove the load off in disposition to this duty, to quicken our deadness therein, to enlarge our hearts in desires after the God of all grace, to strengthen us to wrestle for a blessing. And truly God is not to be prevailed with but

by the mediation of His Son, and by the strength of His own Spirit.

4. We should pray always because Satan is always forward to assault us. Satan is compared to a lion in Scripture. And Elian observes, concerning the lion, that if at any time he is beaten back, he retires with his face towards you as being ready upon the least encouragement to make another attempt. In like manner, Satan watches, has his eye always upon us, and is very forward to tempt. And should not we be ever forward to pray? Our whole life is a time of temptation. Wicked spirits are continually engaged against us. "We wrestle, says the apostle, with principalities and powers, with the rulers of the darkness of this world, with spiritual wickedness in high places." These enemies are invisible, so it is more difficult to withstand them. They are too subtle and too strong for us. We need, therefore, to pray without ceasing, since they cease not endeavouring to bring us both to sin and ruin.

5. We should pray always because corruption will quickly recruit and recover strength upon the least neglect of prayer. Had David been praying when he was sleeping so long in the day time, or after his sleep had been ended; had he gone to the throne of grace instead of idly walking upon the roof of his palace; nay, when first he cast his eyes on Bathsheba, if he had immediately looked up to heaven and cried, then that spark of concupiscence might have been extinguished before it set him in a flame. His foul fall, and the doleful consequences of it, might have been prevented. But duty was neglected, and sin took the advantage of neglect. He was hurried into two sins almost as heinous can possibly be committed, 2 Samuel 11. Experience

shows us that if we omit or are slight in prayer, in that
day our passions are more easily stirred and our lusts
get ground. Thus Amaleck prevailed when Moses'
hands began to hang down. But when they were held
up to heaven, Israel had the better.

V. The Application. The Christian's security lies so
much in praying always.

USE 1. OF INSTRUCTION. This concerns the extreme danger that prayerless souls are in. It will be
faithfulness and kindness to make such sensible of
their danger. Therefore, I shall a little stay upon it, and
manifest their peril in these particulars.

1. Those who are strangers to prayer, God is against
them. O dreadful! What is God? And who are they?
Who can stand before His indignation? Who can defend himself against that arm that is omnipotent? "The
mountains quake, the hills melt, the devils tremble before this God; the whole world compared with him, is
but as the drop of the bucket, and the small dust on
the balance, and all the sin habitants of the world are
nothing, less than nothing, and vanity," Isaiah
40:15,17. Surely it is fearful to have so glorious and
great a God as an enemy. But an enemy He is unto all
that count not His lobe and Saviour worth the praying
for. Those that will not entreat Him to be reconciled, it
is when they neither value His love, nor fear His wrath;
and they are unquestionably under wrath.

2. Those who are strangers to prayer, their mercies
are not mercies indeed to them. That threatening is
fulfilled upon them, Malachi 2:2, "I will send a curse
upon you, and I will curse your blessings." Prayer will
turn curses into blessing. Afflictions are part of the

curse inflicted because of sin, but prayer alters the nature of them. For the sanctification of them being begged and granted, they work together for the good of them that feel them. Affliction yields "the peaceable fruits of righteousness to them that are exercised thereby," says the Apostle. On the other side, where prayer is not, blessings are a snare, and the good things which are received work together for the harm and ruin of those that do enjoy them. There is a spirit of slumber that has seized on them in the midst of their enjoyments. Their table, their plenty, their abundance becomes a snare "and a trap, and a stumbling block, and a recompense to them," Romans 11:8,9.

3. Those who are strangers to prayer, Satan is endeavoring their ruin and there is none to hinder him. Satan is said, in Scripture, to fill the hearts of the ungodly, to keep possession of them, and to work in the children of disobedience. The devil has come down with great wrath. Like a roaring lion, he walks about, seeking whom he may devour. And truly he finds abundant prey, for most watch not at all, pray not at all against him. Those who pray not are led captive by Satan at his pleasure. They do not care or desire to have his snare broken, nor themselves recovered.

4. Those who are strangers to prayer, how certain is it that continuing as they are, they will miss those great things revealed in the Gospel, since they count them not worth their seeking! The gospel informs us of the one thing needful, of the pearl of great price, of the kingdom of God and His righteousness. And this is the law that is established, that they who would have these things must seek them. They that seek them not understand not their worth nor their own need, and,

therefore, certainly and justly go without them.

5. Those who are strangers to prayer are in danger of meeting with a deaf ear when cries are extorted by calamity. O read and tremble, Proverbs 1:26-28, "I will laugh at your calamity, I will mock when your fear cometh, when your fear cometh as desolation, and your destruction as a whirlwind; when distress and anguish cometh upon you, then shall they call upon Me, but I will not answer; they shall seek me early, but they shall not find Me." The meaning is this, that when cries are extorted merely by distress, and only the removal of calamity is desired, there being no true humiliation for sin, nor desire to be reformed, all such cries will be neglected. If you will not seek the Lord while He may be found, nor call upon Him while He is near, when you cry in extremity, He may be far off from you.

6. Those who are strangers to prayer should consider that quickly the accepted time, which they improve not, will be past, and then they shall beg but must certainly be denied. We read in Scripture of calls that no heed was given to. When the foolish virgins came after the door was shut, and said, "Lord, Lord, open unto us;"—alas, they spoke too late. The door was not opened, but the reply was, "I know you not whence you are." When the rich man begged for a drop of water to cool his tongue, being tormented in the flame, this was not granted to intimate that not the least mitigation of torment in hell is to be looked for. All at last will be ready to pray, "Lord, open the door that lets me into Thy kingdom and glory! Lord, vouchsafe a little ease and respite in the midst of our excessive agonies and sorrows!"

But, oh, God's ear, as well as heaven's gate, will be

shut eternally. His mercy will be clean gone for ever! What madness is it, then, to waste all our accepted time, and not to come to the throne of grace before the day of grace comes to an end!

USE 2. OF CAUTION. Two things you are to be cautioned about:

1. Take heed of resting in prayer itself, in the bare duty done. Prayer is your security, not in itself considered, but because it leads you to the rock that is higher than you, Psalm 61:2. Prayer puts you under the Lord's wing, and you are covered with His feathers—His truth becomes your shield and buckler. They that rest in the mere form, vainly imagining that speaking the words of prayer will help them, use prayer like a charm, and are unacquainted with the right manner of praying.

2. Take heed of thinking that any kind of prayer will secure you and engage God for you. Unbelieving prayers, where Christ is not relied on for audience; cold and careless prayers, where the things prayed for are not praised; hypocritical prayers, where the heart is not indeed engaged—these will neither reach God's ear nor fetch the blessing. Sin's bow will not fetch the blessing. Sin's bow will abide in strength, notwithstanding these prayers. Nor will the strong hoods of Satan be thrown down by them.

USE 3. OF EXHORTATION. The third use shall be of exhortation unto this duty of prayer. The arguments to persuade you are these following:

1. Scripture commands are very frequent which require this duty. How often is prayer called for. And not only the Lord's authority in these commands is to be

regarded but also His goodness. He does not require prayer that He may receive from us, for He is so much above us that He needs us not, nor our performances. And He is so infinitely perfect that there can be no addition to the perfection of His being or His blessedness. Therefore the Lord calls us to pray always, Luke 21:36; to pray everywhere, 1 Timothy 2:8; to continue instant in prayer, Romans 12:12; and in everything, by prayer and supplication, to make our requests known unto God, Philippians 4:6. He is willing to give what we need, and to communicate that mercy without which we must be miserable.

2. The efficacy of prayer should persuade to prayer. He that bids you seek His face, if your hearts echo back, "Thy face, Lord, will we seek," will in nowise hide His face from you, nor put you away in anger, Psalm 27:8,9. By prayer, you may prevail with God for His love. And, being interested in that, nothing will be denied. That the efficacy of prayer may be evident, I shall imitate the apostle (speaking concerning faith, Hebrews 11) and reckon up the wonders that have been the effects of prayer.

By prayer Abraham had saved Sodom, though the cry of their sins was so loud and great if there had been ten righteous persons in it. By prayer, he obtained a son from God, when his wife Sarah was past child-bearing.

By prayer, Jacob was delivered from the wrath of his brother Esau; Jonah, by prayer, out of the whale belly; and the three children out of the seven-times heated Babylonish furnace.

By prayer, David stayed the plague, so that it seized not on Jerusalem, and caused the sword of the destroying angel to be put up into the sheath again.

By prayer, Elias stayed the rain for three years and six months, and by the same means opened the clouds of heaven so that the earth brought forth her fruit. By prayer, he brought down fire which consumed the two captains and their fifties that came to take him.

By prayer, Joshua commanded the sun and it stood still in Gibeon, and the moon in the Valley of Aijalon. For the Lord hearkened to the voice of a man and fought for Israel.

By prayer, Daniel stopped the mouths of lions and came untouched out of the den. By prayer, Peter, Paul, and Silas were delivered out of prison, shackles and iron gates being but weak things to the power of supplications.

And what shall I more say, for time would fail me, as the Apostle speaks, if I should tell of Samuel, of Samson, Jehoshaphat, and of the prophets and apostles, who, by prayer procured thunder to destroy their enemies; out of weakness were made strong; turned to flight the mighty hosts of adversaries; the dead they raised to life again; made the lame from the womb to walk and leap; healed diseases beyond the skill of art to cure. Behold prayer's efficacy, though performed by men of like passions with ourselves! This should persuade us to the love and practice of the duty.

3. Who is it that would hinder you from prayer? Who stands at your right hand to resist you? Certainly it is an enemy, who is unwilling you should draw nigh to God because he knows it is so good for you, Psalm 73. Your own hearts also are ready to draw back, but this argues their egregious folly and desperate wickedness.

4. What has followed upon the omission of prayer? Has not this omission ushered in sins of commission? Have you not, when you have neglected to cry for strength in your souls, found yourselves, like Reuben, unstable as water? Have you not easily been induced to do that which has filled the face of God with frowns and the mouth of conscience with reproaches? On the other side, has not prayer been with success sometimes? Have you not found encouragement and grace at the mercy seat? Oh, do that which both bitter and sweet experience prompts you to!

5. Prayer is an honorable employment. In this duty you have admittance to the ear of the King of Heaven—how high is your company? Your fellowship is with the Father and with His Son Jesus Christ, 1 John 1:3. Though the Lord is high, yet He has respect unto the lowly. He will regard the prayer of the most destitute and not despise it. He allows you a freedom to pour out your complaints and to make known before Him your troubles. And what honor is this, to have to do immediately with God, to have Him so nigh to you in all that you call upon Him for? (Deuteronomy 6:7)?

6. Frequency and fervency in prayer will be a great evidence of your regeneration and adoption. The child, when born, cries; and the sinner, when born again, prays. Of Paul it was said, as soon as he was converted, "Behold he prayeth," Acts 9:11. It is the spirit of adoption that makes us cry, "Abba, Father." If we cannot be satisfied unless we approach unto God, and value His favor and fellowship above all earthly things, and are chiefly desirous of those blessings which He never takes away again, we may conclude from our spiritual breathing, our spiritual life. Now, a good evi-

dence of regeneration, what will it be worth in a day of trouble, in a dying hour?

USE 4. OF ENCOURAGEMENT TO BELIEVERS.

1. Their prayers are God's delight. "The sacrifice of the wicked is an abomination to the Lord, but the prayer of the upright is His delight," Proverbs 15:8. "O my dove, that art in the clefts of the rock, in the secret place of the stairs, let me see thy countenance, let me hear thy voice, for sweet is thy voice, and thy countenance is comely," Song of Solomon 2:14. We are pleased with the talk and requests of our children, though their language is lisped and broken. God is infinitely more indulgent than earthly parents are or can be, and much more willing to give good things than they, Matthew 7:11.

2. There are many reasons why the God whom believers pray to should answer them:

1.) They are His chosen ones. God pitched His love on them before the foundation of the world was laid.

2.) They are His Son's purchase. He has bought them with a price, shed His blood for the remission of their sins, given His life for their ransom.

3.) They are in covenant with God. He has engaged to be their God, and surely He will be their guard also.

4.) They are vessels of mercy, in whom He deigns to glorify His grace and love for ever. Surely, then, He will heed these when they pray; He will give them the good they need, and save them from the evil which makes them fly to Him for shelter. I have done with the first doctrine, that a Christian's security lies very much in praying always.

Doctrine 2

All Prayer

All prayer is of concernment to be used; "praying always with all prayer," says the text. Prayer is a duty of very great extent. The parts of it are admirably suited to the present state and condition of a Christian and the divers kinds of prayer very well agree with the various circumstances wherein we are. All the ways of seeking God shall be to purpose if He is but sought diligently, and according as He Himself has appointed. For He tells us plainly that He says, "Not to the seed of Jacob, seek ye me in vain," Isaiah 45:19.

Two things I shall here insist on. First, I shall speak concerning the parts of prayer, and show how all these parts are to be used. Second, I shall mention the several kinds of prayer, and endeavor so to persuade and direct you to each kind that this duty may be performed in its utmost latitude.

I begin with the parts of prayer, and they are these:

1. One part of prayer is a humble compellation, or naming of God. Those titles that are given Him in Scripture we must be acquainted with, and such should be used as are most suitable unto the matter of our prayers, and which have the greatest tendency to excite those gracious and spiritual affections which are required in our supplications. If we consult the prayers of saints which are recorded in the Bible, we shall find

that God is called sometimes "Lord," sometimes "Father," sometimes "the Great and Mighty and Terrible God," sometimes "the King of Glory," sometimes "the High and Lofty One that inhabits eternity, whose name is holy," sometimes "the God and Father of Christ," and likewise "the Father of Mercies, and God of all Comforts." It is not amiss to add unto God's title those attributes, the consideration whereof may help towards such a frame of spirit as becomes prayer.

Would we have our heart in a holy awe and filled with reverence and godly fear? Mention, then His omnipresence, greatness, His holiness, and jealousy. Would we have our hearts broken for sin? Mention His anger and hatred for iniquity, and, withal, His goodness, forbearance, and readiness to be reconciled, for "the riches of His goodness and long-suffering strongly lead unto repentance," Romans 2:4. Finally, would we in our requests have our desires enlarged, our faith encouraged, and be also forward to praise? Mention, then, the freeness of God's love, the superabundance of His grace, as He is the Father of Jesus Christ. As of old He was called, "the Lord that brought Israel out of Egypt," and afterwards, "the Lord that delivered Judah from the North country," namely, out of the Babylonish captivity. So likewise, in the New Testament, He is called "the God and Father of our Lord Jesus Christ," Ephesians 1:3; 1 Peter 1:2; 2 Corinthians 1:3. Christ is the only prevailing advocate in prayer, and His relation to God is the ground of our hope and expectations.

2. A second part of prayer is acknowledgment and confession of sin. This confession God requires. Only acknowledge your iniquity that you have transgressed against the Lord your God. To confess sin has been the

practice of the penitent. God has been honored when offending Him has been acknowledged to be most unreasonable and heinous. Confession has had a great influence in making sinners humble and ashamed—and upon it how quickly has forgiveness followed! "While I kept silence (that is, while I excused and extenuated my sin and refused ingenuously to acknowledge it), my bones longed, for day and night Thy hand was heavy upon me, my moisture was turned into the drought of summer. I acknowledged my sin unto Thee, my iniquity have I not hid. I said, I will confess my transgressions unto the Lord, and Thou forgavest the iniquity of my sin," Psalm 32:3-5.

This confession of sin in prayer should be particular—general acknowledgments move but little. The very root of sin must be dug up and bewailed. Paul cries out that he was a "blasphemer, and persecutor, and injurious," 1 Timothy 1:13, and laments "the law in his members," the body of death that made him so forward unto evil, Romans 7. David particularized his uncleanness and blood-guiltiness and traced these abominable streams unto the fountain whence they issued forth: the corruption of his nature. "Behold I was shapen in iniquity, and in sin did my mother conceive me," Psalm 51:5. Our despising the remedy which Christ offers in the gospel should also be confessed with special sorrow. For herein we go beyond the very devils, who never had one offer of pardon and grace made to them. And finally, as there is abundant cause, we should fall to judging and condemning ourselves. One that is truly penitent is, as a certain author expresses it, "a faithful pleader for God against himself." We must unclasp the book of conscience and spread it before the Lord. We must hold up our hands and cry, "Guilty, guilty!" and say we can lay claim to nothing as our due but severity and punishment.

3. A third part of prayer is deprecation, or praying against what we have deserved and are afraid of. We ought, with great solicitude, to pray against the anger and hatred of God. "He, even He, is to be feared: who can stand in His sight when once He is angry?" Psalm 76:7. The anger of God expresses itself several ways: the lightest expressions of it, namely, in temporal and outward calamities, are sometimes very terrible. Pestilence, famine, the sword of war, which devours flesh and drinks blood—how intolerable are they to look upon? But spiritual judgments are worse than these and argue hotter displeasure. When the Lord gives sinners up to blindness of mind—searedness of conscience, strong delusions, vile affections, and hardness of heart—this shows He is extremely angry. The others may, but these judgments especially should be deprecated.

But the worst of all is to come in the other world, and that is the vengeance of eternal fire! Oh how importunate should we be to be delivered from wrath to come; so that we may not be sentenced to depart with a curse at the great day, that hell may not be our eternal home! How importunate should we be that we may not, in utter darkness, be gnawed by the worm that never dies, that we may not dwell with devouring fire, nor inhabit everlasting burnings!

4. A fourth part of prayer is petition. Here God gives us leave to be bold and large. And, when we have asked never-so-much, He is ready to do exceeding abundantly above all that we can ask or has entered

into the heart of man to conceive. We should petition
for pardon, for we highly need it. And the Lord has
said, "Though we have made him to serve with our
sins, and wearied him with our iniquities, yet he will
blot out transgressions for his own sake, and remember
our sins no more," Isaiah 43:24-25. Till a pardon is obtained, nothing else can be expected. But when once
God in Christ is reconciled and becomes a Father,
nothing will be denied. His love, therefore, and the
sense of it, should be entreated with our whole heart.
And since the Lord has promised to give both grace
and glory, Psalm 84:11, we may be bold to be petitioners for both. We should be earnest that grace and holiness may be wrought in truth in our hearts, that grace
may be continually increased, and that we may persevere and be faithful to the very death—and at length
attain that glory, honor, and immortality which is
promised unto patient continuance in well doing.
Temporal blessings also we have leave to ask, for the
Lord considers our frame, and is in every way ready to
encourage us unto our duty.

5. A fifth part of prayer is intercession for others.
Not only those should be remembered by us that stand
in a near relation to us but we should be concerned for
the whole city, for the whole nation—nay, for the
whole church of Christ militant upon earth. We should
prefer Jerusalem before our chief joy. We should not
keep silence, we should "give the Lord no rest till He
establish, and till He make Jerusalem a praise in the
earth," Isaiah 62:6-7. We should in nowise hold our
peace "till the righteousness thereof go forth as
brightness, and the salvation thereof as a lamp that
burneth;"—that is, till the church is both reformed

and delivered from oppressing adversaries.

In prayer, we are to have regard to ourselves, to others, to the Lord Himself, and to Christ His Son. We are to beg that His name may be hallowed from the rising of the sun to the going down of the same, that His kingdom may come, and that all on earth may do His will and submit unto the sceptre of His Word.

6. Another part of prayer is imprecation. Some are such that we are to desire that the Lord would fight against them. We may pray that the Lord will rebuke the evil angels, and pull down that kingdom of darkness under which the most of men are held in bondage. In reference to men, we must be much upon our guard against wishing them personal evil. David and the other prophets are not examples for us to follow in this matter. For they knew by a prophetic spirit God's intentions concerning the persons that they prayed against.

The general rule which we ought to follow is this: "But I say unto you, love your enemies; bless them that curse you, do good to them that hate you; pray for them that despitefully use you and persecute you," Matthew 5:44. This is to resemble God, who "maketh His sun to rise on the evil and the good." We are to beg rather the conversion than the confusion of our enemies. And supposing they are implacable and incorrigible, we must desire rather that they may be hindered from doing harm by their designs and power than that harm may come to them. Even when we pray against antichrist, whom we find devoted in Scripture to destruction, we must have no private grudge against the persons of any, but our eye must be fixed on Christ's honor (which Popery so much injures) and on the advancement of His kingdom in the world.

7. A seventh part of prayer is thanksgiving. The Lord's prayer ends with a doxology, or giving honor unto God: "For Thine is the kingdom, and the power, and the glory, for ever," Matthew 6:13. To praise is to "speak with the tongues of angels." All the creatures that are visible are mute except man. He is the world's high-priest who should offer this sacrifice of praise for all. He is the tongue of the creation which should be sounding forth God's goodness towards all. How much does the Lord let forth unto us! And shall we deny Him the revenue of praise? His mercies are without number, and His love without motive and without measure. When praise is offered, He accounts Himself glorified, Psalm 50. Therefore, in everything we should give thanks, for this is the will of God in Christ Jesus concerning us, 1 Thessalonians 5:18. Thus have I gone over the parts of prayer, and none of these parts are needless.

The Several Kinds of prayer

Prayer is twofold: vocal (when the voice and heart are joined together) and mental (when the heart only is engaged). We shall look first at vocal prayer.

I. Vocal Prayer. Vocal prayer is when tongue and heart go together in this duty.

There are several reasons why the tongue is to be made use of in prayer.

With our tongues we are to honor God, and when they are thus employed speaking to Him, or of Him, or for Him, then they are our glory. As there are sins of the tongue, so there are duties of the tongue too. And as the tongue of the swearer, blasphemer, filthy and foolish talker is harsh and hateful to God, so the tongue of him who prays sincerely is pleasant. Christ told His spouse that her voice was sweet and her countenance comely.

In praying with others, words are necessary. Some must be the mouth of the rest unto God.

Words, especially Scripture language, help to excite and stir up the affections, and they serve to keep the heart more intent upon the duty.

Vocal prayer is threefold: first, prayer in the closet; second, prayer in the family; and third, prayer in the public congregation and assembly. Of all these I shall speak in order.

Prayer in the Closet

That secret prayer is the Lord's ordinance is very evident. "But thou when thou prayest enter into thy closet, and when thou hast shut thy door, pray unto thy Father which is in secret," Matthew 6:6. And as our Lord gave this precept, so He is our example in regard of secret prayer. "And in the morning, rising up a great while before day, He went out and departed into a solitary place and there prayed," Mark 1:35. Jacob was left alone wrestling with God, and had the name of Israel given him, for as a prince he had power with God and prevailed, Genesis 32:24-30. Now, if you would be fully informed what this wrestling was, compare the forecited place with Hosea 12:3-4. "By his strength he had power with God, yea, he had power over the angel, that is, an Angel of the covenant, and prevailed. He wept and made supplication to him."

Now for the better managing of this sort of prayer, let these rules be observed diligently:

1. Study privacy—be as secret as possible. Though we are not to be ashamed of any duty, and though our light is to shine before men that they, seeing our good works, may glorify our Father in heaven, yet a Christian is to do much out of the sight of others. As long as God's ear is open to the most whispering prayers, what need is there that any other ear should hear a word which we speak? When there is a desire that men should take notice of our prayers, God takes no notice of them, unless it is to abominate the hypocrisy in them. Therefore, we have that caution from the Lord Jesus, "And when thou prayest, thou shalt not be as the hypocrites are, for they love to pray standing in the synagogues, and in the corners of the streets, that they may be seen of men. Verily, I say unto you, they have their reward," Matthew 6:5.

2. Take the fittest time for secret prayer. The morning especially is to be chosen, though once more in a day, at least, it should be your ordinary practice to pour out your hearts in private before the Lord. "My voice shalt Thou hear in the morning," says David, Psalm 5:3. "In the morning, O Lord, will I direct my prayer unto Thee, and will look up." If the soul is serious in its address unto God in the beginning of the day, it is likely to have more grace and strength to resist temptations, and to walk with God all the day long. It is better to be shorter in the evening duties and larger in the morning. Then the spirits are fresher and more abundant, and the soul does not have such clogs in its actings as it meets with when the body is spent and tired. But if something unavoidable falls out so

that you cannot pray at the time you desire and were wont, be sure to lay hold of some other opportunity, and neglect not the duty altogether.

3. Let the Word of God be looked into and meditated on when prayer is made. The Word will direct you, quicken and encourage you, unto prayer. By the Word, God speaks to you; by prayer, you speak to Him. If you do not regard God's voice, how can you expect He should mind yours? If you will not hear and obey, He will not hear and grant what you request of Him. The Word should dwell richly in you, Colosians 3:16. Your delight should be in the law of the Lord, and in that law should you meditate day and night. The Scriptures should be searched, which shows they are deep, and all is not discovered at your first looking into them. You must seek here as for silver, and search here as for hidden treasure, if you would understand the fear of the Lord and find the knowledge of God. How enlightening, how enlivening, how cleansing and transforming is the Word of God! How sweet and desirable are the Lord's testimonies! When the Spirit becomes the Expositor of Scripture, opens the eyes to behold wondrous things out of God's law and affects the heart, oh, then, there is such efficacy, profit, and sweetness as is beyond comparison!

4. Be liberal in this duty of secret prayer. Pray with an enlarged and with a free spirit. Do not grudge the time you spend here, for this is the best way of returning time unto a good account. Be sensible how good it is to draw nigh to God, for the promise is, if you draw nigh to God, He will draw nigh to you. "Draw nigh to God and He will draw nigh to you; cleanse your hands, ye sinners; purify your hearts, ye double-minded,"

James 6:8. Now God's drawing near implies His being reconciled to us; His manifesting His power and grace for our help and supply. Oh, therefore, go unto God with a holy eagerness, who is so ready to meet you, to satiate the weary soul and replenish every sorrowful soul. We must be much and often with God, for this is the way to come to an acquaintance with Him. And the better we are acquainted with Him, the more we shall love Him and be sensible of His love to us. Listen to what is said, Job 22:21, "Acquaint now thyself with Him, and be at peace, thereby good shall come unto thee."

5. In secret prayer be very particular. Ease your consciences by a particular enumeration of your iniquities and the aggravations which have heightened them. Make known all your wants before that God who has called Himself God All-sufficient. Fear not that the Lord will be weary of hearing, or be backward to give a gracious return. When you are alone with God, you may use the greater freedom of speech. This particular will contribute much unto your brokenness of heart, with which the Lord is well-pleased, and also unto a sense of your manifold wants, and making of you meet to be supplied.

6. Look after secret prayer. Stand upon your watchtower and observe what answer is given. The merchant inquires after the ships that he sends to sea. When a petition is presented to a prince, you wait to see what answer will be returned. Be this wise in prayer. If you speed not, find out the impediment; if you do speed, be encouraged to exercise faith in God and to persist in prayer. "Because He has inclined His ear unto me, therefore, will I call upon Him a long as I live," says David, Psalm 16:1. And let answers of prayer be a mat-

ter of praise, that Satan and conscience may not accuse you of, and God may not be angry at, your ingratitude.

PERSUASIONS TO SECRET PRAYER

Thus of the rules concerning secret prayer. Now follow the arguments to persuade unto it.

1. Consider, God sees in secret. In secret places God sees, for He fills both heaven and earth. His omnipresence is an evident demonstration of His omniscience. As He cannot be confined to any place, so neither can He be excluded. "All things are open and naked before Him," Hebrews 6:13. And as His seeing in secret is matter of terror to the ungodly, so of joy unto the righteous. David speaks both with wonder and with gladness, Psalm 89:7-10, "Whither shall I go from Thy Spirit, or whither shall I flee from Thy presence? If I ascend up into heaven Thou art there; if I make my bed in hell, behold Thou art there; if I take the wings of the morning, and dwell in the uttermost part of the sea, even there shall Thy hand hold me, and Thy right hand shall hold me." In whatever secret corner you are, God is with you; all your sighs and groans, your complaints and desires, are taken notice of.

2. Frequency in secret prayer is a great argument of uprightness and sincerity. It is a sign you seek God Himself when none but God knows of your seeking Him. What the apostle speaks of the Jew may be applied unto the Christian. He is not a Christian who is one outwardly, but he who is one inwardly—not so much openly as in secret. The praise of such is not of men but of God.

3. Secret prayer is a marvelous way to thrive in

grace, and to grow rich towards God. By this means, faith will grow exceedingly, love will abound, and our souls will prosper. Some tradesmen keep a shop and drive a trade there, but they have a secret way of trading which is not observed. And by this they grow wealthy in a short space. A Christian who is much in secret with God, O how much does he gain! How good does such a one find the Lord! How ready both to forgive and to give! And he can set his seal unto that truth, that "God is plenteous in mercy unto all that call upon Him," Psalm 86:5.

4. Secret prayer is a means to fit for public ordinances. They who are most upon their knees in the closet will get the most benefit in the sanctuary. The preparation of the heart is from God, and He must be sought unto in secret to fit our spirits for solemn worship. Those that, before they come to hear, pray that the gospel may come to them not in word only, but in power also, and the Holy Ghost, and much assurance, are likely to find the gospel working effectually, and that it is the power of God to their salvation. Those who, before they come to the table, examine themselves alone and beg that God would search them and are importunate for strength against every corruption, for all the fruits of Christ's sufferings and for all the graces of the Spirit, are not likely to be sent away empty.

5. Secret prayer is a means to keep the impression of public duties upon the heart, after the duties themselves are ended. Your work is not over when public ordinances are over. Has any sin been discovered and reproved? You must go in secret and bewail it, and cry out, "Lord, let not this nor any iniquity have the do-

minion over me." Has any duty been made manifest? You should go in secret and cry, "Incline my heart unto Thy testimonies, and make me to go in the path of Thy commandments." Have any gracious and holy resolution, by the motions of the Spirit with the Word, been made? You must go alone and beg, "Keep this, O Lord, forever in the imagination of the thoughts of my heart, and establish my heart unto Thee."

6. Secret prayer is the way to have special tokens of God's love, and those joys that a stranger does not intermeddle with. Oh the sweet meltings and thawings of the heart for sins, as it is an abuse of mercy, that are experienced in secret prayer! Oh the visits that the great Physician of souls then makes! How suitably and gently He deals with the wounded spirit! What assurance He gives, that He will in nowise cast out, but give rest unto the weary and heavy-laden! Oh what peace is spoken to the saints in answer to prayer! What sweet intimations are given, and sometimes what a rich and full persuasion of their interest in that love, which is unchangeable and everlasting! Surely "the secret of the Lord is with them that fear Him, and He will show them His covenant."

7. Consider, God will reward openly. This argument Christ uses, Matthew 6:6, to enforce secret prayer: "Thy Father which seeth in secret shall reward them openly." As all secret wickedness shall at last be detected and punished, so all secret piety and godliness shall be made manifest before the whole world at the judgment day, and the reward will be exceeding great and everlasting. So much, then, concerning prayer in the closet.

Family Prayer

Second, prayer in the family is to be insisted on.
And that family prayer is a duty may be evidently
proved by these arguments.

1. The Apostle in the text enjoins all prayer, and
family prayer is one kind that holy men have used.
Joshua resolved that he and his house would serve the
Lord. And prayer is so principal a part of divine service
that in Scripture it is sometimes put for the whole.
"Then began men to call upon the name of the Lord;"
that is, in a more public manner to worship Him. So of
Cornelius it is said that "he feared God with all his
house and prayed unto the Lord always," Acts 10:2.

2. Parents are called to bring up their children in
the nurture and admonition of the Lord, to teach
them in the way wherein they ought to go, and to be a
pattern to them of the discharge of every Christian
duty. But how can they more effectually furnish them
with such an example than by bowing their knees
along with them before the throne of grace, imploring
in their presence the best of blessings upon them? Few
things are more calculated to impress the minds of
children and of servants than hearing these prayers of
the head of the family. And where they are seconded
by a consistent example, a signal blessing has often accompanied them.

3. The family stands in need of blessings, which
they are to beg for together, and to deprecate family
evils. And, for encouragement, Christ has promised
that where two or three are gathered together in His
name, He will be in the midst of them. Now, in family
duties, two or three are gathered together in Christ's

name, and His presence may, without presumption, be expected.

4. Wrath is threatened upon prayerless families. "Pour out thy fury upon the families that call not upon Thy name," Jeremiah 10:25. I grant indeed that the word "families" is of such a latitude that it extends unto countries and kingdoms. But if there is an obligation upon countries and kingdoms to join in calling upon God, surely, then, families more strictly taken are in nowise exempted.

DIRECTIONS FOR FAMILY PRAYER

Having proved family prayer a duty, I shall lay down some directions as to the performance of it.

1. Be sensible that prayer is a business of greater concernment than any worldly business whatsoever. You are indeed to be diligent to your callings that are particular, but your general callings are of greatest weight. The general calling is that which all are called to. And what are all called to? They are called to serve and glorify God, and to work out their own salvation. Prayer is a part of your homage to the King of heaven. Much spiritual and eternal benefit is to be obtained by it; therefore, do it not as a bye-business, neither let every small matter cause the omission of it.

2. Believe that success in your callings depends upon the Lord's blessing. "The blessing of the Lord maketh rich," says Solomon, and "He addeth no sorrow with it," Proverbs 10:22. With this, it is in vain to rise up early, and to sit up late, and to eat the bread of carefulness. Now prayer for this blessing is the way to fetch it. I grant indeed that many thrive in the world without prayer. But then wealth is a curse and a snare

to them. It is a weight that hinders them from ascending into the hill of the Lord, and helps to sink them into destruction and perdition.

3. Let prayer be ordinarily twice a day—as under the old law there was a morning and evening sacrifice. And let the whole family join in it if it is possible, since there are none who do not need prayer and may not receive advantage by it.

4. Let the Word of God be read when prayer is made that not only you, but your households after you, may be acquainted with the mysteries of the gospel, and with the will of God. Abraham communicated what he had learned from the Lord unto his family. He used his authority "and commanded his children, and his household after him, to keep the way of the Lord," Genesis 18:19.

5. Take heed of customariness and formality in family worship. Engage always with a serious spirit, and in every duty stir up yourselves to take hold on God.

MOTIVES TO FAMILY PRAYER

I conclude with the motives to persuade you to family prayer.

1. You that are governors have a charge of the souls that dwell under your roof, and must answer for them. Therefore, you are to pray with them, to pray for them. Otherwise, you will incur the guilt of the blood of souls, and that will lie heavy. You provide food for your households, for you are unwilling it should be said you are so much worse than infidels as to suffer and to starve that dwells with you. Oh, what unmercifulness is it patiently to suffer those of your household to go on in the way that leads to damnation, and not to call

upon the Lord, in their hearing, that they may be saved!

2. Families are the seminaries both of church and state. And, therefore, as you desire the church may be pure and the state righteous, look well unto your families and let religion flourish in them. Reformation indeed must begin with persons. And if every one would mend one, all would be reformed. But from persons it must proceed to houses. And if these were but once leavened with godliness, what holy cities and what a happy nation would there be!

3. Consider, family worship has been woefully neglected of late in these declining times. How many large consciences, loose principles, and loose practices are there to be found among us! We match Laodicea in lukewarmness. And what was said of languishing Sardis may be applied to us, that we have "a name to live, but are dead." In many families, all are dead as a stone, and there is a most impious and gross neglect of God and duty. In other families, all are ready to die. Lively services are rarely to be found. Oh, it is high time to awake, and vigorously to endeavor that in our houses the Lord may be served by all and that with all their heart, all their soul, all their mind, and all their strength.

I have finished with family prayer.

Public Prayer

Third, prayer in the public congregation and assembly is to be spoken of. God's temple of old was called the "house of prayer" because there His people met together to seek His face. Public prayer is a great

ordinance and, when rightly managed, of great efficacy.

Now, the rules concerning public prayer are these:

1. These prayers must be performed in a known
tongue, that all may understand and be edified, 1 Corinthians 14. They should be well expressed. Nothing
that is crude, unseemly, or that borders upon nonsense
or impropriety should be brought forth in the assembly.

2. Come at the very beginning. To come late is
both offensive to God and to serious spirits, and it is to
cheat and defraud your own souls. And when you are
there, let your gesture be reverential, for God expects
worship and adoration from your whole man—internal
from soul and external from the body.

3. Take heed of distraction when there are so many
objects to divert you and your hearts are so exceeding
slippery. Remember, God's jealous eye is fixed upon
you, and as He cannot be deceived so He cannot endure to be mocked by you, Galatians 6:6.

4. Take heed of carnal designs in your public duties. Let not your supplications be like those of the
Pharisees and Scribes, of whom Christ says they made
"prayers only for a pretence and show," Luke 20:47.
The hypocrites are like the birds of prey which, though
they soar never so high towards heaven, yet their eye is
still downward that they may catch something. Be not
seemingly devout in the congregation, that you may
the more unsuspectedly be unjust in your shops, and
secretly intemperate and unclean. But be very sincere
in your public addresses unto God; as knowing you
have to do with Him that sees not as man sees, that
judges not according to outward appearance, but tries

the heart and reins.

And, to persuade you to this public prayer, consider:

God is hereby acknowledged and honored. His people hereby testify to the world that there is a Lord in heaven whom they worship, and from whom they have their expectation. And, indeed, this is one reason of public institutions, that we may make a profession to the world whose we are and whom we serve.

The Lord vouchsafes something to His people in the sanctuary that elsewhere is not to be found. David was in an admirable frame when he was in the wilderness of Judah: God was liberal to him both of grace and of comfort. But he was not satisfied because he was deprived of the public ordinances that were administered in the tabernacle. Therefore, he cries out, "My soul thirsteth for Thee, my flesh longeth for Thee, to see Thy power and Thy glory so as I have seen Thee in the sanctuary," Psalm 63:1-2.

The united prayers of many saints together are stronger and more apt to prevail. Much fire together gives the greater heat, and many waters joined run with more violence. And in like manner, when a great congregation joins together as one man to wrestle with God in prayer, how successful are they likely to be! Abraham alone would likely have prevailed for Sodom. But suppose there had been an assembly of righteous ones belonging to Sodom that had joined with Abraham in prayer. Surely the city would have been spared.

I have dispatched vocal prayer, which I divided into three kinds, secret, family, and public.

II. Mental Prayer. In the second place, I come to speak of mental prayer, which is when the heart alone without the tongue is engaged. Now this mental prayer is twofold: first, more solemn; and secondly, more sudden and ejaculatory. It is lawful and possible to pray alone with the heart in a more solemn manner, and truly, in some places and in some circumstances, words may not be so conveniently uttered. But where it is convenient, words should be used, because it is difficult to pray anything while only in the heart. And do it without roving.

But mental prayer is more sudden and ejaculatory, which I shall a little dilate upon. In this kind of prayer, the soul lifts up itself to God in some short desire and request. Thus "Moses cried unto God," Exodus 14:15 and yet we do not read of a word uttered. Thus Nehemiah prayed when King Artaxerxes was speaking to him, Nehemiah 2:4. These holy ejaculations are the very breathings of the new creature. They mightily help to keep down the lustings of the flesh and to preserve us unspotted by the world, or the unclean god of it. But the heart hereby is kept close to the God of heaven.

Concerning this mental ejaculatory prayer, let these directions be observed:

1. Let the heart frequently be sending up desires to God. All true desires are observed, are pleasing to Him and shall be satisfied. Let these desires, therefore, be strong, and principally after the greatest, that is to say, spiritual blessings.

2. In all your civil employments, let your hearts ever and anon be thus engaged. This will make and keep you spiritual. It will hinder your estrangement from

God, and your being ensnared by the unrighteous mammon.

3. Let every temptation at the very first be resisted by this kind of prayer: "Watch and pray that ye enter not into temptation," Matthew 26:41. Oh sigh and groan to the God of all grace when you find Satan assaulting, and a sinful and deceitful heart ready to yield, "that you may have grace to help in the time of need," Hebrews 4.

4. Let this prayer begin and end every duty. Sigh before for assistance and sigh afterwards for acceptance, that infirmities, through Christ Jesus, may be passed by, and that you may obtain some spiritual advantage by every ordinance.

5. Begin and end every day with mental prayer. As soon as ever you awake, there are many watching for your first thoughts. Satan, sin, and the world will have them if your souls are not lifted up to the Lord. Let Him be last likewise in your thoughts. This is the way to lie down in peace and safety, Psalm 4.

6. Especially upon the Sabbath day, ejaculatory prayer should be abundant. You must not then think your own thoughts nor find your own pleasures. Holy desires should issue forth continually. Sabbaths would be gainful seasons, indeed, were they but thus improved.

7. Mix mental prayer and praise together. Let your souls, and all that is within you, bless the Lord upon any manifestation of His goodness, while you desire blessings from Him.

And thus have I gone over the parts and kinds of prayer. Much work indeed I have told you of, but the more work the better, for the more grace is to be expected in order unto the performing of what is required. I shall conclude with a very brief application in two words.

How sharply are they to be reproved, and how melancholy is their condition, who, instead of praying with all prayer, use no prayer, but live in the total neglect of this duty!

Let the disciples of Christ be persuaded to pray with all prayer. All prayer that God has appointed He is ready to hear. In all prayer, the name of Christ must be used, as it is only for His sake we can expect acceptance. And the promises of God, which are sure, exceeding great and precious, may be pleaded. And how glad may we be that the Lord has appointed so many successful ways of seeking Him, wherein He has consulted the variety of our conditions and necessities! So much for the second doctrine.

Doctrine 3

Supplication in the Spirit

Prayer, when rightly performed, is supplication in the Spirit. Indeed, all our worship of God, who is a Spirit, must be in spirit and in truth, else it is in fact no worship. As the body without the spirit is dead, so duties without spirit are dead also.

In the handling of this point I shall, first, open to you what it is to pray in the Spirit. Second, I shall lay down the reasons of the doctrine. Third, I shall answer some cases of conscience about praying in the spirit. Last, I shall make application.

1. What it is to pray in the Spirit.

This, as I have already intimated, refers both to the spirit of him who prays and to the Spirit of God, who helps to pray.

This praying in the spirit refers to the spirit of him who prays, and several things are here included.

1. To pray with our spirit implies to pray with understanding. I will "pray with the spirit, and I will pray with understanding also," 1 Corinthians 14:15. We must not only understand the words that are spoken, but also, and that principally, the worth of those things which we petition for. We must likewise, in some measure, be acquainted with the all-sufficiency and faith-

fulness of that God whom we pray to, and with our own
indigency who are the petitioners. The Athenians had
an altar dedicated "to the unknown God," and they are
said "ignorantly to worship him." And truly all their
worship degenerated into superstition. We must know
the Lord and ourselves, what His promises and our
own needs are, else prayer will be of no account.

2. To pray with our spirit implies to pray with judgment, discerning between things that differ. There is as
vast a difference between sin and holiness as there is
between deformity and beauty: There is as vast a difference between the creature and the Creator as there
is between the broken cisterns that can hold no water
and the fountain of living waters. "Be astonished, O ye
heavens at this, and be horrible afraid; be ye very deso-
late, saith the Lord, for My people have committed two
evils, they have forsaken Me, the Fountain of living waters, and hewed them out cisterns, broken cisterns that
can hold no water." There is as vast a difference between a state of grace and a state of wrath as there is
between heaven and hell. Now he that prays must be
apprehensive of all this. And a believing apprehension
of it will make him earnest for the loving-kindness of
the Lord, that he may taste more and more of the
Fountain of living waters and be cleansed from all de-
filements.

3. To pray with our spirits implies to pray with intention of mind. Abraham drove away the fowls that lit
upon his sacrifice. And so should we drive away the impertinent, sinful, and troublesome thoughts that arise
or are injected into our hearts when we engage in
prayer. Our hearts cannot wander in the least but they
are espied by Him, whose "name is jealous." We

should, therefore, desire that the Lord Himself, who holds the wind in His hand, would seize upon our more unruly hearts and keep them close to Himself in duty, especially considering there are some kinds of distractions that nullify and make void prayer—distractions that are not regarded, not lamented, not watched, or striven against.

4. To pray with our spirits implies to pray with spiritual affections. The affections are the wings of the soul. And the soul is carried either to or from any thing, according as the affections are inclined. The Apostle, exhorting to seek the things that are above, presently adds, "set your affections on things above," Colossians 3:1-2. He intimates that we shall never seek the things above in good earnest unless our affections are placed on them. Those affections that have evil for their object must spend their strength upon sin, which is the worst of all evils. Sin must be hated most perfectly. Sin must cause the deepest sorrow. Sin must be most feared. And against sin the heart should rise with the greatest indignation. Those affections that have good for their object—love, desire, and the like—should run with a full stream towards God and those great things that are brought to light by the gospel and promised in the covenant of grace. The stronger and more spiritual our affections are in prayer, the better success will follow: It is said of Judah, 2 Chronicles 15:15, that "they sought the Lord with their whole desire, and He was found of them."

The Work of the Spirit of God in Prayer

This praying in the Spirit refers to the Spirit of God

who helps to pray. The Apostle Jude exhorts us to build up ourselves in our most holy faith, and to "pray in the Holy Ghost," Jude 20; and so to keep ourselves in the love of God, looking for the mercy of our Lord Jesus Christ unto eternal life. Now, the operation, or working of the Spirit of God in prayer, I shall explain in these particulars.

1. The Spirit of God teaches believers what to pray for. He opens their eyes to understand the Word and to know what the will of the Lord is. "We know not," says the Apostle, "what we should pray for as we ought, but the Spirit maketh intercession for the saints according to the will of God," Romans 8:27.

2. The Spirit removes impediments to prayer. He turns that love that naturally is in the heart to sin into hatred. He causes the world that was idolized to be condemned. He cures that infidelity, in reference to the excellency of spiritual things, that the unrenewed soul is full of—and also that enmity against God and holiness, which was in the mind all the while it was carnal. Where the "Spirit of the Lord is, there is liberty," 2 Corinthians 3:17. The fetters are knocked off, the clogs removed, the soul is brought out of prison and is made free, both unto the performance of duty and free in the performance of it.

3. The Spirit encourages unto prayer. He lets believers understand that now is the accepted time, that now is the day of salvation. "Wherefore," he said, "I have heard thee in a time, behold, now is the day of salvation," 2 Corinthians 6:2. Though the Lord should have been sought much sooner, yet it is not too late to seek Him now. He will be found by the hearty seeker. Such seeking shall not be in vain. "But if from thence

thou shalt seek the Lord thy God, thou shalt find Him, if thou seek Him with all thy heart, and with all thy soul," Deuteronomy 6:29.

4. The Spirit enables believers to exercise those graces that are required in prayer. There are four graces especially that should be exercised: humility, faith, love, and patience.

<u>Humility</u>. The Lord has a special regard to the humble, whereas the proud He knows afar off, and He has threatened to resist the proud. The humble soul has high and awful apprehensions of God in prayer, and mean, very mean, thoughts of itself. Abraham was humble when he said, "behold, I have taken upon me to speak unto the Lord, who am but dust and ashes." Job was humble when he said, "Mine eye seeth Thee, wherefore I abhor myself." The good angels themselves are humble, though never in the least offenders. The cherubims cover their faces with their wings, and cry out, "Holy, holy, holy is the Lord of Hosts, the whole earth is filled with His glory." How vile, then, should we be in our own eyes who, by our guilt, are so obnoxious, who have so many foul spots and stains upon your souls, which are the effects of sin, nay, whose very righteousnesses are but filthy rags (Isaiah 64:6)?

<u>Faith.</u> Faith is to be exercised in prayer. And truly we may come with confidence to the throne of grace if we consider the power of God, which is not only most mighty, but almighty. "I am God Almighty," said the Lord to Abraham, the father of the faithful. He can do more for us than we can desire should be done for us. Nothing is too hard for Him, and, although all other helps fail, He does not need them. His arm, when alone, can bring salvation. This power of God may

safely be relied on, for He is also full of mercy. "God hath spoken once, twice have I heard this, that power belongeth unto God, also unto Thee belongeth mercy," Psalm 62. David was encouraged by this in his supplications, Psalm 25:6, "Remember, O Lord, Thy tender mercies, and Thy loving-kindnesses, for they have been ever of old." And we have not only an intimation of God's merciful nature, but in His covenant, He has promised to show, for this He delights in. And Christ is the Mediator of this covenant, so that it is most sure. Hear the Apostle, Hebrews 8:10-12, "This is the covenant that I will make, saith the Lord, I will put My laws in their minds, and write them in their hearts. I will be to them a God, and they shall be to Me a people; for I will be merciful to their unrighteousness, and their sins and iniquities I will remember no more."

Love. Love is to be exercised in prayer. There must be a love to our neighbor, and they must from the heart be forgiven who have trespassed against us. Shall we think much of a few pence when we are debtors of many thousands of talents? But principally, there must be love to the Lord expressed in prayer. His favor and fellowship with Him must be longed for. The soul must thirst for God, for the living God, as the chased hart after the waterbrooks. And, when He does manifest Himself, He must be rejoiced and delighted in, and His grace admired, whatever is received.

Patience. Patience is also to be exercised in prayer. There must be a patient waiting in this duty, a right understanding of God's wisdom and faithfulness—that He knows what and when to give, and will do it in the best time and measure. This will be a great means to cure our over-hastiness. David is to be imitated, who

said, "I waited patiently for the Lord," and he lost
nothing by it. For it follows, "He inclined his ear unto
me, and heard my cry." These are the graces which the
Spirit enables believers to exercise in prayer.

5. The Spirit directs believers unto Christ as the
sole prevailing advocate. We are said to have access to
the Father by the Spirit and through the Son,
Ephesians 2:18. The Spirit leads us to Christ as the
Mediator, who is the way unto God. The Spirit shows
that God, having given Christ, has opened, through
Him, the treasures of His grace, and for His sake will
give freely all things. The Spirit still is turning the eye
of the believer towards the Lord Jesus, and in prayer
instructs us how to improve His relation to us who is
bone of our bone, flesh of our flesh, and has become a
Head and Husband to us; also how to improve His sufferings by which all that we need has been procured;
how to improve His intercession, which, as it is inces-
sant, so it is never denied; and, finally, how to improve
His power and authority, for He can do what He will,
both in heaven and in earth. He is the Prince of Peace,
and the Lord of life and glory. He can give peace and
life and glory to whom He please.

6. The Spirit makes believers sincere in their aims
when they pray. They design the hollowing and honor-
ing of God's name, as well as their own welfare. They
beg for pardon and grace, not only because it is good
for themselves to have these, but likewise, because the
Lord glorifies His grace, mercy, and goodness in forgiving, healing, and saving those that cry to Him.

Thus you see what it is to pray in the Spirit. And,
consequently, it does not lie barely either in fluency of
utterance, in variety of expressions, or in multitude of

words.

2. The reasons of the doctrine.

Now follow the reasons of the doctrine, and they are of two sorts: first, why our own spirits should engage in prayer.

1. Because God is a Spirit. Our Lord assigns this as a reason why worship should be in spirit, because God is a Spirit who is worshipped.

2. He principally requires our spirits. "My son, give Me thy heart," Proverbs 23:26. And truly, He narrowly observes where our hearts are when we are at prayer; and no wonder, for our spirits are most capable of serving Him. To admire, fear, love, trust in Him, these are the principal ways of worshipping Him, and this is done with the heart.

3. Without our spirits, prayer is but a mockery. If the Lord is honored with the mouth, and the heart is far from Him, God says, "In vain do they worship Me, and I will not hold them guiltless." And this you may observe, that when our hearts are not engaged in prayer, they are commanded by the Lord's enemies. Sin, the world, and Satan, detain them.

The second sort of reasons are why we must pray by help of the Spirit of God. His assistance is necessary:

1. Because of our darkness. We, of ourselves, do not know not God, nor His will, nor our own greatest needs, nor wherein lies our great interest and truest happiness.

2. Because of our deadness. Active we are as to sin, but unto prayer indisposed. The dead man must be lifted and carried, for, of himself, he cannot stir. We that naturally are without strength, nay, without life,

cannot lift up our souls to God unless the Spirit lift them up to Him.

3. Because of the opposition that is made by the evil one. When we come to the mercy seat, the devil makes nothing of taking our right hand. He is ready to resist us as he did Joshua the high-priest, Zechariah 3:1. And we are not able to withstand him unless the Spirit of God, who is infinitely stronger, rebukes him for us.

4. The Spirit's assistance is necessary in prayer because of that natural averseness in our own hearts unto what is good. Whereas we should hate the evil and love the good, we hate the good and love the evil. Nay, in the very best, there is a law in the members which wars against the law of the mind, and evil is present. If the Spirit were not also mightily and graciously present, there would be an utter inability to prayer, or any duty which God requires.

3. Cases of conscience. In the third place, I am to answer some cases of conscience concerning the spirit of prayer.

CASE 1. Do all believers have the spirit of prayer?

ANSWER 1. All true believers have this spirit, for the spirit of grace, which all saints have received, is also a spirit of supplication, Zechariah 12:10. And the Apostle expressly says, "If any man have not the spirit of Christ, he is none of His."

CASE 2. Do only believers have the spirit of prayer?

ANSWER 2. The spirit of prayer is peculiar to believers, for where the Holy Ghost helps the heart to pray, He cleanses the heart from what before defiled it, and turns the heart and the desires of it towards God.

So this is now its language: "Whom have I in heaven but Thee, and there is none on earth I desire besides Thee," Psalm 73:25.

CASE 3. Can the spirit of prayer be lost?

ANSWER 3. The Spirit may be grieved by our corruptions when they prevail, and when we grow slothful and heedless how we enter into temptation. And, being grieved, He may withdraw His quickening and assisting influences. But the Spirit is never quite lost by those that have been truly renewed by Him. He abides forever where He has consecrated any to be His temple, John 14:16. David, after his fall, says, "Restore unto me the joy of Thy salvation," to show that his joy was lost. But he prays, "take not Thy Holy Spirit from me," to signify that the Spirit was not quite departed, though that departure was deserved and feared.

CASE 4. May not persons excel in the gift of prayer who yet are void of the spirit?

ANSWER 4. I answer in the affirmative. The gift of prayer may only serve to puff up professors with pride. How are such pleased in reflecting upon the reputation they have gained by their enlargedness in expression! And this pride is not checked, is not abhorred. The words of prayer may be used and a carnal worldly design carried on. Hypocrites aim at an eminency in gifts that they may pass for godly persons. Under the cloak of religion, they cover their wickedness. In their most enlarged supplications, they aim at their own profit or fame, and are prodigiously destitute of the fear of God. It is certain the gift of prayer may be in the unsound-hearted. For even the gift of prophecy, which the Apostle prefers before other gifts, we find in Matthew 7:21-22, "Many will say unto Me in that day, Lord, Lord, have we not prophesied in Thy name? Then will I profess unto them, I never knew you; depart from Me, ye workers of iniquity."

CASE 5. May not some that have the spirit of prayer be very weak in the gift of utterance?

ANSWER 5. I answer, yes. There was much of the spirit of prayer in Hezekiah when he "chattered like a crane or swallow, and mourned like a dove," Isaiah 39:14. The Lord regards not so much the expression as affection; and the heart may be sincere in its desires when not only because of the strength of these desires, but also through confusion, there lacks utterance. Let not those, therefore, that are but weak in expression be discouraged. For the heart may highly value mercy and grace, and obtain both when prayer is but lisped and stammered forth by the tongue. Now follows the application.

Application

USE 1. OF REPROOF.

1. To those who pray in form but whose heart and spirit does not pray with them. They put the Lord off with bended knees, stretched-forth hands, lifted-up eyes, the labor of their lips, the fruit of their invention—but all this while their hearts are not with Him, and their affections run a-whoring after their vanities and iniquities. The prayers of such dissemblers are dead prayers, and truly are to be numbered among

their dead works. And their prayers, not being minded by themselves, how should God have regard to them, unless it is to hate and punish them?

2. They are to be reproved who make light of the Spirit of God, and of His assistance in this duty of prayer. They account the aid of the Holy Ghost a needless, notional, and imaginary thing. Such never knew what it is to wrestle with God, what it is to sigh and groan, and be, as it were, in travail till the blessings begged for are obtained. Oh how impossible is it that nature should rise this high, till the spirit renews and elevates it!

USE 2. OF TRIAL. Whether we have the spirit of prayer or not? And this may be discerned by these following signs.

1. Those that have the spirit of prayer have been convinced of sin by the Spirit, John 16:8. He has revealed sin, broken their hearts for it, and it is now become a load to them though before they loved it never so extremely. Before they hid sin; now they lay it open in prayer. Before they excused it; now they aggravate it and judge themselves worthy of hell and wrath because of it.

2. Those that have the spirit of prayer are made to look unto Christ crucified. "I will pour out upon the house of David, and the inhabitants of Jerusalem, the spirit of supplication: Then shall they look upon Him whom they have pierced, and mourn for Him, and be in bitterness as one is in bitterness for the loss of a first-born," Zechariah 12:10. Christ crucified is looked upon by such with a weeping eye—because their sin was the cause of His sufferings—and with an eye of de-

pendence, for all their expectation of grace, peace, and life is through Him alone.

3. They that have the spirit of prayer are earnest for the fruits and graces of the Spirit—that love, joy, peace, long-suffering, gentleness, goodness, faith, meekness, temperance. All which the Apostle enumerates, Galatians 5:22-23, may be in them and abound. And they are restless in prayer for the mortification for the deeds of the flesh, for they considered what is said, Romans 8:13, "If ye live after the flesh, ye shall die; but if ye through the Spirit mortify the deeds of the body, ye shall live."

4. They that have the spirit of prayer are enabled to go unto God as unto a father. "And because ye are sons, God hath sent forth the spirit of his Son into our hearts, crying, Abba, Father," Galatians 4:6. Not but that doubts and fears may be in those that have the spirit. Witness the Psalmist who cried out, "Will the Lord cast off for ever; and will He be favorable no more? Is His mercy clean gone for ever; and doth His promise fail for evermore? Hath God forgotten to be gracious; hath He in anger shut up His tender mercies?" Psalm 77:7-9. But at length, and truly it may be long before, faith gets the better of unbelief. Many that are the children of God cannot always call him "Father." Yet even then they go to Him and are not quite beat off from Him. There is a secret trust that He has some gracious respect to them, and by this they are encouraged still to persist in prayer.

USE 3. OF EXHORTATION. Prize and value the spirit of prayer. As without His help you cannot pray to any purpose, so He can make prayer mightily prevail-

ing. The Spirit will create a holy gladness in your access
to the throne of grace. He will enlarge your hearts in
this duty, which enlargements are not without sweetness and great satisfaction. The Spirit will draw up and
indite such petitions for you as will not be denied, and
give some encouraging intimation of your being accepted and answered in the beloved.

Directions to Have the Spirit of Prayer

Now, if you would have the spirit of prayer, follow
these directions.

1. Rest not in the bare gift of prayer. Let it not satisfy you that you have a praying tongue and no more.
All your supplications are but as flattering the Lord
with your lips, and lying unto Him with your tongues,
while your hearts are not right with Him.

2. Be sensible of your need of the Spirit. Light and
liberty, life and liveliness, are the effects of the Spirit—
good motions, holy affections, are His offspring.
Without Him, you will be like Pharaoh's chariots when
the wheels were taken off, and drive on heavily. But He
can make your souls like the chariots of Amminadab.

3. Part with every thing that grieves the Spirit.
Foster not any lust or inordinate affection that may
render your hearts an unpleasant habitation to Him.

4. Frequently beg for the Spirit, and especially in
secret. This will be a sign that you indeed desire Him.
Plead the promises which you find, Luke 11:13, "If you
then being evil, know how to give good gifts to your
children, how much more shall your heavenly Father
give the Holy Spirit unto them that ask Him?" And
what God has promised, Christ died that He might

purchase. Nay, Christ has prayed that the Spirit might be bestowed. And, therefore, you may pray with the greater encouragement and assurance. Thus concerning the third doctrine.

Doctrine 4

Watch in Prayer

In prayer, watching is a necessary ingredient. Watching is a duty which the great Prophet Christ Himself frequently pressed. The injunction is general, "What I say unto you, I say unto all, Watch," Mark 13:37. He knew that a spiritual lethargy is a disease most incidental. But if at any time, surely in holy duties this heedlessness and sleepiness reveals itself, we need, therefore, to rouse up our spirits that are so sluggish naturally. Deborah speaks to herself four times: "Awake, awake; Deborah, awake, awake; utter a song," Judges 5:12. We need thus again and again to call upon our souls to awake and be watchful when about to utter a prayer. Watching and prayer are joined in Scripture. And not only so, but watching is required in prayer, Colossians 4:2, "Continue in prayer, and watch in the same with thanksgiving." So 1 Peter 4:7, "But the end of all things is at hand, be ye therefore sober, and watch unto prayer."

In the handling of this doctrine, I shall first show what we are to watch against in prayer; second, what we are to watch over; third, what we are to watch for; fourth, what manner of watching is required in prayer; fifth, give the reason why watching is so necessary; and, lastly, make application.

202

1. What we are to watch against in prayer.

In the first place, I am to tell you what we are to watch against in prayer.

1. We must watch against indwelling corruption. There is a law in our members that wars against the law of our minds, and the law in our members commands quite contrary to the Law of God. This law says "do not pray at all," but especially forbids seriousness and fervency in prayer. And if we are not watchful, this law will sway and over-rule us and bring us into captivity to the law of sin. We need to look to ourselves, for when we have thought of doing good, evil will be present with us. And if care is not taken, the evil will hinder our doing of the good. Oh, how deep is the corruption of our nature! How desperately wicked is the heart of man! How great are the remainders of sin in those that are most renewed! Since the remaining flesh still lusts against the Spirit, this flesh is to be narrowly eyed, that it may be weakened and checked, else it will spoil all our services.

2. When praying, we must watch against the evil one. Satan does not like to see us at the throne of grace because he knows and has felt the sufficiency of that grace that believers obtain there. "I besought the Lord," says the Apostle, "when buffeted by the messenger of Satan," 2 Corinthians 12:8. And the power of Christ so rested upon him that Satan had no power, unless it were full sore against his will, to keep him humble, and to hinder his being exalted above measure. The devil, therefore, with might and main withstands us in prayer. And how many are his wiles that he may keep us off from this most advantageous duty! Sometimes he objects the difficulty of prayer. Some-

times he says it is needless to spend so much time
therein. Sometimes he says it is fruitless and that little
comes of all our cries and tears. Sometimes he pro-
poses other business to be done, that we may be di-
verted from engaging with that fervor and devotedness
we ought to feel in this duty. How busy our adversary,
the devil is! We should be acquainted with and watch
against his wiles, and do our duty without crediting or
regarding his instigations.

3. When praying, we must watch against the cares
of this world. Our Lord cautions against over-solici-
tousness about what we shall eat, what we shall drink,
and wherewithal we shall be clothed as things which
would hinder us from seeking the kingdom of God
and His righteousness, Matthew 6:32-33. Earthly care
will allow but little or no time for prayer, and very
much distracts the heart in that duty. Worldly projects
are bold to come into the thoughts, and secular business and employments are minded even then when the
Lord seems to be worshipped. Surely it is our wisdom
to take heed to the Apostle, Philippians 4:6, "Be careful for nothing, but in every thing by prayer and supplication with thanksgiving, let your requests be made
known unto God." Prayer is an antidote against this
care, as this care is an impediment unto prayer.

4. When praying, we must watch against the pleasures of this life. There is a strange proneness to those
pleasures wherewith the senses are gratified to bewitch
the heart. And if these are loved and admired, prayer
will be irksome and unpleasant, and we shall easily be
drawn wholly to neglect that which we do not at all
like. She that continued in prayer and supplication was
not one that lived in pleasure, 1 Timothy 5:5-6. Watch

against pleasures which are but for a season and, when ended, are followed by torments that will never end. We read of that rich man in the gospel who was clothed in purple and fine linen, who fared sumptuously and deliciously every day. We read, I say, that he feasted, but not that he prayed, till he was in the place of torment. Pleasure before hindered prayer; torment forced him to pray. But alas! It was then too late. Despise sensual pleasures, and, when they are presented to entice you, scorn them. In the Lord, and in prayer, infinitely truer and more solid delight is to be found.

5. When praying, we must watch against deceitful riches. Christ says we cannot serve God and mammon. If the love of money is the root of evil, as the Apostle affirms, then it must be a hinderance to duty. Moses had low thoughts of the treasures of Egypt. Nay, he looked upon the very reproach of Christ as greater riches, Hebrews 11. If any are deceived by such treasure and grow eager after it, it will certainly hinder them from seeking Him who is invisible, especially from diligently seeking Him. One great reason why many pray so seldom and so coldly is worldly-mindedness. They are altogether for growing rich in the world, so their desires are small of growing rich towards God. Luther was a man much and mighty in prayer. He spent three hours a day constantly herein. But he was also eminent for his contempt of riches. And, therefore, when one said, "Why don't they stop Luther's mouth against the Pope by some preferment?" it was answered, "That German beast" [he should have said, "that German saint"] does not care for silver."

6. When praying, we must watch against the sins

that most easily beset us. The sin of our constitution, the sin of our calling, the sin which has naturally the greatest interest in our love, is the arch-rebel against God and our chief enemy. Upon the least unwatchfulness, this sin will prevail; upon its prevailing, backwardness to prayer and deadness in it will be the consequence. But not only the sin that so easily besets us, but every weight must be laid aside if we would, with freedom, converse with God in prayer. Every iniquity allowed defiles the soul and separates between the Lord and us, and makes us unfit for communion with Him. Therefore, we must watch and strive against all sin without exception.

2. What we are to watch over in prayer.

In the second place, I am to inform you what we are to watch over in prayer.

1. In prayer, we are to watch over our thoughts. It is a proverb, but none of Solomon's, nor a wise one, that "thoughts are free." God sees the thoughts, and the wicked must forsake not only his way but his thoughts if he will return to the Lord and partake of mercy, Isaiah 55:7. If thoughts are not watched over, there may be as many thoughts as sins, and guilt thereby vastly increased. Thoughts are very quick and fleet things, and great is the natural vanity, impertinence, confusedness, and sinfulness of them. If there is no eye to them, nay, if the eye is not very careful, prayer may be made and God prayed to and not thought on all the while. Right prayer is hard labor, and the labor lies very much about the thoughts in fixing them upon God, keeping out vain imaginations, and expelling them as soon as notice is taken of their intrusion.

2. In prayer, we are to watch over our reasoning faculty. There are certain reasonings which the Apostle calls high things that exalt themselves against the knowledge of God, which must be brought into captivity, 2 Corinthians 10:5. We must not be peremptory in arguing and determining that this, that, and the other thing is good for us, but rather we must refer ourselves to His wisdom and good pleasure who does all things for His people both well and wisely. As we must not lean to our own understanding in judging what temporal mercies are most convenient, so neither are we to grow so bold and presumptuous as to reason against any of the attributes or promises of God nor any part of His will which He has revealed.

The Lord has proclaimed Himself gracious to His people and terrible to His enemies. We must pray on and believe this, though enemies are high and His church never so much oppressed, though providences seem never so much to thwart God's promises. We must pray and wait for their accomplishment. Finally, we must not reason against any part of His will. But though His commands are never so strictly holy, we must approve of them and beg grace to keep them.

3. In prayer we are to watch over our hearts. "Keep thy heart with all diligence," Proverbs 4:23. Heed must be taken that there be no jarring between our wills and the will of God, for His will is holy, right, and good. Ours, therefore, should always comply with His. As the echo answers and returns the voice, so should our wills, complying, answer God's will commanding. This you may observe in David, a man after God's own heart. The Lord says, "Seek ye My face." David's heart echoes back, "Thy face, Lord, will I seek." So it is in Psalm

114:4-5. The Lord commands to keep His precepts
diligently. David's echo is, "O that my ways were directed, that I might keep Thy statutes!" We must see to
our hearts in prayer, that they are sincere in hating
what the Lord abhors and in choosing what He offers
in the gospel and also promises to bestow.

4. In prayer, we are to watch over our consciences
so that they perform their offices faithfully. Their
office is to observe and condemn every miscarriage, to
urge unto a more spiritual manner of praying, and to
be restless and unquiet if prayer is omitted upon any
slight pretense or "the male in the flock be not offered
to the Lord, but a corrupt thing." A tender conscience
is a blessing that can never be sufficiently valued. This
will cause the vest to be given unto God. This will not
be satisfied till God approves and commends. And
what a heaven follows upon prayer when the Lord
Himself and His officer—conscience—are both
pleased! But if we grow unwatchful over our consciences and suffer them to fall asleep and become
seared, a thousand faults in prayer will be winked at;
nay, we shall be but little reproached for the total
omission of it.

5. In prayer, we are to watch over our affections.
The more affection in prayer, the more pleasing the
duty will be to God and the more pleasant to him that
performs it. There is enough in the Lord to draw forth
the very strength of our affections. How great is His
goodness! How able and powerful in His hand to save!
How unsearchable are the riches of His grace! "Eye has
not seen, ear has not heard, neither has it entered into
the heart of man what He has prepared for those that
wait upon Him," Isaiah 114:4. We are inexcusable if all

this move not our affections. We should watch and observe when our affections begin to incline towards former lovers, and then compare those lovers and the Lord together that other things may be condemned and our souls may even break for longing after God.

6. In prayer, we are to watch over our outward man. Our tongues and senses must be looked to. Our tongues must speak reverently, considering God is in heaven and we are on earth, Ecclesiastes 5:2. And we must have warrant from God's own Word for the words we utter before Him. Our senses must be guarded, else at the ear or eye especially something or other may enter that may disturbs prayer, and hinders it from being so fervent and effectual.

You see what we must watch over.

3. What we must watch for in prayer.

In the third place, I am to show what we must watch for in prayer.

1. We must watch for fit seasons to pray. There are some times and seasons in which God is nearer than others and more ready to be found of them that seek Him. This the prophet intimates, "Seek ye the Lord, while He may be found; call ye upon Him, while He is near." Those seasons of grace and love are carefully to be observed and improved to the uttermost. When the Lord came so near to Jacob as to suffer him to take hold of Him, that was a special season. Jacob was sensible of it and wrestled long,and with a holy vigor. He kept his hold and would not let go till he had the blessing, Genesis 32:29. That also was a special opportunity when the Lord spake unto Moses, face to face, "as a man speaketh to his friend," Exodus 33:11. Moses im-

proved this and begged for the Lord's presence with
them and with the people of Israel. And, having prevailed for his, he adds further, "Lord, I beseech thee,
show me Thy glory," 5:8. Hereupon the Lord made His
goodness to pass before him, and proclaims, "The
Lord God, merciful and gracious, long suffering,
abundant in goodness and in truth, keeping mercy for
thousands, forgiving iniquity, transgression, and sins."

2. We must watch for admonitions from conscience
unto prayer. When conscience says, "You have not yet
prayed in secret," then go and pour out your heart before Him who sees in secret. "You have not yet prayed
in your family," then call all of your household together and join in begging that the Lord would have
mercy upon all. Conscience is by no means to be disre-
garded, but its admonitions should be taken.

The authority the Lord allows to conscience is
great, and its office is of a large extent. Conscience is a
witness, a judge, and a monitor. As a witness, it takes
notice of the evil we do, of the good we refuse to do,
and likewise observes when we are careful of our duty.
As a judge, it acquits or condemns, according as we
have been either good or faithful, or evil and slothful
servants. As a monitor, it tells us beforehand of our
duty. And, as we would avoid its accusations and reproaches, we should not venture upon any sin which it
cries out against, nor neglect prayer, or any other duty
which it charges us to perform, as we will answer for it
before God.

3. We must watch for the motions of the Spirit unto
prayer. When the Holy Ghost moves to this duty and
His motions are heeded and obeyed, we are to conclude that the same Spirit which moves to prayer will

assist in prayer. It is a wonderful privilege that the
Spirit is sent unto the churches, and is speaking and
striving for their good. Every one should have an ear to
hear what the Spirit says, Revelation 3. When the Spirit
speaks, concerning sin, "this is not the way," therefore
avoid it. "Oh, do not this abominable thing which God
hates." We must by no means consent to evil. When the
Spirit says concerning duty, "This is the way, walk ye in
it," Isaiah 30:31, we must by all means yield unto that
which is good. If the Lord by His Spirit says, "Seek My
face," with the greatest eagerness we should reply, "Thy
face, Lord, I will seek," and He will not then hide His
face from us nor put His servants away in anger.

The motions of the Spirit unto prayer are twofold-
ordinary, extraordinary.

There are more ordinary motions unto prayer. It is
the mind and will of the Spirit that our usual times for
prayer of all sorts should be observed. And though
deadness and indisposition be never-so-great, and our
hearts draw back from the throne of grace, yet we must
go there. Experience teaches that where deadness at
the beginning of prayer has seemed invincible, yet all
of a sudden it has been removed and the duty has been
carried on and concluded with more than ordinary enlargements. The Israelites were commanded to go forward when they came to the Red Sea. They might have
answered, "What, would you have us march into the
water, and be drowned?" Well, but forward they went,
and the water was dried up before them, Exodus 14. So
truly, many times, when we are about to pray, there is
great listlessness and many discouragements. Yet we
must go forward and engage in our duty, and the sea is
dried up before us. These discouragements are re-

moved.

There are more extraordinary motions of the Spirit unto prayer: upon some remarkable providence, either cross or kindness; upon the hearing of some more than ordinary affecting truths; upon some special manifestations by way of quickening and peace. And upon all these, the Spirit may move unto more than ordinary plying of this work of prayer. And the iron is by all means to be struck while it is thus hot. An extraordinary motion of the Spirit raised David out of his bed at midnight: "At midnight I will arise to give thanks unto thee, because of thy righteous judgments," Psalm 119:62. So we read also, Acts 16:25, that at midnight, Paul and Silas prayed and sang praises unto God, and the prisoners heard them. Here let it be observed that when the Spirit of God thus extraordinarily moves to pray, He sweetly and strongly inclines the heart to comply with His motions. There is a quickening heart that goes along with His persuasions to engage in this duty.

4. We must watch for all manner of encouragements in prayer. And truly the Lord is not backward to give if we are heedful and forward to take encouragement. The Lord encourages to prayer various ways.

First, by making us sensible what a privilege access to the mercy-seat is. He causes us to be satisfied and delighted in His presence. And our hearts cry out, "Oh how good is it for us to be here! This is none other than the throne of grace, and this is indeed the gate of heaven. "It is good for me to draw nigh to God," says holy David, Psalm 73.

Second, the Lord encourages to prayer by melting the heart for sin. He thaws the ice by the beams of His love. A sense of unkindness, and unsuitable carriage towards the Father of mercies, causes plenty of godly sorrow. And the heart hereby is exceedingly alienated from its iniquity.

Third, the Lord encourages to prayer by enlarging the desires after Himself, making the soul enamored of Him and altogether unsatisfied till it tastes and sees His goodness.

Fourth, the Lord encourages to prayer by intimations of audience. The Lord said unto Daniel at the close of his prayer, "O man, greatly beloved," Daniel 9:23. Christ answers the woman of Canaan, "Great is thy faith; be it unto thee even as thou wilt," Matthew 15:28. When God, after we have been earnest for pardon, for sanctification, for grace to honor and to please Him, causes a peace and calmness in our spirits, we have a hint that our petitions are according to His will and will be granted. Here is great encouragement in prayer. Now such encouragements should be watched for and laid hold on, with the greatest thankfulness.

5. We must watch for the returns of prayer. The Psalmist had been praying, and he resolved that he would hearken what God the Lord would speak, that is, by way of answer, Psalm 85:8. In like manner, the Church, concluding that the Lord would at last hear, resolved to wait for Him: "Therefore will I look unto the Lord, I will wait for the God of my salvation; my God will hear me," Micah 7:7. If you do not watch for returns of prayer, you do not consider what you do, or with whom you have to do in prayer. When you pray, you take the name of God into your mouths; and shall that be taken in vain? When you pray, you engage in

an ordinance of God—and shall that be used in vain? What, do you imagine that God's hand is shortened, or His ear heavy, and His bowels straitened? Not looking after your prayer dishonors Him more than you are aware of. He speaks to you and does for you in vain. This is the ready course to provoke Him to keep silence and to shut His hand. You are, therefore, with the prophet, to stand upon your watchtower, and to observe what God says to you, Habbakuk 2:1.

A Case of Conscience

Here one grand case of conscience is to be proposed and resolved. How shall we know whether prayer is answered "Yes" or "No," and the blessings we have begged given as a return to our requesting them?

I answer that blessings are of two sorts: those that are peculiar to saints and those that are common to the ungodly.

There are blessings that are peculiar to the saints, such as the sense of God's love, strength against corruption, righteousness and true holiness, peace of conscience, power to run in the ways of God's commands without weariness, and to walk without fainting. If such blessings as these are prized and earnestly desired in prayer, and after prayer are bestowed, they may be concluded the fruit of supplication. "In the day when I cried Thou answeredst me," said David, "and strengthenedst me with strength in my soul," Psalm 138:3. He prayed for grace and spiritual strength, and received it, and concluded that his prayer was answered. It is only the children of God who long and beg for such blessings. And, if the Lord's hand is open and gives the blessings begged, we may also conclude that His ear was open to the begging.

There are blessings that are common to the ungodly, such as health, food, raiment, relations, prosperity, removing of afflictions, and mercies of the like nature. It is more difficult to know when these are given or continued as return to prayer. But yet this may be known in these particulars:

1. Temporal blessings are the fruit of prayer, when they were begged not only *of* God but *for* God, that they might be employed in His service and to His praise. Joshua begged for victory over the Canaanites, but he had an eye to God's great name, which he knew would be dishonored if Israel were overthrown, Joshua 7:9. When we desire some estate that we may do good with it, and honor the Lord with our substance, when we desire health and strength that we may be the more useful, and serve our generation according to the will of God—when we desire such things and our desires are bestowed, surely prayer is heard.

2. Temporal blessings are the fruit of prayer when they are begged with a humble and holy submission and not asked as the principal things. When we pray for daily bread and the meat that perishes in such a measure as the Lord sees most meet to deal forth to us, but our greatest hunger and thirst is after higher things, even that meat which endures to everlasting life, and the waters of that fountain that is always flowing, and yet ever full.

3. Temporal blessings are obtained by prayer when they prove as cords to draw the heart nearer to God and effectually engage unto obedience. David was brought very low. The sorrows of death compassed

him. He called upon the name of the Lord for deliverance, Psalm 116:3-4. Well, deliverance was granted, and what effect did it have? It made him admire divine mercy, it strengthened his faith, it made him cry out, "Truly I am Thy servant," and resolve to "walk before God in the land of the living." Surely this deliverance came by prayer, and so he was persuaded, verses 1-2, "I love the Lord, because He hath heard my voice and supplication, because He hath inclined His ear to me; therefore will I call upon Him as long as I live."

I have showed you what we are to watch for in prayer.

4. What manner of watching is required.

1. Our watch must be very strict, and this strictness will be acknowledged as reasonable if we consider that prayer is a business of weight. Life or death, blessing or cursing will follow according as we speed well or ill in prayer. When we come to the throne of grace, we entreat for no less than the forgiveness of millions of offences; the least of which, if unpardoned, is sufficient to expose us to eternal condemnation. We entreat for no less than grace and glory. We deprecate no less than anger of the Almighty, and everlasting torments. Surely we should be watchful and full of care, by all means, to speed in a duty of such vast concernment.

2. Our watch must be continued. It must be before, in, and after prayer, and all little enough.

We must watch before prayer, that every thing may be avoided and removed that may hinder the heart from preparing to have to do with God. It is not easy to enter rightly upon this duty.

We must watch in prayer. Prayer is expressed in

Scripture by the metaphor of wrestling. If the wrestler watches not he prevails not, but is easily foiled. If we are not very vigilant all the while we are praying, God, whom we wrestle with, will withdraw, and we shall miss the blessing; and Satan that wrestles against us, will presently overcome us.

We must watch after prayer. We must trace our hearts, and mark how they have behaved themselves; we must observe and bemoan our failings, and be thankful for assisting grace. We must be the same upon our legs that we were upon our knees, and lie according to our prayers.

5. Why watching is so necessary in prayer.

1. God watches how this duty is performed, and has denounced a curse on those who do the work of the Lord negligently. He narrowly observes where the thoughts are and how much of the heart and affection is in every prayer. Hearken to the Apostle, "Neither is there any creature that is not manifest in His sight, but all things [even the thoughts and intents of the heart, whereof he had spoken in the foregoing verse] are naked and open unto the eyes of Him with whom we have to do," Hebrews 4:13.

2. Satan watches. In a time of war, there is the stricter watch. Now our life is a warfare, therefore we should be ever vigilant. Our adversary the devil goes about, 1 Peter 5:8, endeavouring to do all the mischief and to hinder all the good he possibly can. Satan is very busy about us in prayer. And if our unwatchfulness gives him but the least encouragement and advantage, he presently spies and takes it.

3. Unless we watch, our hearts will deal treacher-

ously. They will start aside from God like deceitful bows, and the arrow of prayer will be far from hitting the mark. But our supplications will degenerate into mere formality whereas, if we are intent and serious and mind our business while we are at prayer, we shall undoubtedly make something of it. I come at last to the application.

6. Application.
USE 1. OF REPROOF. Two sorts of persons deserve, and highly need a reprehension.

The careless hypocrite is to be reproved. The Scripture—which has this pre-eminence above all other laws: that it binds the very heart and conscience—speaks very terribly against hypocrisy, which is the heart's dissimulation and going away from God, even while the external part of devotion is yielded to Him. The folly in the praying hypocrite will appear in these things:

His conscience is fast asleep in prayer and lets him do even what he pleases. But this sleeping lion will at length awake. At farthest, hell will awaken his conscience, and then it will bitterly reproach him, and never cease reproaching.

The hypocrite does not regard the God he is praying to. He is not awed by the Lord's majesty, nor affected with His mercy, neither is he afraid of provoking Him to jealousy, but presumes upon God as if He were altogether such an one as himself. "These things hast thou done, and I kept silence; and thou thoughtest I was altogether such an one as thyself; but I will reprove thee, and set them in order before thine eyes. Now consider this, ye that forget God, lest I tear you in pieces, and these be none to deliver," Psalm 50:21-22.

The hypocrite regards not the things he is praying for nor himself that is concerned in prayer. He is not concerned for his soul, which is most truly himself. And though he prays for the favor of God, for the kingdom of God, and deliverance from everlasting fire prepared for the devil and his angels, yet he is cold and heedless, as if he were indifferent whether heaven or hell were his eternal abode.

The drowsy and declining saints are also to be reproved. These having been once so thoroughly awakened are more without apology if they grow again unwatchful.

The prayers of unwatchful saints have very bad mixtures. Oh the forgetfulness, fearlessness, weariness, and mocking of the Lord, that believers under their declinings are to be charged with! How near do they come to the borders of unregeneracy! How like are they to the unsound-hearted!

The prayers of unwatchful saints are very unprofitable. Children they are, but alas! They do not improve their relation nor make serious application to their Father. The Spirit is in them, but they accept not His strength and grace. Prayer is not totally laid aside, but little comes of it because they do not vigorously engage in it.

The prayers of unwatchful saints are uncomfortable. The Spirit is grieved by their carelessness, and how can it be expected He should be a Comforter to them? Conscience is dissatisfied and continually grudging because they do not stir up themselves to lay hold on God when they call upon Him, Isaiah 64:7. Much fear, much bondage, many secret gripes of spirit follow upon careless praying.

The prayers of unwatchful saints are so offensive that they may mostly fear some stroke from God, some smarting rod to awaken the spirit of prayer in them. "I will be unto Ephraim as a lion, and as a young lion to the house of Judah. I, even I, will tear and go away: I will take away, and none shall rescue him," Hosea 5:14. Now what was the reason of this severity? It follows verse 15, "In their affliction they will seek Me early." He thrust the spur in their side and made them bleed to make them mend their sluggish pace in duty. He chastened them that He might hear louder cries, and have more serious prayers from them.

USE 2. OF EXHORTATION. Be persuaded to watch in prayer. Those that watch not at all pray not at all in God's account. Those who watch most make most of prayer. These arguments I shall further use to second this exhortation.

1. The more watchful you are in prayer, the better you will understand the devil's enmity. You will perceive his envy and his hatred, and how loath he is that you should receive any distinguishing mercies, especially at the hand of God. Therefore, he so stirs himself that he may resist you. And the better you know this enemy, the better armed you will be.

2. The more watchful you are in prayer, you will be more acquainted with yourselves and your own hearts. You will more fully understand your wants and your spiritual plagues. And the understanding of these is one good step to the supply and cure.

3. The more watchful you are in prayer, the more experimentally will you understand the loving-kindness

of the Lord. You will find that he deals bountifully.
"Return unto thy rest, O my soul, for the Lord hath
dealt bountifully with thee," Psalm 116:7. God is certainly willing to give. They who watch in prayer take
notice what they receive, and great joy it is to behold
the prayers that as messengers we dispatched to heaven
then return loaded with mercy. "Ask and you shall receive, that your joy may be full." So much then, for the
fourth doctrine.

Doctrine 5

Persevere in Prayer

We must persevere if we would speed in prayer. Or, prayer must be with all perseverance. The words of the text are not without emphasis. Not only perseverance, but *all* perseverance is required by the Apostle. There should not be the least fainting but a vigorous persisting in our supplications. Observe how the Apostle speaks in other places. Colossians 4:2, "Continue in prayer." Romans 12:12, "Rejoicing in hope, patient in tribulation, continuing instant in prayer."

In speaking to this doctrine, I shall first tell you what it is to persevere in prayer; second, what kind of perseverance is required; third, give you the reasons of this perseverance; and, last, make application.

1. What it is to persevere in prayer.

1. This perseverance in prayer implies resolvedness of spirit against all opposition. The resolution is not to be made in our own strength but in the power of grace. And then it will be firm and hold. He that perseveres in prayer resists Satan's endeavors to hinder him in his duty. Though this lion roars upon him by fearful, blasphemous thoughts; though this adversary buffets him by confused, amazing, and affrighting imaginations; yet all his skill does not beat him off from prayer. The more busy he finds Satan, the more need

he perceives of calling upon God. As the devil cannot
prevail by his more irksome temptation so as to cause
an omission of prayer, in like manner, on the other
side, the more pleasing temptations are withstood. The
devil speaks big words concerning sports and pastimes
and pleasures of sense. He talks at a high rate of
worldly advantages that are to be pursued that he may
divert and draw away the heart from prayer. Yet he that
perseveres in this duty believes this lying and deceitful
spirit in nothing.

Nay, he retorts upon Satan and answers that therefore he prays that he may find true joy and greater
sweetness in God than the creatures can possibly yield.
Therefore he prays because he has a mind to be rich,
indeed, and to have a treasure in heaven where neither
moth nor rust corrupts and where thieves cannot
break through nor steal.

And as for that opposition he meets with from
within from the corruption of his heart (which is indeed the greatest), he bewails it, struggles with it, and
cries out for the Spirit of life to quicken and help him.
He is convinced of the necessity of prayer, and the excellency of what prayer is for. And opposition is but a
whet to him that he may stir up himself to lay hold on
God.

2. This perseverance in prayer implies getting
through all discouragements. The more that blind
Bartimeus was discouraged by the people, the louder
he cried, "Jesus, thou Son of David, have mercy upon
me." And his cry was heard. According to his desire, he
had his sight restored.

The woman of Canaan, who came to Christ that her
daughter might be dispossessed of a devil, met with

great discouragements but overcame them all,
Matthew 15:21-29. When first she uttered her request,
Christ answered her not a word. This, one would have
thought, might have struck her dumb and made her
conclude it vain to have spoken any more. But, no—
still she cried after Him, whereupon the disciples inter-
ceded for her. Christ answered that He was sent to the
lost sheep of the house of Israel. Here was a second
repulse, but neither did this discourage her. She came
and worshipped Him and said, "Lord, help me!" Christ
said "It is not meet to cast the children's bread unto
the dogs." This was a third repulse, and worst of all;
and yet she did not give over, but pleaded that, though
she were indeed no better than a dog, crumbs might
be given her. She succeeded, and whatever she had a
mind to was granted.

He who perseveres in prayer will not be discouraged. Is his guilt great? He replies that the Lord's
mercy will be the more magnified if he obtains a pardon. Is he much distempered? He replies that the
more will the skill of the great Physician be shown in
healing his spiritual diseases. Is he very unworthy? He
replies that the prodigal upon his returning found his
father's doors and his father's arms open, though he
came home in rags, having wasted all his substance
among the harlots in riotous living. Though he is
wretched, miserable, poor, blind, and naked, yet he
says that Christ has eye-salve to make him see, gold
tried in the fire to make him rich, and white raiment to
cover him, Revelation 3:17-18. It is a mercy-seat, it is a
throne of grace he goes to. And, therefore, discouragements are not invincible.

3. This perseverance in prayer implies continual

importunity. Importunity is many times troublesome to
man, but God is delighted with it. Humility, indeed becomes us in our addresses to Him. But we are allowed
to be urgent, to be instant, to be pressing in these
things which are according to the will of the Lord. And
He loves to see us so, for it argues that we value highly
what we beg with importunity. The unjust judge was
prevailed with by the widow's importunity. And will the
Lord neglect importunate prayer, who has commanded and encouraged importunity, and who is so
righteous and gracious? He that perseveres in prayer
follows the Lord with his request. He will not let Him
alone till he has a pardon—and that pardon sealed. He
will not let Him alone till his lusts, which are the worst
of spiritual enemies, are killed, till more grace is
granted of which he cannot have too great a measure.
Take notice of David's importunity in Psalm 69:145-
147, "I cried with my whole heart; hear me, O lord, I
will keep Thy statutes. I cried unto Thee, save me, and
I shall keep Thy testimonies; I prevented the dawning
of the morning, and cried, I hoped in Thy word; my
eyes prevent the night watches." He cried and cried
and cried again, before the dawning of the morning
and in the night watches. Behold how urgent he was in
prayer.

4. This perseverance in prayer implies an holy insa-
tiableness after God, and desiring still more, though
never so much is obtained. Indeed, there is a great
obligation upon us to be thankful for the least measures of grace. But we are not to be contented with the
greatest but still longing for more. Though David enjoyed much of God, and had such a sense of His loving-kindness which was better than life, and experi-

enced that communion with the Lord which was more satisfying than marrow and fatness, yet we find him still following hard after God. "My soul followeth hard after Thee, Thy right hand upholdeth me," Psalm 113:8. And indeed, the more we taste and see how gracious the Lord is, it cannot but increase our longing and raise our thirst to a greater vehemency. Though the Apostle Paul had attained to so much, yet he said, "I forget those things that are behind; and reach forth unto these things that are before, and press towards the mark, for the prize of the high calling of God," Philippians 3:13-14.

5. This perseverance in prayer implies a continuing to engage in all kinds of prayer. There should be a constant and daily course of prayer, even unto the end of life; and if at any time, by weakness or otherwise, the course is necessarily interrupted, our hearts at least should then be working towards God, being sensible that He is our all, that all our hope is in Him, and that all our help is from Him. It is a happy thing so to habituate and accustom ourselves to prayer as to make it become natural to us, and to esteem it as necessary as our very breath.

2. What kind of perseverance is required.

1. In this perseverance there should be no interruptions. Daniel, rather than his course of praying before his God in giving thanks should be interrupted, chose instead to adventure the loss of dignity, of his prince's favor, and his own life besides. And that God whom he served continually delivered him. Daniel resolved to open his mouth in prayer. God sent His angel and stopped the mouths of the lions so that they did

not hurt him. And as carnal fear should not cause the omission of prayer, so neither should any prevailing corruption and deadness. Still the Lord is to be sought and served.

2. In this perseverance there should be a continual endeavor to excel and do better—to pray with more and more spirituality and liveliness. It is a sad sight to see children as weak now as they were several years ago. We conclude there is some bad humor that oppresses nature and causes that weakness, and is an impediment to their growth. It is this and more sad to see Christians stand at a stay and perform duties no better now than some years ago they used to perform them. If there is still the same deadness, the same unbelief, the same worldly-mindedness and distractions which were wont to be, it argues that the Spirit is kept under by the flesh and its prevalency. We are not only to do more than others but to do more than ourselves. The Lord requires us, and truly gives ample encouragement, to be not only steadfast and unmoveable but also to abound in the work of the Lord. "The path of the just should be like the shining light, that shineth more and more unto the perfect day," Proverbs 4:18. All our duties are motions homeward, and heaven is our home. And the nearer home, the swifter should our spiritual motions be.

3. Why prayer should be with perseverance.

1. Divine commands are very express, not only to perform the duty but to continue in the duty. In the text, not only praying is enjoined, but praying always and with all perseverance. And, 1 Thessalonians 5:17, "Pray without ceasing." God's command should cause

us perpetually to stand in awe. We must not dare to cease doing that which He would have us without ceasing, be employed in.

2. The Lord perseveres in attending and encouraging. Therefore, we should persevere in praying. His eye is continually upon His people. Eye, ear, heart, and hand are all open, and if we open our mouths wide, we shall be filled, Psalm 81:10.

3. The Lord is as worthy to be sought unto still as sought to at all. Therefore, we should continue seeking Him. Though our expectation from other things is never so high, yet upon trial we shall discover their emptiness and vanity. But the more we know God, and the greater experience we have of Him, the more we shall behold His fulness, and how good it is to draw near to Him. Israel went astray after other lovers but found her mistake and resolved to return to her first husband, for then it was best with her, Hosea 2:7. God's service is such as no fault at all is really to be found therein. And, therefore, to leave that service is very unreasonable.

4. We are far from attaining all that is attainable by prayer. Clearer discoveries there may be of God. There may be much larger communications of grace. There may be more of peace and joy. Therefore, it concerns us to wait on the Lord still, and not to grow weary of our attending.

5. This present world is full of enemies and snares. Therefore, we should continually have recourse to the God of all grace that grace may be proportioned to our work and to our danger. The world is evil, and the evil one is very active to draw us to evil. And he has a strong and numerous party within our own souls, even all the

remaining corruption. Surely, unless we persevere in prayer and thereby engage Him for us who is able to keep us from falling and to present us faultless before the presence of His glory with exceeding joy, Jude 24, we shall not persevere to the end and be saved. The application follows.

4. Application.
USE 1. OF REPROOF:

1. To those who pray in a time of distress and affliction, but after that is removed and their slavish fear allayed, they quickly give over. When God slew the children of Israel, then they sought Him. They returned and inquired early after God, they remembered that God was their Rock and the high God their Redeemer. But as soon as the Lord ceased smiting, they ceased crying. They flattered with their tongues and were unstedfast in His covenant, Psalm 78:23-37. This is the way to have affliction quickly return again— and that with more of gall and wormwood—or to have spiritual judgments, which are a great deal worse, succeed temporal ones.

2. Reproof belongs to those who pray for a little while, while the conviction is fresh and strong and the exhortation to this duty is still sounding in their ears. But by degrees the conviction wears off, and the exhortation is forgotten. And then, oh, how their hearts depart from God, and what a task and tedious thing is prayer to them! But those foregoing convictions will very much aggravate their omisssions—these omissions having been give way to, especially at first, with much violence offered to their own consciences and resisting the holy Ghost, who strives to make them persevere in

supplication.

3. Reproof belongs to apostates that somewhile made a great profession, and none more forward to pray than they but who now have thrown off this and other ordinances of Christ, being carried away either by a profane or erroneous spirit.

Many are carried away by a profane spirit. And, having restrained prayer, even restraining grace is taken from them. They run out to all excess of riot. They are abominable, vicious, intemperate, unclean, and unrighteous. They declare to all that seven unclean spirits are entered into them and that their last end is likely to prove worse than their beginning. They once, indeed, knew the whole commandment but are now turned from it. And it happens to them according to the proverb, "The dog is turned to his vomit again, and the sow that was washed, to her wallowing in the mire," 2 Peter 2:21-22.

Many are carried away from prayer by an erroneous spirit. These not only break the Lord's commands but persuade themselves that they do well in it, and endeavor to draw others to the like transgression. And hereby their guilt and danger is the greater. Every one that speaks against prayer or any other ordinance of Christ, as he strikes at Christ's authority, who is King of the church, so he is deceived and made use of by the devil to injure souls by drawing them away from God and their duty.

But it may be objected that the Apostle himself says, Colossians 2:20, "Why are ye subject to ordinances?"

I answer, the 21st verse following shows what ordinances the Apostle speaks of: the ceremonial ordinances—"Touch not, taste not, handle not." He is not to be understood concerning the ordinances of Christ's institution for in this very epistle he commands that the Word of God should dwell richly in them, that they sing psalms with grace in their hearts to the Lord, and that they should continue in prayer.

4. Reproof belongs to those who limit God and conclude that, if they are not heard presently, they shall never be answered. In effect they say, "Why should we seek the Lord any longer?"

Vile and sinful creatures should not be so quick with God. What if we tarry some time before we have the grace and comfort we beg? If it comes at last, is not the Lord gracious to a wonder? Besides, the Lord knows when it is fittest to answer prayer. Therefore, it becomes us patiently to wait for His right timing of His benefits, if not the smallest part of them.

USE 2. OF DIRECTION. How you may persevere in prayer:

1. Be exceeding jealous and afraid whenever you find deadness and formality seizing upon you. You know not whether it may grow. The prognostic signs of an approaching distemper easily persuade you to take preventing medicine. Oh, when you find your hearts out of order, fear and go to your Physician to heal your hearts, and reduce them to the right praying frame!

2. Take heed of quenching the Spirit. Let your ears be open to hear what He says to the churches in Revelation 2. Deliver up yourselves wholly unto the Spirit's conduct and guidance. Be led to Him, from what ways and in what ways He pleases, else He will be grieved and withdraw. And if He does so, alas, your Helper will be gone and your infirmities will hinder

your perseverance in prayer!

3. Be sensible that all your prayers will be lost if now you should totally and finally give over. That previous righteousness will be reckoned as none at all. It will be just like the morning cloud and as the early dew that vanishes away. Pray on, therefore, that all may not be in vain.

4. Labor to be acquainted with the sweetness of prayer that you may have experience of those quickenings, those enlargements, those supports, those ravishing delights that the saints have found sometimes in prayer. And then you will like the duty so well that you will not be drawn off from it.

5. Depend upon Him that gives power to the faint, and increases strength in them that have no might. He faints not, neither is He weary, and He alone can keep you from being weary in well doing. As He only can help you when you cry, so He alone can help you to hold on in crying.

6. Cheer up yourselves with this consideration, that if you persevere in prayer but a little while longer, in heaven all your prayers will be fully answered. Remember that if prayer lasts as long as time lasts, time will quickly be succeeded by eternity, and prayer will end in everlasting raises. So much, then, for the fifth doctrine.

Doctrine 6

Supplication for all Saints

The sixth and last doctrine is this. Our spirits must be so public as to supplicate for all saints as well as for ourselves. Therefore, the Apostle adds in the text, "and supplication for all saints."

Here I shall first show what saints the Apostle speaks of, and, second, why we should pray for them all, and then give you the uses.

First, what saints the Apostle speaks of. The saints are of two sorts: triumphant in heaven, and militant on earth.

1. Triumphant in heaven—these do not need our prayers. We need not pray that they may be eased of their loads, for their burdens are removed, and they are entered into perfect rest. We need not pray that God would manifest Himself to them, for they see Him as He is and not as here in a glass darkly. Nor that they may be freed from sorrow, and defended from enemies, for their joy is full. All tears are wiped away, and they are past all danger. "They are made pillars in the heavenly temple, and they shall go no more out," Revelation 3:12. In all the Bible we find not one petition for departed saints. They are with the Lamb crowned above, and are above our supplications.

2. Militant saints on earth—of these the text speaks, and to these the words are to be confined. And truly all

233

of them claim a share in our supplications.

    1.) We are to pray for saints of all nations. Prayer may reach them though never so far, and the God we pray to is acquainted with every saint in particular throughout the universe. He knows what they all want and how to supply all their needs.

    2.) We are to pray for all saints of all persuasions, as long as they hold the Head and are dear to Christ, notwithstanding their differences from us in opinion. Surely, notwithstanding this difference, they should be upon our hearts to desire their good. Oh that there were less quarreling and disputation and more praying and supplication one for another! And this would be a great means to unite and heal our breaches.

    3.) We are to pray for saints of all conditions, high and low, rich and poor, bond and free, male and female. Every saint is a jewel, and a jewel is not to be condemned, though it lies upon a dunghill. The meanest saints are precious in the Lord's eyes, and we should have regard to them.

Why our Supplications should be for all Saints

    The reasons why our supplications should be for all saints are these:

1. Because of their relation to God. They are all His children, and He has the love of a Father to them. Nay, He is a thousand times more full of affection than earthly parents can be. If God loves them, so should we. And we should show our love by our wishing their good, especially considering how much the honor of God is concerned in them and how much His name is

glorified in their preservation.

2. Because of their relation to our Lord Jesus. Should not we pray for them, since Christ died for them? He bought them with the price of His own blood, and they are all espoused to Him. Nay, they are His members—those for whom He ever lives to make intercession. Surely, then, we also should intercede in their behalf.

3. We should pray for all saints because of our relation one to another. We are all begotten by the same seed. We are all members one of another. So "we being many, are one body in Christ, and every one members one of another," Romans 12:5. We are all animated by the same Spirit, one of whose principal fruits is love. And love should be expressed in prayer. Finally, we are all heirs to the same inheritance. Oh, how importunate should we be, that we may come all safely thither!

4. We should pray for all saints because all are engaged in the same war and are wrestling with the same enemies. We should beg, therefore, that all may be kept from the evil of the world, that Satan may be trod under the feet of all, that sin may be subdued in all, and that all may at last be made more than conquerors.

5. All saints are carrying on the same design: the glory of God and the advancement of the kingdom and interest of Christ. We should help one another by prayer that this great end may be attained.

USE 1. OF CONSOLATION. Saints have more prayers going for them than they are aware of. Those that you never saw, nor shall see in this world, are concerned for you and are desiring that you may have that

grace and strength you need, considering the difficulty
of your work and your many adversaries. As every one
should pray for all, so all are praying for every one.
And this is matter of great encouragement.

USE 2. OF REPROOF. To those who are of a selfish
spirit, who are all for themselves but do not look after
Zion. These have neither love to Christ nor to their
own souls upon a right footing. If they loved the Head,
they would be solicitous for the welfare of the body. If
they truly desired the good of their own souls, they
would have pity on the souls of others that are of equal
value.

USE 3. OF EXHORTATION. Be more frequent
and fervent in praying for all the saints. This will be a
great argument that you are indeed members of the
body of Christ when all your fellow-members are loved,
when you feel their sorrows and are concerned for
their welfare.

Pray for the saints' unity, that they may be knit together in love. Their beauty lies much in their agree-
ment and their strength, in their being united. But if a
house or kingdom is divided, division has tendency to
destruction. Christ prayed that His disciples might be
one, as that which would serve very much to convince
the world that God had sent Him. For the division of
saints is not the least cause of prevailing infidelity and
of men's questioning the very truth of Christianity.

Pray for the saints' purity, that the Church may be
more and more cleansed and conformed to the holy
Head, the Lord Jesus.

Pray for the saints' prosperity, especially for those

glorious and peaceable times after antichrist's ruin and the calling home of the Jews, when the kingdoms of the world shall become the kingdoms of the Lord and of His Christ.

Pray for the saints' increase. And, in thus doing, you are kind unto the world. Beg that the prince of darkness may lose and that Christ may gain more and more subjects every day, and that out of the quarry of mankind more may be taken to be made living stones in the Lord's temple.

Pray for the saints' support under all oppressions, for their perseverance to the end, and that the Lord Jesus would hasten His second appearing, when all His church shall be triumphant, when devils and the reprobate world shall be confined to hell, and all the elect shall join together in shouting forth "hallelujahs" unto Him that sits upon the throne and to the Lamb for ever.

Thus have I finished this argument of prayer. What are now your resolutions? Shall there be prayerless families still or any strangers unto secret duty, notwithstanding all that has been spoken? May pardon, grace, life, and salvation be all obtained for asking? And will you not do this much? Will you neither be earnest for others nor for yourselves? Shall none of the directions that have been given be followed? Shall all the arguments that have been used be unsuccessful?

Oh, Thou that commandest and hearest prayer! Oh Thou that helpest Thy people to pray! Pour out the sprit of grace and supplication, that Thy throne of grace may be surrounded with supplicants, that there may be a great flocking to the mercy-seat, and grace may be imparted abundantly to Thy own glory, through Jesus Christ the great High Priest, who is passed into the heavens and is at Thy right hand for ever. Amen.

Secret
Prayer
Successfully
Managed

by

Rev. Samuel Lee
Minister of St. Botolph's, Bishopsgate

Biographical Sketch

The Rev. Samuel Lee, A.M.,
of Wadham College, Oxford,
Minister of St. Botolph, Bishopsgate.

The Rev. Samuel Lee was born in London in 1627. His father was an eminent citizen, greatly esteemed for his private virtues, who lived to a good old age. He appears to have been a man of considerable property. Leee was educated at St. Paul's School under Dr. Gale and then entered Wadham College, where he studied under the direction of Dr. Wilkins, afterwards the excellent Bishop of Chester. He made great attainments in knowledge and piety and was so highly esteemed as to be chosen fellow of his college and proctor of the university. There can be no doubt entertained respecting his religion or literature, when it is stated that he served as proctor in 1656 when John Owen was Vice- Chancellor.

In the following year, he composed his Temple of Solomon, which he printed in folio at the request and expense of the University. His reputation as a preacher led him to London, and he was inducted to the living of St. Botolph, the rectory of which was £40 per year. Here he labored with usefulness and acceptance to his parish until his ejectment in 1662 by the Bartholomew act. Mr. Lee was, in his view of church discipline, a Congregationalist, but he was eminent for the display of charity and catholic spirit. After this trial, we find him the minister of an independent congregation at Newington Green near London. But the persecution of the Church party continuing, he determined to escape from the tender mercies of the cruel, and, in 1686, he embarked for New England. Here he was received with attention and respect and soon became pastor of the Church at Bristol, R.I., where he labored for three years. Hearing of the glorious revolution of 1688, however, and wishing to enjoy its fruits and obtain for himself a valuable estate, he became so desirous to return that he embarked with his family in mid-winter. He sailed from Boston for England in the Dolphin, under Capt. John Foy. The passage was very tedious, owing to the prevalence of easterly winds, and, at length, on the coast of Ireland, they fell in with a French privateer. After a severe resistance, and in great danger of sinking, they were compelled to surrender, and the Dolphin was carried as a prize to St. Maloes in France.

After some detention, his wife and daughter and two servants were sent to England by the king's order, while he was retained a prisoner. Grief at the loss of his family and his solitary condition in a strange land brought on a fever, of which he died in a few days, aged 64.

Secret Prayer
Successfully Managed

"But thou, when thou prayest, enter into thy closet, and when thou hast shut thy door, pray to thy Father which is in secret, and thy Father who seeth in secret, shall reward thee openly." Matthew 6:6

We have here our blessed Lord's instructions for the management of secret prayer, the crown and glory of a child of God.

I. The direction prescribed for our deportment in secret duty is in three things: (1) Enter your closet. This word signifies a secret or recluse habitation, and sometimes it is rendered a hiding place for treasure. (2) "Shut thy door," or lock it, as the word intimates. The Greek word furnishes the term "key," as appears by Revelation 3:7 and 20:1-3, implying that we must bar or bolt it. (3) "Pray to thy Father which is in secret." Tertullian notes this name "father" as intimating both piety and power, "thy Father" denoting intimacy and propriety.

II. A gracious promise which may be branched into three parts: (1) For your Father sees you in secret. His eye is upon you with a gracious aspect when you are withdrawn from all the world. (2) He will reward you. The word used here is sometimes translated by "rendering," Matthew 22:21; Romans 2:6 and 13:7; by "delivering," Matthew 27:58 and Luke 9:42; by "yield-

ing" or "affording," Hebrews 12:11 and Revelation
22:2. All which comes to this: He will return your
prayers, your requests, amply and abundantly into your
bosom. (3) He will do it openly, manifestly, before the
world sometimes, and most plentifully and exuberantly
before men and angels at the great day. Secret prayers
shall have open and public answers.

III. Here is a demonstration of sincerity, from the
right performance of the duty set forth by the antithe-
sis in the fifth verse, "But thou shalt not be as the hypocrites, for they love to pray standing in the synagogues and in the corners of the streets, that they may
be seen of men." Enter not your house only or your
common chamber, but your closet, the most secret and
retired privacy, that others may neither discern you
nor rush in suddenly upon you. God will answer you
and perform your request as a gracious return to your
secret sincerity. God is pleased, by promise, to make
Himself a debtor to secret prayer. It brings nothing to
God but empty hands and naked hearts, to show that
reward, in Scripture sense, does not flow in on the
streams of merit but of grace. It is monkish divinity to
assert otherwise; for what merit strictly taken can there
be in prayer? The mere asking of mercy cannot merit it
at the hands of God, Malachi 2:3. Our most sincere petitions are impregnated with sinful mixtures. We halt,
like Jacob, both in and after our choicest and strongest
wrestlings. But such is the grace of our heavenly
Father, who spies that little sincerity of our hearts in
secret, that He is pleased to accept us in His beloved,
and to smell a sweet savor in the fragrant perfumes and
odors of His intercession.

Though I might draw many notes hence, I shall

treat but one containing the marrow and nerves of the text: that secret prayer duly managed is the mark of a sincere heart and has the promise of a gracious return.

Prayer is the soul's colloquy with God, and secret prayer is a conference with God upon admission into the private chamber of heaven. When you have shut your own closet, when God and your soul are alone, with this key you open the chambers of paradise and enter the closet of divine love. When you are immured as in a curious labyrinth, apart from the tumultuous world, and entered into that garden of Lebanon in the midst of your closet, your soul, like a spiritual Daedalus, takes to itself the wings of faith and prayer, and flies into the midst of heaven among the cherubims.

I may call secret prayer the invisible flight of the soul into the bosom of God. Out of this heavenly closet rises Jacob's ladder, whose rounds are all of light. Its foot stands upon the basis of the Covenant in your heart. Its top reaches the throne of grace. When your reins have instructed you in the night season with holy petition, when your soul has desired Him in the night, then with your spirit within you will you seek Him early. When the door of your heart is shut and the windows of your eyes are sealed up from all vain and worldly objects, up you mount, and your have a place given you to walk among angels that stand by the throne of God, Zechariah 3:7.

In secret prayer, the soul, like Moses, is in the back side of the desert talking with the angel of the covenant in the fiery bush, Exodus 3:1. Here's Isaac in the field at eventide, meditating and praying to the God of his father, Abraham, Genesis 24:63. Here's

Elijah, under the juniper tree at Rithmah in the wilderness, and anon in the cave hearkening to the still small voice of God, 1 Kings 19:4, 12. Here's Christ and the spouse alone in the wine-cellar. The banner of love is over her and she utters but half words, having drunk of the sober excess of the Spirit, Canticles 2:4 and Ephesians 5:18. Here we find Nathaniel under the fig-tree, though it may be at secret prayer, yet under a beam of the eye of Christ, John 1:48. There sits Austin in the garden alone, sighing with the Psalmist, "How long O Lord," and listening to the voice of God, "Take up the Bible and read" (Confessions, 1st book, 8th chapter). It is true, hypocrites may pray, pray alone, pray long, and receive their reward from such whose observations they desire. But a hypocrite takes no sincere delight in secret devotion. He has no spring of affection to God. "But O my dove," says Christ, "that art in the clefts of the rock, let Me hear your voice, for the melody thereof is sweet."

A weeping countenance and a wounded spirit are most beautiful prospects to the eye of heaven, when a broken heart pours out repentant tears like streams from the rock smitten by the rod of Moses' law in the hand of a mediator. Oh how amiable in the sight of God is the cry, "Out of the depths have I cried unto Thee," which Chrysostom glosses thus to "draw sighs from the furrows of the heart." Let your prayer become a hidden mystery of divine secrets, like good Hezekiah upon the bed with his face to the wall so that none might observe him, or like our blessed Lord, that grand example, who retired into mountains and solitude apart, and saw by night the illustrious face of His heavenly Father in prayer.

The reasons why secret prayer is the mark of a sincere heart are as follows: A sincere heart busies itself about heart work to mortify sin, to quicken grace, to observe and resist temptation, to secure and advance his evidences; therefore, it is much conversant with secret prayer. The glory of the king's daughter shines within, arrayed with clothes of gold, but they are the spangled and glittering hanging of the closet of her heart, when she entertains communion with her Lord. The more a saint converses with his own heart, the more he searches his spirit. He labors to walk before God, as being always in His sight, but especially when he presents himself at the footstool of mercy. An invisible God is delighted with invisible prayers, when no eye sees but His. He takes most pleasure in the secret glances of a holy heart. But no more of this, let us descend to the question deducible from the text, a question of no less importance than daily use, and of peculiar concern to the growth of every Christian.

QUESTION. How shall we manage secret prayer that it may be prevalent with God to the comfort and satisfaction of the soul?

ANSWER. For method's sake, I shall divide it into two branches.

How to manage secret prayer, that it may prevail with God.

How to discern and discover answers to secret prayer, that the soul may acquiesce and be satisfied that it has prevailed with God.

Before I handle these, I would briefly prove the duty and its usefulness, leaving some cases about its attendants and circumstances towards the close.

As to the duty itself, the text is plain and distinct in the point. Yet further observe in Solomon's prayer that if any man beside the community of the people of Israel shall present his supplication to God, he there prays for a gracious and particular answer. And we know Solomon's prayer was answered by fire, and so we learn a promise given first to personal prayer, 1 Kings 8:38-39; 2 Chronicles 6:29-30, and 2 Chronicles 7. Besides the many special and particular injunctions to individual persons, as Job 22:27 and 33:26; Psalm 32:8 and Psalm 1:15. Wives as well as husbands are to pray apart, Zechariah 12:14, solitary, by themselves, James 5:13.

We may argue this point from the constant practice of the holy saints of God in all ages but especially of our blessed Lord. And it is our wisdom to walk in the way of good men and keep the paths of the righteous, like Abraham, Eliezer, Isaac, Jacob, Moses, Hannah, Hezekiah, David, Daniel. The time would fail me to bring in the cloud of witnesses. Our Lord, we find sometimes in a desert, in a mountain, in a garden, and at prayer. Cornelius was in his house and Peter was upon the housetop in secret supplication to God.

There is the experience of God's gracious presence and answers sent in upon secret prayers, as in the stories of Eliezer, Jabez, Nehemiah, Zechariah, Cornelius, and Paul. For this cause, because David was heard, shall every one that is godly pray unto Him.

I might urge the usefulness, nay in some cases the necessities, of secret applications to God.

1. Are we not guilty of secret sins in the light of God's countenance that cannot, ought not, to be confessed before others, insomuch that near relations are

exhorted to secret and solitary duties? Zechariah 12:12 and 1 Corinthians 7:4.

2. Are there not personal wants that we would prefer to God alone?

3. Are there not some special mercies and deliverances that concern our own persons more peculiarly, which should engage us to commune with our own hearts and offer the sacrifices of righteousness to God?

4. May there not be found some requests to be poured out more particularly in secret, as to other persons, and as to the affairs of the church of God, which may not be commodiously insisted upon in common?

5. Do not sudden and urgent passions spring out of the soul in secret, that would be unbecoming in social prayer?

6. To argue from the test, may not the soul's secret addresses about inward sorrows and joys be a sweet testimony of the sincerity and integrity of the heart, when the heart knows its own bitterness and a stranger intermeddles not with his joy? Perhaps a man has an Ishmael, an Absalom, a Rehoboam to weep for, and therefore gets into an inward chamber where, behold, his witness is in heaven and his record on high. And when others may scorn or pity, his eye pours out tears unto God.

To end this, when a holy soul is close in secret, what complacency does it take when it has bolted out the world and retired to a place that none knows of to be free from the disturbances and distractions that often violate family communion? When the soul is in the secret place of the Most High, and in the shadow of the Almighty, Oh how safe, how comfortable!

Nor can I insist upon secret prayer under the variety of mental and vocal, nor enlarge upon it as sudden, occasional, or ejaculatory, referring somewhat of this toward the end. I must remark that there are some things which aptly belong to secret prayer; yet, being coincidental with all prayer—public, social, and secret—it is proper to treat those which are important to our present duty and must, therefore, refer to a double head.

I. How shall we manage secret prayer, as it is coincident with prayer in general, so that it may prevail?

1. Use some preparation before it. Rush not suddenly into the awful presence of God. Sanctuary preparation is necessary to sanctuary communion. Such suitable preparatory frames of mind come down from God. It was a good saying of one, "He never prays ardently that does not premeditate devoutly." It is said of Daniel, when he made that famous prayer, he *set* his face to seek the Lord, Daniel 9:3. Jehoshaphat also set himself to seek the Lord, 2 Chronicles 20:3. The church in her soul desires the Lord in the night, and then in the morning she seeks Him early. Desires blown are meditations, are the sparks that set prayer in a light flame.

The work of preparation may be cast under five heads, when we apply to solemn, set prayer.

1.) The consideration of some attributes in God that are proper to the intended petitions.

2.) A digestion of some peculiar and special promises that concern the affair.

3.) Meditation on suitable arguments.

4.) Ejaculations for assistance.

5.) An engagement of the heart to a holy frame

of reverence and keeping to the point in hand. That was good advice from Cyprian, "Let the soul think upon nothing but what it is to pray for," and he adds that, therefore, the ministers of old prepared the minds of the people with "let your hearts be above." For how can we expect to be heard of God when we do not hear ourselves, when the heart does not watch while the tongue utters? The tongue must be like the pen of a ready writer, to set down the good matter which the heart indites. Take heed of ramblings. To preach or tell pious stories while praying to the great and holy God is a branch of irreverence and a careless frame of spirit, Hebrews 12:28.

2. Humble confession of such sins as concern and refer principally to the work in hand. Our filthy garments must be put away when we appear before the Lord who has chosen Jerusalem, Zechariah 3:4. "Look upon my afflictions," says David, and "forgive all my sins." There are certain sins that often relate to afflictions. First "deliver me from transgression, then hear my prayer, Oh Lord." This is the heavenly method. He first forgives all our iniquities and then heals all our diseases, Psalm 103:3. A forgiven soul is a healed soul. While a man is sick at heart with the qualms of sin unpardoned, it keeps the soul in dismay that it cannot cry strongly to God. And, therefore, in holy groans he must discharge himself of particular sins. Thus did David in that great penitential psalm, Psalm 51. Sin, like a thick cloud, hides the face of God so that our prayers cannot enter, Isaiah 59:2. We must blush with Ezra, and our faces must look red with the flushings of conscience if we expect any smiles of mercy, Ezra 9:6. Our crimson sins must dye our confessions, and the

blood of our sacrifices must sprinkle the horns of the golden altar before we receive an answer of peace from the golden mercy seat. When our persons are pardoned, our suits are accepted, and our petitions crowned with the olive branch of peace.

3. An arguing and pleading spirit in prayer. This is properly wrestling with God: humble yet earnest expostulations about His mind toward us. "Why hast Thou cast us off forever; why doth Thy anger smoke? Be not wroth very sore, O Lord: remember not iniquity forever; see, we beseech thee, we are Thy people," Psalm 74:1; Isaiah 64:9. If so, why is it thus? as affrighted Rebekah flies out into prayer, Genesis 25:22. An arguing frame in prayer cures and appeases the frights of spirit and then inquires of God. The temple of prayer is called the soul's inquiring place. I must refer to Abraham, Jacob, Moses, Joshua, David, and Daniel, how they used arguments with God.

Sometimes, it is from the multitudes of God's mercies; Psalm 5:7, 6:4, and 31:16; from the experience of former answers, Psalm 4:1, 6:9, and 22:4. Sometimes it is from their trust and reliance upon Him, Psalm 9:10 and 16:1; from the equity of God, Psalm 17:1; from the shame and confusion of face that God will put His people to if not answered, and that others will be driven away from God, Psalm 31:17 and 34:1; and lastly from the promise of peace, Psalm 20:5 and 35:18. These and many like pleadings we find in Scripture for patterns in prayer which, being suggested by the Spirit, kindled from the altar and perfumed with Christ's incense, rise up like memorial pillars before the oracle.

Let us observe, in one or two particular prayers, what instant arguments holy men have used and pressed in their perplexities. What a working prayer did Jehoshaphat make, taking pleas from God's covenant, dominion and powerful strength, from his gift of the land of Canaan and driving out the old inhabitants—ancient mercies! From his sanctuary, and promise to Solomon; from the ingratitude and ill requital of his enemies, with an appeal to God's equity in the case and a humble confession of their own impotence. Yet in their anxiety, they fixed their eyes upon God. 2 Chronicles 20:10. You know how gloriously it prevailed when he set ambushes round about the court of heaven and the Lord turned his arguments into ambushes against the children of Edom. Yes, this is set as an instance how God will deal against the enemies of His church in the latter days, Joel 3:2. Another instance is that admirable prayer of the angel of the covenant to God for the restoration of Jerusalem, Zechariah 1:12, wherein he leads from the length of time and the duration of his indignation for threescore and ten years, from promised mercies and the expiration of prophecies, and behold, an answer of good and comfortable words from the Lord. Observe that when arguments in prayer are very cogent upon a sanctified heart, such being drawn from the divine attributes, from precious promises and sweet experiments of God's former love, it is a rare sign of a prevailing prayer. It was an ingenious remark of Chrysostom concerning the woman of Canaan: the poor distressed creature was turned into an acute philosopher with Christ, and disputed the mercy from Him. Oh, it is a blessed thing to attain to this heavenly philosophy of prayer, to argue blessings out of the hand of God. Here is a spacious field. I have given but a small

prospect where the soul like Jacob enters the list with
omnipotence and, by holy force, obtains the blessing.

4. Ardent affections in prayer, betokening a heart
deeply sensible, are greatly prevalent. A crying prayer
pierces the depths of heaven. We read not a word that
Moses spoke but God was moved by his cry, Exodus
14:15. I mean not an obstreperous noise, but melting
moans of heart. Yet sometimes the sore and pinching
necessities and distresses of spirit extort even vocal
cries, not unpleasant to the ear of God. "I cried to the
Lord with my voice, and he heard me out of His holy
hill." And this encourages David to a fresh onset,
"Hearken to the voice of my cry, my King and my God;
give ear to my cry; hold not Thy peace at my tears."

Another time he makes the cave echo with his cries.
"I cried, attend to my cry, for I am brought very low."
And what is the issue? Faith gets courage by crying. His
tears watered his faith so that it grew into confidence,
and so he concludes, "Thou shalt deal bountifully with
me, and the righteous shall crown me for conqueror,"
Psalm 142:1, 5-7. Plentiful tears bring bountiful mercies, and a crying suitor proves a triumphant praiser.
Holy Jacob was just such another at the fords of
Jabbok. He wept and made supplication, and prevailed
with the angel. The Lord told Hezekiah He had heard
his prayer, for He had seen his tears. Such precedents
may well encourage backsliding Ephraim to return and
bemoan himself, and then the bowels of God are troubled for him.

Nay, we have a holy woman also weeping sorely before the Lord in Shiloh and then rejoicing in His salvation, 1 Samuel 1:10 and 2:1. The cries of saints are like
vocal music joined with the instruments of prayer:

They make heavenly melody in the ears of God. The bridegroom calls to his mourning dove, "Let me hear thy voice, for it is pleasant." What Gerson says of the sores of Lazarus we may say of sighs, "as many wounds, so many tongues." Cries and groans in prayer are so many eloquent orators at the throne of God.

5. Importunity and assiduity in prayer are highly prevalent. Not that we should lengthen our prayer with tedious and vain repetitions, as the heathen did of old, but we should be frequent and instant in prayer. As Christ bids us to pray always, and the Apostle Paul bids us to pray without ceasing, we learn the duty of constancy in prayer. As the morning and evening sacrifice at the temple is called the continual burnt offering, Numbers 28:4, 6; as Mephibosheth is said to eat bread continually at David's table and Solomon's servants to stand continually before him—that is, at the set and appointed times, so it is required of us to be constant and assiduous at prayer, and to offer our prayers with perseverance.

When the soul perseveres in prayer, it is a sign of persevering faith, and such may have what they will at the hand of God when praying according to divine direction, John 16:23. Nay, urgent prayer is a token of a mercy at hand. When Elijah prayed seven times, one after another for rain, the clouds presently marched up out of the sea at the command of prayer, 1 Kings 18:43. "Ask of Me things to come, and concerning the works of My hands command ye Me, said the Lord," Isaiah 45:11. When we put forth our utmost strength in prayer, and receive no nay from Heaven, our prayers must be like the continual blowing of the silver trumpets over the sacrifices for a memorial before the Lord,

Numbers 10:10. Such prayers are, as it were, a holy mo-
lestation to the throne of grace, Isaiah 54:7. It is said of
the man who rose at midnight to give out three loaves
to his friend that he did it not for friendship's sake but
because he was pressing, so importunate as to trouble
him at such a season as twelve o'clock at night, Luke
11:8. Our Lord applies the parable to instant prayer.

It was so with the success of the widow with the unjust judge, because she vexed and molested him with
her solicitations, Luke 18:5. But of all, the patters of
the woman of Canaan is most admirable. When the
disciples desired her to be dismissed because she troubled them by crying after them, yet she persisted,
Matthew 15:23. May I say it reverently, Christ delights
in such a troublesome person. Augustine observes, by
comparing both evangelists, that first she cried after
Christ in the streets, but our Lord took to a house. She
followed Him there and fell down at His feet—but as
yet He answered her not a word. Then our Lord went
out of the house again, and she followed with stronger
importunity, and argued the mercy into her bosom,
and Christ ascribed it to the greatness of her faith. To
knock at midnight is deemed no incivility at the gate of
heaven. An energetic prayer is likely to be an effica-
cious prayer. Cold petitioners must have cold answers.
If the matter of prayer is right and the promise of God
fervently urged, you are likely to prevail like princely
Israel who held the angel and would not let him go until he had blessed him.

QUESTION. But can God be moved by our arguments and affected with our troubles? He is the unchangeable God and dwells in the inaccessible light.

With Him is no variableness nor shadow of turning.

ANSWER. I reply, these holy motions upon the hearts of saints in prayer are the fruits of his love to them, and the appointed ushers-in of mercy. God graciously determines to give a praying, arguing, warm, affectionate frame as the fore-runner of a decreed mercy. The reason that carnal men can enjoy no such mercies is because they pour out no such prayers. The spirit of prayer prognosticates mercy near at hand. When the Lord by Jeremiah foretold the end of the captivity, he also predicted the prayers that should open the gates of Babylon. Cyrus was prophesied of to do his work for Jacob his servant's sake, and Israel his elect, but yet they must ask him concerning those things to come, and they should not seek him in vain, Isaiah 45:1-4 and 45:19. The glory of the latter days in the return of Israel is foretold by Ezekiel. But then "the Lord will be inquired of by the house of Israel to do it for them," Ezekiel 36:24,37. The coming of Christ is promised by Himself, "But yet the spirit and bride say, Come, and he that heareth must say, Come." And when Christ says He will "come quickly," we must add, "even so come Lord Jesus."

Divine grace kindles these ardent affections when the mercies promised are upon the wing. Prayer is that chain, as Dionysius calls it, that draws the soul up to God and the mercy down to us. Prayer is like the cable that draws the ship to land, though the shore itself remains unmovable. Prayer has its kindling from heaven, like the ancient sacrifices that were enflamed with celestial fire.

6. Submission to the all-wise and holy will of God. This is the great benefit of a saint's communion with

the Spirit, that He makes intercession for them according to the will of God. When we pray for holiness, there is a concurrence with the divine will, for "this is the will of God, even your sanctification," 1 Thessalonians 4:3. When we pray that our bodies may be presented as a living sacrifice, acceptable to God, we then prove what is that good, acceptable, and perfect will of God, Romans 12:1, 2. In the covenant of grace, God does His part and ours too. When God commands us to pray in one place, He promises in another place to pour out upon us a spirit of grace and supplication, Zechariah 12:10. God commands us to repent and turn to Him, Ezekiel 14:6. In another place, Jeremiah 31:18, "Turn Thou me and I shall be turned, for Thou art the Lord my God." And again, "Turn thou us unto Thee, O Lord, and we shall be turned," Lamentations 5:21. And again, "A new heart will I give you, and a new spirit will I put within you, and cause you to walk in My statutes," Ezekiel 36:26-27. And Paul says, "For this cause I cease not to pray for you, that He would work in you that which is well pleasing in His sight." Colossians 1:9-10, Hebrews 13:21. "Work out your own salvation, for it is God that worketh in you, to will and to do of His good pleasure," Philippians 2:12-13. Precepts, promises, and prayer are connected like so many golden links to excite, encourage, and assist the soul in spiritual duties. But in other cases, as to temporal and temporary mercies, let all your desires in prayer be formed with submission guided by His counsel and prostrated at His feet, acted by a faith suited to the promises of outward blessings. And then it shall be unto you even as you will. Gerson said well, "Let all thy desires as to temporals turn upon the hinge of the di-

vine good pleasure." That man shall have his own will
who resolves to make God's will his. God will certainly
bestow that which is for the good of His people.

One great point of our mortification lies in this: to
have our wills melted into God's. And it is a great token of spiritual growth when we are not only content
but joyful to see our wills crossed that His may be
done. When our wills are sacrifices of holy prayer, we
many times receive choicer things than we ask expressly. It was a good saying, "God many times grants
not what we would in our present prayers, that He may
bestow what we would rather have, when we have the
prayer more graciously answered than we petitioned."
We know not how to pray as we ought, but the Spirit
helps us out with groans that secretly hint a correction
of our wills and spirits in prayer. In great anxieties and
pinching troubles, nature dictates strong groans for re-
lief. But sustaining grace and participation of divine
holiness, mortification from earthy comforts, excita-
tion of the soul to long for heaven, being gradually
wearied from the wormwood breasts of their sublunary,
transient and unsatisfying pleasures, and the timing of
our heart for the seasons wherein God will time His deliverances—these are sweeter mercies than the immediate return of a prayer for an outward good.

What truly holy person would lose that light of
God's countenance, which he enjoyed by glimpses in a
cloudy day, for a little corn and wine? Nay, in many
cases open denials of prayer prove the most excellent
answers, and God's not hearing us is the most signal
audience. Therefore, at the foot of every prayer, sub-
scribe "Thy will be done," and you shall enjoy preventing mercies that you never sought and converting mer-

cies to change all for the best, resting confident in this, having asked according to His will, He hears you.

7. Last, present all into the hands of Christ. This was signified of old by praying toward the temple because the golden mercy seat typified that Christ was there, 1 Kings 8:33 and Hebrews 8:3. He is ordained of God to offer gifts and sacrifices, and, therefore, it is of necessity that He should have something from us to offer, being the high priest over the house of God, Hebrews 10:21. What does Christ do on our behalf at the throne of grace? Put some petition into the hands of Christ. He waits for our offerings at the door of the oracle. Leave the sighs and groans of your heart with this compassionate intercessor, who is touched with the feelings of our infirmities, who sympathizes with our weaknesses. He that lies in the Father's bosom and has expounded the will of God to us, John 1:18, adds much incense to the prayers of all saints before the throne of God. He explains our wills to God, so that our prayers, perfumed by His, are set forth as incense before Him, Revelation 8:3 and Psalm 141:2. He is the day's-man, the heaven's-man, between God and us, Job 10:23. Whatever we ask in His name, He puts into His golden censer that the Father may give it to us, John 15:16 and 16:23. When the sweet smoke of the incense of Christ's prayer ascends before the Father, our prayers become sweet and amiable and cause a savor of rest with God. This I take to be one reason why the prevalency of prayer is so often assigned to the time of the evening sacrifice, pointing to the death of Christ about the ninth hour of the day, near the time of the evening oblation, Matthew 27:46; Acts 3:1 and 10:30.

Hence it was too that Abraham's sacrifice received

a gracious answer, being offered about the going down
of the sun, Genesis 15:12 and 24:63. Isaac went out to
pray at even tide. Elijah at Mount Carmel prays and offers at the time of the evening sacrifice, 1 Kings 18:36.
Ezra fell upon his knees and spread out his hands at
the evening sacrifice, Ezra 9:5. David prayed that his
prayer may be virtual in the power of the evening sacrifice, Psalm 141:2. Daniel at prayer was touched by the
angel about the time of the evening sacrifice, Daniel
9:21. All this is to show the prevalency of our access to
the throne of grace by the merit of the intercession of
Christ, the acceptable evening sacrifice. Yea, therefore,
we are taught in our Lord's prayer to begin with the title of a father. In Him we are adopted to be children
and to use that prevalent relation as an argument in
prayer.

There are some other particulars in respect to
prayer in general, as it may be connected and coincident with secret prayer—stability of spirit, freedom
from distraction by wandering thoughts, the acting of
faith, the aids of the Spirit—all which I pass by, and
come to the following.

Directions, Special and Peculiar, to Secret Prayer

1. Be sure of intimate acquaintance with God. Can
we, who are but dust and ashes, presume to go up into
heaven and boldly to enter the presence chamber and
have no fellowship with the Father or with the Son?
"Acquaint thyself with Him and be at peace; then shalt
thou have thy delight in the Almighty, and lift up thy
face unto God. Thou shalt make thy prayer unto Him,

and He shall hear thee. The decrees of thy heart shall
be established to thee, and the light shall shine upon
thy ways," Job 22:21, 26-28. First, shining acquaintance
and then shining answers. Can you set your face unto
the Lord God? Then you may seek Him by prayer. First
Daniel sets and shows his face to God, and then seeks
Him by prayer and supplication, Daniel 9:3. Does God
know your face in prayer? Do you often converse in
your closets with Him?

Believe it, it must be the fruit of intimate acquaintance with God to meet Him in secret with delight.
Can you come familiarly as a child to a father, considering its own vileness, meanness, or unworthiness, in
comparison with His divine love, the love and bowels
of a heavenly Father. Such a Father, the Father of fathers, and the Father of mercies. How sweetly does the
Apostle join it! God is our Father because He is the
Father of our Lord. And because He is His Father, so
He is our Father. Therefore, He is the Father of mercies, 2 Corinthians 1:2-3. O what generations of mercies flow from this paternity! But we must plead to this
access to the Father through Christ, by the Spirit,
Ephesians 2:18. We must be gradually acquainted with
all three—first with the Spirit, then with Christ, and
last with the Father. First, God sends the spirit of His
Son into our hearts, and then through the Son we cry
"Abba, Father," Galatians 4:6 and Ephesians 1:4. The
bowels of mercy first wrought in the Father to us, He
chose us in Christ, and then sends His Spirit to draw us
to Christ, and by Christ to himself. Have you this access
to God by the Spirit? Bosom communion flows from
bosom affections. If your souls are truly in love with
God, He will graciously say to your petitions, "Be it

unto you according to your love."

2. The times of finding God. A godly man prays in finding seasons. When God's heart and ear are inclined to audience, then God is said to bow down His ear. There are special seasons of drawing nigh to Him when He draws nigh to us; times when He may be found. When your beloved looks forth at the window, and shows himself through the lattice, Psalm 31:2; Isaiah 105:6; Psalm 32:6; and Canticles 2:9. That is a time of grace, when God knocks at the door of your heart by His Spirit. Notions upon the heart are like the doves of the East, sent with letters about their necks. It is said of Bernard that he knew when the Holy Spirit was present with him by the motions of his heart. When God reveals Himself to the heart, He opens the ears of His servants for some gracious message. When God bids us seek His face, then the soul must answer, "One thing have I desired, that will I seek after." Holy desires warm the heart and set the soul on seeking. They are like messengers sent from heavens to bring us into God's presence.

Take heed, then, of quenching the Spirit of God. He that is born of the Spirit knows the voice of the Spirit, John 3:8. When the soul is melted by the Word, or softened by affliction, or feels some holy groans and sighs excited by the Spirit, that is a warm time for prayer. Then we enjoy intimations of the presence of God, Romans 8:27. Or when prophecies are near to expire, then there are great workings and searchings of hearts in Daniel, Zechariah, Simeon, and Anna. Or when some promise comes with applying power, "therefore Thy servant hath found in his heart to pray this prayer unto Thee, for Thou hast promised this goodness unto Thy servant," 2 Samuel 7:27-28. When we find promises dropped into the soul like wine, it causes the lips of them that are asleep to speak, Canticles 7:9.

3. Keep conscience clear and clean from secret sins. With what face can we go to a friend to whom we have given any secret affront? And will you be so bold as to come before the God of heaven when He knows you maintain some secret sin in your hearts? Do you dare to bring a Dalilah with you into this sacred closet? True is that remark of Tertullian, "He that turns his ear from God's precepts must stop his mouth in the dust, if God turns His holy ears from their cry." When our secret sins are in the light of His countenance, we may rather expect to be consumed by His anger and terrified by His wrath, Psalm 90:7-8.

But it is perhaps objected, "Then who may presume and venture into secret communion?"

True, if God should strictly mark what we do amiss, who could stand? David was sensible of this objection, but he answers it humbly, "There is forgiveness with thee, that thou mayst be feared," Psalm 130:4. If we come with holy purposes, God has promised to pardon abundantly, Isaiah 60:7. His thoughts and ways are not as our ways. Guilt makes us fly from His presence, but proclamation of pardoning grace to a wounded soul that comes for strength from heaven to subdue its iniquities sweetly draws the soul to lie at His feet for mercy. Though we cannot as yet be so free as formerly, while under the wounding sense of guilt, yet when He "restores to us the joy of His salvation, He will again uphold us with His free spirit," Psalm 51:12. Yet take heed of scars upon the soul. God knows our foolishness, and our guiltinesses are not hid from Him. Yet we come for purging and cleansing mercy.

A godly man may be under the sense of the divine displeasure for some iniquity that he knows, as the Lord spake of Eli; yet the way to be cured is not to run from God, but like the distressed woman come fearing and trembling, fall at His feet and tell Him all the truth. But if prayer has cured you, sin no more, lest a worse thing come upon you, Matthew 5:33. For if we "regard iniquity in our heart, the Lord will not hear us," but the guilt may stare conscience in the face with great amazement, Psalm 66:18.

It is storied of one who secretly had stolen a sheep, that it ran before his eyes in prayer so that he could have no rest. How strangely will memory ring the bell in the ears of conscience if we have any secret sin, if we look but aside with desires and secret thoughts (after our peace-offering) to meet our beloved lusts again. This is dangerous. God may justly give up such to cast off that which is good, to cleave to their idols, and let them alone. But if the face of the heart is not knowingly and willing spotted with any sin and lust (hating infirmities which he mourns under), then your countenance, through Christ, will be comely in the eye of God, and your voice sweet in His ears. As one said, "he who prays well, lives well," so a holy life will be a walking continual prayer. His very life is a constant petition before God.

4. Own your personal interest with God, and plead it humbly. Consider whom you go to in secret: "pray to thy Father who seeth in secret." Can you prove yourself to be in covenant? What you can prove, you may plead, and have it successfully issued. In prayer, we take God's

covenant into our mouths, but without a real interest. The Lord expostulates with such—what have they to do with it? Psalm 50:15, 16. God never graciously hears, but it is upon interest. This is the argument Solomon presses in prayer: "For they be Thy people and Thine inheritance," 1 Kings 8:51. Thus David pleads, "Thou art my God; hear the voice of my supplication," Psalm 140:94. "Truly I am Thy servant," Psalm 116:16. Asa turns the contest heavenwards, "O Lord, Thou art our God, let not mortal man prevail against Thee; Thou takest me for the sheep of Thy field, and the servant of Thy household, therefore seek me," 2 Chronicles 14:11. When Israel shall be refined as silver and tried as gold, "they shall call on His name and He will hear them. I will say it is My people, My tried, refined, golden people, and they shall say the Lord is my God," Psalm 119:176 and Zechariah 13:9. When you can discern the print of the broad seal of the covenant upon your heart and the privy seal of the Spirit upon your prayers and can look upon the Son of God in a sacerdotal relation to you, you may come boldly to "the throne of grace in time of need," Hebrews 4:16.

5. Be very particular in secret prayer, both as to sins, wants, and mercies. Hide none of your transgressions if you expect a pardon. Be not ashamed to open all your necessities. David argues because he is poor and needy, Psalm 40:17; 70:5; 86:1; 109:22. Four different times he pressed his wants and exigencies before God, like an earnest but holy beggar, showed before Him his trouble, and presented his ragged condition and secret wounds, as Job said he would "order his cause before Him," Job 23:4.

There we may speak out our minds fully and name

the persons that afflict, affront, and trouble us. And woe to them that a child of God, upon a mature judgment, names in prayer. I do not find that such a prayer in Scripture returned empty. Jacob prayed in a great strait, "Deliver me from the hand of my brother, from the hand of Esau," Genesis 32:11. David prayed, in the ascent of Mount Olives, "O Lord, I pray Thee, turn the counsel of Ahithophel into foolishness." 2 Samuel 15:31. Prayer twisted the rope for him at Giloh. Thus Jehoshaphat in his prayer names Ammon, Moab, and Edom conspiring against him, 2 Chronicles 20:10. Thus Hezekiah spreads the railing letter before the Lord, Isaiah 37:14. And the Psalmist takes them all into a round catalogue that counseled against Israel, Psalm 83:6. Thus the church, in her prayer, names Herod Antipas and Pontius Pilate, whereof the first was sent into perpetual banishment and the latter showed himself (Josephus, L. 18, c. 9. Euseb. Chron. L. 2, p. 159). It is of great use in prayer to attend to some special case or single request with arguments and affections suitable. "For this cause," says Paul, "I bow the knee," Ephesians 3:14. Suppose a grace deficient in its strength—"Lord, increase our faith," Luke 17:5. Or a temptation urgent—"For this I prayed to the Lord thrice," Corinthians 12:8. A great reason why we reap so little benefit by prayer is because we rest too much in generals. And if we have success, it is but dark, so that often we cannot tell what to make of the issues of prayer. Besides, to be particular in our petitions would keep the spirit much from wandering, when we are intent upon a weighty case, and the progress of the soul in grace would manifest its gradual success in prayer.

    6. Holy and humble appeals before the Lord in se-

cret when the soul can submissively and thankfully expose itself to divine searching. The soul cannot dwell
in the presence of God under the flashing of defilement. Neither will the Holy Spirit own a defiled soul.
But when a person can humbly, modestly, and reverently say, "Search me and try my reins, and see if there
be any wicked way in me, and lead me in the way everlasting," Psalm 139:23, it will be the means of the ebul-
litions and boilings up of joyful affections and meek
confidence at the footstool of grace, especially in pleas
of deliverance from wicked and proud enemies. When
David can plead in the case stated between his enemies
and himself, "for I am holy," Psalm 86:2,14,17, it shows
him a token for good, or when we plead against the assaults of Satan, can we be conscious that we have
watched and prayed against entering into temptation?

When in the main we can wash our hands in inno-
cency, we may then comfortably compass God's altar
about. In case of opposition and injustice: "He re-
warded me," says David in the point of Saul, "according
to my righteousness and the cleanness of my hands before Him," Psalm 18:20. Or about the truth of the love
that is in the heart to God: "Thou that knowest all
things knoweth that I love Thee," John 21:17. As to
zeal for the worship and ordinances of God, so did
Nehemiah, Nehemiah 13:14-22. As to the integrity of a
well-spent life, so did Hezekiah, Isaiah 38:3. Or if we
cannot rise so high, yet as the church did, "The desire
of our soul is to thy name and to the remembrance of
thee," Isaiah 26:8. Or lastly, when we can unfeignedly
plead the usefulness of a mercy entreated in order to
the divine glory—as when a minister or the church of
Christ for him, prays for such gifts and graces, such

knowledge and utterance—that he may win souls to
Christ, and can appeal that it is his principal aim—this
is glorious! Ephesians 6:19 and Colosians 4:3.

7. Pray for the Spirit, that you may pray in and by
the Spirit. "Awaken the north wind and the south, to
blow upon thy garden, that the spices thereof may flow
forth," Song of Solomon 4:16. Then you may invite
Christ, "Let my beloved come into his garden and eat
his pleasant fruit," that the soul may enjoy Him and
hold sweet communion with Him. All successful prayer
is from the breathing of the Spirit of God, when He in-
spires and indites, when He directs the heart as to matter and governs the tongue as to utterance. God graciously hears the sighs of His own Spirit formed in us.
He sends forth His Spirit, and "the waters flow," Psalm
147:18. The waters of contrition flow upon the breathing of the Spirit, and the soul is, as it were, all afloat
before the throne of grace when these living waters issue from under the threshold of the sanctuary, Ezekiel
47:1. Devout tears drop down from the Spirit's influences. Melting supplications follow the infusions of
grace by the Spirit. "Then they shall mourn for pierc-
ing of Christ," says the prophet, "and be in bitterness
as for a first-born, like the mourning at the town of
Hadadrimmon where Josiah was slain," Zechariah
12:10. Then, in that day, Zechariah 13: 1, 2, 4 and 14:8,
what inundations of mercy shall refresh the church,
when the Lord will extend her peace like a river, and
the glory of the Gentiles like a flowing stream! Great
things to the church, and gracious things to the soul.
Holy sighs in prayer give intelligence of great mercies
to follow. To withstand powerfully all the wiles of
Satan, one means is to consecrate every part of the

spiritual armor by prayer in the Spirit, Ephesians 6:18.

8. Apply special promises to special cases in prayer; for God has, and will, magnify His word of promise above all His name. When we are under the word of command for a duty, we must seek for a word of promise and unite them in prayer, John 12:28. When a promise of aid suits the precept, it renders prayer victorious and obedience pleasant. When we come with God's own words into His presence, when we take His words with us that He would "take away all iniquity," He will "receive us graciously," Hosea 14:2. Jacob urges that God had bid him return from his country and kindred, Genesis 32:9. Solomon urges the word of promise to David, 1 Kings 8:24. Jehoshaphat urges the word of promise to Solomon, 2 Chronicles 20:8-9. Daniel fills his mouth with the promise given to Jeremiah. He reads, and then applies it in prayer, Daniel 9:2-3. First search the Bible and look for a promise and, when found, open it before the Lord.

Paul teaches us to take the promise given to Joshua, and then to say the Lord is our helper, Hebrews 13:5-6. The special ground of the answer of prayer lies in the performance of a promise, Psalm 50:15 and 65:24. Simeon lived upon a promise and expired sweetly in the arms of a promise, in the breathings of a prayer, Luke 2:29. Sometimes the soul depends for an answer by virtue of the covenant in general, as in "I will be thy God," Genesis 17:7. Sometimes the great Remembrancer draws water out of some well of salvation, John 14:26. But, in both, God's faithfulness is the soul's surety. Hence it is that David in prayer so often argues upon the veracity and truth of God, and the church in Micah is so confident that the mercy promised to

Abraham and confirmed in truth to Jacob should be
plentifully performed to His people Israel, Micah 7:20.

9. Sober and serious resolutions before God in
prayer. The 119th Psalm is full of these. "I will keep
Thy statutes. I will run the way of thy testimonies. I will
speak of thy testimonies before kings. I have sworn and
will perform it, that I will keep thy righteous judgments." And elsewhere: "quicken us and we will call
upon Thy name," Psalm 80:18. "O when wilt Thou
come unto me? I will walk within my house with a perfect heart," Psalm 101:2. Thus the soul makes holy
stipulations and compacts of obedience to God. Thus
Jacob said, "if God will be with me, then shall the Lord
be my God," and resolved upon a house for God, and
reserving the tenth of all his estate to his service and
worship, Genesis 28:22. And this conjunction "if" is not
to be taken for a single condition, as if God did not bestow what He asked. God should not be his God; and
that would be a great wickedness. But it is a rational
setting forth of order and time. Because, or since, God
is graciously pleased to promise, I will acknowledge
Him to be the God whom I adore by erecting a temple
and paying tithes to maintain His worship. But whatever it is that the soul in distress does offer to God in
promise, be not slack to perform, for many times answers of prayer may delay till we have performed our
promises, Psalm 96:13,19. David professes to pay what
his lips had uttered in trouble, for God had heard him.
If we break our words to God, no wonder if we feel
what the Lord threatened to Israel, that they should
know His breach of promise, Numbers 14:34.

10. A waiting frame of spirit in prayer. "I waited patiently for the Lord; He inclined to me and heard my

cry," Psalm 40:1. The Hebrew word signifies, "I expected with expectation." He walked up and down in
the gallery of prayer. This is set forth by hope till God
hears, "In thee, O Lord, do I hope; Thou wilt hear, O
Lord my God," Psalm 38:15. Say with Micah, "I will
look unto the Lord; I will wait for the God of my salvation," Micah 7:7. Hoping, expecting, trusting, living
upon the promise and looking for an answer of peace,
as when an archer shoots an arrow he looks after it
with his glass to see how it hits the mark. So, says the
soul, I will attend and watch how my prayer flies toward
the bosom of God and what messages return from
heaven. As the seaman, when he has set sail, goes to
the helm and compass and stands and observes the sun
or the pole-star, how the ship works, and how the land-
marks form themselves aright according to his chart, so
do you when you have been at prayer. Mark your ship,
how it makes the port, and what rich goods are laden
back again from heaven. Most men lose their prayers
in the mists and fogs of non-observation or forgetfulness. And thus we arrive at the second question.

II. How to discover and discern answers to secret prayer, that the soul may be satisfied that it has prevailed with God?

Let us now consider the condition to prayer in the
test. He will return it into your bosoms. This is so when
the mercy sought for is speedily and particularly cast
into your arms, Psalm 104:28; 147:9. Like the irrational
creatures in their natural cries seek their meat from
God and gather what He gives them and are filled with
God. When God openly returns to His children, there
is no further dispute. For the worst of men will ac-

knowledge the divine bounty when He fills their hearts with food and gladness, Acts 14:17. But when cases are dubious:

First, observe the frame and temper of your spirit in prayer—how the heart works and steers its course in several particulars.

1. A holy liberty of spirit is commonly an excellent sign of answers, a copious spirit of fluentness to pour out requests as out of a fountain, 2 Corinthians 1:17. As God shuts up opportunities, so He shuts up hearts when He is not inclined to hear. The heart is sometimes locked up that it cannot pray. Or if it does and will press on, it finds a straitness, as if the Lord had spoken at once to Moses, "Speak no more to Me of this matter," Deuteronomy 3:26. Or as God spake to Ezekiel, though Noah, Daniel, and Job should entreat for a nation when the time of alarm is come, there is no salvation but for their souls, Ezekiel 14:2 and 7:11. When God intends to take away near relations, or any of His saints unto Himself, it often happens that neither the church of God nor dear friends have apt reasons or hearts to enlarge. The bow of prayer does not abide in strength. God took away gracious Josiah suddenly, 2 Chronicles 35:25. The church had time to write a book of lamentation and to make it an ordinance in Israel, but no time for deprecation of the divine displeasure in it. But in Hezekiah's case, there was both a reason and a heart enlarged in prayer, and the prophet crying for a sign of the mercy, 2 Kings 20:11.

Holy James might be quickly dispatched by the work of Herod Agrippa, but the church had time for supplication in behalf of Peter, Acts 12:2,12. When the Lord is graciously pleased to grant space of time and enlargement of heart, it is a notable sign of success. "Thou hast enlarged me when I was in distress," says David, Psalm 4:1. Though it is meant of deliverance, yet it may be applied to prayer, as the holy prophet seems to do. Yea, though the soul may be under some sense of displeasure and in extremities, yet it lifts up a cry, Psalm 18:6. When conscience stops the mouths of hypocrites, they shun and fly the presence of God.

2. A blessed serenity and quiet calmness of spirit in time of prayer, especially when the soul comes troubled and clouded at first while it pours out its complaints before the Lord. But, at length, the sun shines forth brightly. It is said of Hannah, she was no more sad; her countenance was no longer in the old hue, cast down and sorrowful because of her rival. Thus the Lord dealt with David, though not fully answered, yet filled with holy fortitude of spirit, and revived in the midst of his trouble, 1 Samuel 1:18. Prayer dispels anxious solicitude, and chases away black thoughts from the heart, Psalm 138:3,7. It eases conscience and fills the soul with the peace of God, Philippians 4:6-7.

3. A joyful frame of spirit. God sometimes makes His people not only peaceful but joyful in His house of prayer. Thus sped Hezekiah, Isaiah 56:7, when his crane-like chatterings were turned into swan-like songs, and his mournful elegies into glorious praises upon ten-stringed instruments in the house of the Lord. The lips of Habbakuk quivered and his belly trembled, but before he finished, his voice was voluble in holy songs and his fingers nimble upon the harp, Habbakuk 3:16. Thus it was at Solomon's prayer: When the fire came down, the people were warmed at worship and went away glad and merry at heart, 2 Chronicles 7:1,10.

David's experience of this sent him often to the house of God for comfort, and thus chides his soul when cast down at any time. "I am going to the altar or God, to God my exceeding joy; why art thou disquieted within me?" Psalm 43:4-5. His old harp that had cured Saul of his malignant dumps, being played upon with temple songs, now curds his own spiritual sadness.

When we look upon God with an eye of faith in prayer, it enlightens our faces with heavenly joy. When Moses came out of the mount from communion with God, how illustrious was his face from that heavenly vision. Wherefore, prayer for divine mercy and comfort sometimes exhibits itself in this language, "Make Thy face to shine upon us, and we shall be saved," Psalm 83:3. And on this wise the priests of old were to bless the children of Israel, "The Lord make His face to shine upon thee, and be gracious to thee," Numbers 6:25. These, and the like expressions in Scripture, import that sometimes the Lord was pleased to give forth a shining glory from the oracle, and thereby made known His presence unto His people and filled them with awful impressions of His majesty and mercy, Exodus 40:34, Leviticus 9:23, Numbers 16:19. This joyful light of God's countenance is like the sun rising upon the face of the earth. It chases away the dark fears and discouragements of the night. Such heavenly joy shows the strength of faith in prayer, and the radiant appearances of God. Yea, to this end all prayer should be directed, that our joy may be full, John 16:24.

4. A sweetness of affection to God. When the soul has gracious sentiments of God in prayer, clouds of jealousy and suspicions of the divine mercy (as if God

were a hard master) are marvelously unbecoming a
soul that should go to God as a father. And hence,
from such unsuitable thoughts of infinite mercy, to restrain prayer is greatly provoking. Whereas the apprehension of God's excellent goodness should work the
heart into lovely thoughts of God. Man, but especially a
saint, is an accumulated heap of divine favors, and the
gifts of divine mercy should attract our hearts. And
when the soul comes to perceive that all flows from the
fountain of his eternal love, it makes prayer to be filled
with holy delight and joy. The ecstasies of love often
rise upon the soul in secret, and such divine affection,
that it carries the soul beyond itself. Let the profane
world say what they will, when spiritual ardors like so
many fragrant spices flow out of the soul. "I love the
Lord, for He hath heard my supplication," Psalm
116:1. As answers of prayer flow from the love of the
Father, so suitable workings of holy affections flow
from the hearts of children, John 16:27. When the soul
is filled with gracious intimations, like those of the an-
gelical voice to Daniel, "O Daniel, greatly beloved," or
like that to the Holy Virgin, "Hail, thou that art highly
favored," how greatly does it enflame the heart to God,
Daniel 10:11, Luke 1:28!

5. Inward encouragements sometimes spring in
upon the heart in prayer from remembrance of former
experiments, which mightily animate the soul with fervency. When Moses calls to mind that God had forgiven and delivered from Egypt, there immediately follows a sweet intimation of mercy, Numbers 14:19-20.
When the soul considers the days of old, the years of
ancient times, and calls to remembrance its former
songs in the night, he draws an argument out of the

quiver of experience, "Will God be favorable no more? can He forget to be gracious? Can He in anger shut up His tender mercies?" Psalm 77:5-10.

6. A ready heart for thankfulness and service. The heart is brimming and ready to flow over in grateful memorials of His mercy. "What shall I render to the Lord for all His benefits towards me?" Psalm 106:12. As of old at temple sacrifices there was music, so it ought to be now while the mercy is praying for, the heart must be winding up, and tuning for praise, Revelation 5:8, Psalm 107:1. The vials full of the odors of prayer are joined with harps for heavenly melody. When the heart is fixed or prepared, then follow songs and praise. This streams from a sense of divine love. And love is the fountain of thankfulness and all sprightly and vigorous services. The prayer that does not end in cheerful obedience is called by Cyprian, "barren and unfruitful, naked and without ornament." And so we may glance upon the expression of James, 5:16, the effectual, fervent prayer, a working prayer within will be working without, and demonstrate the labor of love.

Second, observe the principal subject matter of prayer. Mark that the arrow of prayer is shot at the scope it aims at. There is usually some special sin unconquered, some untamed corruption, some defect, some pressing strait that drives the soul to prayer and is the main burden of the spirit. Take notice how such a sin withers, or such a grace flourishes, or such a need is supplied upon the opening our hearts in prayer. Watch unto prayer, watch to perform it, 1 Peter 4:7, and then, to expound the voice of the divine oracle and to know that you are successful, cry to your soul by way of holy soliloquy, "Watchman, what of the night?"

Isaiah 21:11.

Third, observe ensuing providences. Set a vigilant eye upon succeeding circumstances; examine them as they pass before you. Set a wakeful sentinel at the ports of wisdom. "His name is near, His wondrous works declare," Psalm 75:1. His mane of truth, His glorious title is that of a prayer-hearing God.

When prayer is gone up by the help of the Spirit, mark how all things work together for good, Romans 8:28. And note the connection there. The working of things together, follows the intercession of the Spirit for all saints, Romans 8:27. God is pleased often to speak so clearly by His works, as if He said, "Here I am, I will guide you continually, and you shall be like a watered garden whose waters fail not," Isaiah 63:9-11. Secret promises animate prayer and often providently expound it. Cyrus was promised to come against Babylon for the church's sake, Isaiah 45:4,11,19. But Israel must ask it of God, and they had a word for it that they should not ask His face in vain. Then follows Babylon's fall in the succeeding chapter.

When we cry to the Lord in trouble, He sends his word of command and heals us, Psalm 107:19-20. There is a set time of mercy, a time of life. When Abraham had prayed for a son, the Lord told him, "at the time appointed I will return," Genesis 5:2 and 18:14. In a great extremity, after the solemn fast of three days by the Jews in Shusan, and the queen in her palace on the fourth day, at night the king could not sleep, and must hear the chronicles of Persia read. Then follows Haman's ruin, Esther 4:16 and 6:1.

Prayer has a strange virtue to give quiet sleep, sometimes to a David, and sometimes a waking pillow

for the good of the church, Psalm 3:4-5; Genesis 24:15.
When Jacob had done wrestling and the angel was
gone at the springing of the morning, then the good
man saw the angel of God's presence in the face of
Esau. Sometimes Providence is not so quick. The mar-
tyr's prayer, as to a complete answer, is deferred for
season, Revelation 6:11. But long white robes are given
to every one, a triumphant frame of spirit, and told
they should wait but a little season till divine justice
should work out the issue of prayer. The thunder upon
God's enemies comes out of the temple. The judgments roar out of Zion, the place of divine audience.
Revelation 11:19 and Joel 3:16. But the means, methods, and times of God's working are various. Submit all
to His infinite wisdom; prescribe not, but observe the
embroidery of providence. It is difficult to spell its
characters sometimes, but it is a rare employment,
Isaiah 5; Psalm 111:2; Ecclesiasties 3:11. His works are
searched into by such as delight in His providences, for
all things are beautiful in His season.

Fourth, observe your following communion with
God. Inward answers make the soul vegetate and lively,
like plants after the shining of the sun upon rain, 2
Samuel 23:4, lift up their heads and shoot forth their
flowers. A saint in favor does all with delight. Answered
prayer is like oil to the spirits, and beauty for ashes.
The sackcloth of mournful fasting is turned to a wed-
ding garment. He grows more free and yet humbly fa-
miliar with heaven. This is one I would wish you to pick
acquaintance with, that can come and have what he
will at court, John 16:23. As the Lord once told a king
by night that Abraham was a prophet, and would pray
for him, he was acquainted with the King of heaven,

Genesis 20:7. O blessed person! I hope there's many
such among you whose life is a perpetual prayer, as
David that gave himself to prayer, Psalm 109:4.

The Hebrew expression, "but I pray," is very
forcible. He is all over prayer, prays at rising, prays at
lying down, prays as he walks—he is always ready for
prayer. Like a prime favorite at court that has the
golden key to the privy stairs and can wake his prince
by night, there are such, (whatever the besotted, profane world dreams) who are ready for spiritual accents
at all seasons, besides the frequency of set commu-
nions. His wings never weary, his willing spirit is flying
continually, and makes God the rock of his dwelling,
into which he may, upon all assaults, have holy retire-
ments.

Some Particular Queries

But enough for the main question with its
branches. There are many particular queries of some
weight that may attend the subject. To such I shall
briefly reply.

QUESTION 1. What is the proper time for secret
prayer?

ANSWER. Various providences, different tempera-
ments and frames of spirit, motions from heaven, opportunities, dictate variously. Some find it best at
evening; others in the night, when all is silent; others
at morning, when the spirits are freshest. I think with
respect to others that conscientious prudence must
guide in such cases, but it should be when others are
retired and the spirit in the best frame for communion.

QUESTION 2. How often should we pray in secret?

ANSWER. If we consult Scripture precedents, we find David at prayer in the morning, Psalm 5:3. Our blessed Lord, early in the morning, Mark 1:35. Chrytsostom advises, "Wash your soul before your body, for as the face and hand are cleansed by water, so is the soul by prayer." At another time, our Lord went to secret prayer in the evening, Matthew 14:23, and Isaac went out at eventide to meditate, Genesis 24:63. David and Daniel prayed three times a day, Psalm 55:17 and Daniel 6:10. And once it is mentioned that David said, "Seven times a day will I praise Thee;" that is, "often will I do it," Psalm 69:164.

Such cases may happen that may require frequent accesses to the throne of grace in a day. But I humbly think we should go there at least once a day, which seems to be imported by that passage in our Lord's prayer, "Give us this day our daily bread." For after our Lord's appointment of secret prayer in the text, He gives this prayer as a pattern to His disciples.

QUESTION 3. When persons are under temptations of disturbance by passion, is it expedient then to pray?

ANSWER 3. Since we are enjoined to "lift up holy hands without wrath," 1 Timothy 2:8, I judge it is not so proper to run immediately to prayer, except to exercise some praying ejaculations for pardon and strength against such exorbitancy. And when in some measure cooled and composed, then speed to prayer, and take heed that the sun does not go down upon your wrath without holy purgation by prayer, Ephesians 4:26. Though I must confess that a Christian should always endeavor to keep his course and heart in such a frame as not to be unfit for prayer upon small warnings. The very consideration of our frequent communion with God should be a great bar to immoderate and exuberant passions.

QUESTION 4. Whether we may pray in secret when others must take notice of our retirement?

ANSWER 4. I must confess, in a strait house and when a person can many times find no seasons but such as will fall under observation, I think he ought not to neglect secret duty for fear of the notice of others. We must prevent it as much as may be, and especially watch our hearts against spiritual pride, and God may graciously turn it to a testimony and example to others.

QUESTION 5. Whether we may be vocal in secret prayer, if we can't so well raise or keep up affection, or preserve the heart from wandering without it?

ANSWER 5. No doubt; but yet a great deal of wise caution must be used about extending the voice. Tertullian advises that both hands and countenance and voice should be ordered with great reverence and humility. And what else do we by revealing our prayers than if we prayed in public? Yet if we can obtain some very private place, or when others are away from home, such may lawfully improve it to their private benefit.

QUESTION 6. How to keep the heart from wandering thoughts in prayer?

ANSWER 6. Although it is exceedingly difficult to attain so excellent a frame, yet by frequent remembering and reflecting upon the eye of God in secret, by endeavoring to fix the heart with all possible watchfulness upon the main scope of the prayer in hand, by being very sensible of our wants and indigences, by not studying an impertinent length but rather being more frequent and short considering God is in heaven and we upon the earth, and by the exercise of holy communion, we may, through the implored assistance of the Spirit, attain some sweetness and freedom, and also more fixedness of spirit in our addresses before the Lord.

QUESTION 7. What if present answers seem not to correspond to our petitions?

ANSWER 7. We must not conclude it to be a token of displeasure, and say with Job, "wherefore dost Thou contend with me?" Job 10:2. Instead we must acknowledge the sovereignty of divine wisdom and love in things which seem contrary to us in petitions for temporal mercies and submit to the counsel of Elihu, since He gives no account of any of His matters, Job 33:13. Neither can we find out the unsearchable methods of His holy ways to any perfection.

There are other cases and scruples that might be treated of. As regarding prescribed forms of prayer in secret prayer—to which I need say but little, since such as are truly converted, Galatians 4:6, have the promise of the Spirit of God to assist and enable them, and they need not drink of another man's bucket that have the fountain, nor use stilts and crutches that have spiritual strength; neither are words and phrases, but faith and holy groans, the nerves of prayer, Romans 8:26; Zecheriah 12;10; Acts 9:11. Yet, for some help to young beginners, it is of use to observe the study or the Spirit, as well as the heavenly matter of several prayers in the Holy Scriptures.

Neither need I press frequency to a holy heart that has fallen in love with spiritual communion, for he delights to be continually with God. The thoughts of God are so precious to him that his soul is even sick of affection, and prays to be stayed with more of "the flagons," and comforted with "the apples" in greater abundance, Song of Solomon 2:5. To some, but I fear very few, it may be needful to say how far it may be expedient to withdraw from prayer for the necessity of the frail body in this vale of tears. It may be said to such, the Lord is very pitiful and gracious to our frailties, that He would rather have mercy than sacrifice in some cases. Though I doubt these phoenixes are very rare that are in danger of expiring in prayer as martyrs of holy love, as Gerson expresses it.

Having now finished with what brevity I could the foregoing queries, I should treat of short, sudden, occasional prayers commonly called "ejaculations," but indeed that requires a set discourse. Yet, because of a promise before recited, I shall give a few hints and then conclude with some application.

Ejaculatory Prayer

Ejaculatory prayer is a sudden, short breathing of the soul toward heaven upon instant and surprising emergency. In holy persons, it is quick and lively, rising from a vehement ardor of spirit, swifter than the flight of eagles, keeping pace with a flash of lightning. It flies upon the wings of a holy thought into the third heavens in the twinkling of an eye, and fetches auxiliary forces in time of need.

There are many precedents recorded in sacred page upon great and notable occasions with strange success. When good magistrates are busy in the work of reformation, let them imitate Nehemiah when redressing the profanation of the Sabbath, "Remember me, O my God, concerning this," Nehemiah 13:14,22. When captains and generals go forth to war, observe Israel's appeal to God rather than acclamations to men. "The Lord thy God be with thee, as He was with Moses," Joshua 1:17. In times of battle, or pursuit of the enemy, valiant Joshua darts up such a prayer as this: "O that the Lord would lengthen this triumphant day," Joshua 10:12. And the Lord heard his voice. The tribes beyond Jordan in a battle with the Hagarites, 1 Chronicles 5:10,20. When Jehoshaphat was in a sore strait, 2 Chronicles 18:31. Samson ready to perish at Lehi with thirst, and when blind exposed to contempt in the temple of Dagon, Judges 15:18 and 16:28. Elisha at Dothan encompassed with a Syrian host, "Lord, open this young man's eyes," 2 Kings 6:17. David near being stoned at Ziklag, 1 Samuel 15:31. In the midst of lawful and laborious callings, Boaz said to the reapers, "The Lord be with you," Ruth 2:4. It sanctifies the plow, as Jerome said of the fields of Bethlehem. The tillers of the fields and the dressers of the vineyards, sang David's psalms. It keeps the shop, and inclines the hearts of customers, it bars the doors, it quenches fires, it blesseth your children within you, it preserves your going out and coming in.

Jacob found it to rest upon his children going on a journey to Egypt, Genesis 43:14. It closes the eye with sweet sleep, Psalm 3:5, gives songs in the night, and wakens the soul in the arms of mercy, Job 40:10 and Psalm 139:18. It sits at the helm when the storm rises at sea, gives strength to anchors in roads, and prosperous gales to the venturous merchant, Psalm 57:28 and Jonah 1:6. When in the palace at dinner, Nehemiah presented the cup to his prince. He presented also a Michtam, a golden prayer, to the King of Heaven, Nehemiah 2:4.

At the reading of the law, Josiah was heard as to some secret cries to Heaven, 2 Chronicles 34:27. At a holy conference in a journey, the disciples prayed, "Lord, increase our faith," Luke 17:5. Jacob, on his dying pillow, predicting future events to his children, fell into a holy rapture. "I have waited for Thy salvation, O Lord," Genesis 49:18. At sacred death, in martyrdom, Zechariah cries out, "The Lord look upon it and require it," 2 Chronicles 2:4. And Stephen, under a shower of stones, melted into prayer for the stony hearts that flung them, "Lord, lay not this sin to their charge," Acts 7:60. And our blessed Savior, in His greatest agonies, made a tender-hearted prayer,

"Father, forgive them," Luke 23:34. And lastly, in the distresses of others, Eli puts up a sudden prayer for Hannah, "The God of Israel grant thy petition," 1 Samuel 1:17.

In these, and many like cases, the Holy Word stores us with patterns for ejaculation in all extremities, which I cannot now digest and improve. Only in a few words let us take a view of the usefulness of such a sudden flight of the soul to heaven.

1. It helps us to a speedy preparation for all duties. With such an ejaculation let us lift up our hands to God in the heavens, Lamentations 3:41.

2. It is a guard against secret sins in the first rising and the first assaults of temptation.

3. It suffers not divine mercies to slip by unobserved in a wakeful Christian and proves a fruitful mother of gratitude and praise.

4. It sanctifies all our worldly employments. It fastens the stakes in the hedge of divine protection, and turns every thing to a blessing, 1 Timothy 4:4-5.

5. It is a saint's buckler against sudden accidents, a present antidote against frights and evil tidings. It is good at all occasions, and consecrates to us not only our meals, but every gasp of air.

6. It is a sweet companion that the severest abridge us of. Outward ordinances and closet duties they may cut off. The little nail in the holy place they may pluck out, Ezra 9:87. But no labyrinth, no prison, not the worst of company can hinder this. In the very face of adversaries, we may lift our souls to God.

Let us conclude with some uses.
USE 1. To convince such of their dangerous state

that neglect secret duties, that have no heart communion, that draw no water out of the sealed fountain. All they do is in public only. It is a suspicious token of hypocrisy, since the kernel and soul of religion lies so much in the heart and closet. Mark the phrase in the text. God's eye is open upon you in the closet, and if your eye be open upon Him, you may see a glorious beauty. The excellence of grace lies in making conscience of secret sins and secret duties.

USE 2. To examine such as perform secret duty but not from a sincere principle—like Amaziah who prayed, but not with a perfect heart, 2 Chronicles 25:2. Like Ahab, they mourn with but crocodile tears. Such do it only because they find precept or example for it. And, therefore, to quiet conscience, they converse only in the shell and trunk of a duty. They rest in the naked performance but matter not whether they taste of the sweet streams that flow in from heaven in the golden pipe of an ordinance. What account can such render who go into their closet, but like Domitian, to catch flies only, and when the doors are shut to the world, their hearts are shut to heaven and communion with God? He that sees in secret beholds the evil frame of such a heart and will one day openly punish it.

USE 3. To excite and awaken all to this excellent manner. Would you live delightfully? Would you translate heaven to earth? Then keep up communion in secret prayer, to know *Him*, to discern *His* face, to behold the lustre of *His* eye that shines in secret. Remember the glorious Person that meets in your closet. All the world yields no such glittering beauty as a gracious person sees when he is in a happy frame at secret prayer. Shut your eyes when you come out, for all other objects are but vile and sordid and not worth the glances of a noble soul. Oh, the sweetness of the hidden manna that the soul tastes when in lively communion with God! It is a part of that which is laid up for saints in glory. Let us a little relish our souls with it.

Things On Which To Meditate

1. Consider what affectionate agonies the soul delights to conflict with in secret: fears that raise confidence, humility that exalts, tremblings that embolden, bright clouds that shine upon Israelites in the night, darkness that enlightens, solitudes full of heavenly company, tears brimful of joy, and holy sighs like a cooling wind in harvest, sick fits that are symptoms of health, holy faintings that are the soul's cordials, a weariness to the flesh that is the healthful exercise of it, vigor to the spirit, and continual motion that never tires. As Austin said of divine love, "It is the weight of my soul, it carries me up and down in all that I speak and aim at."

2. Its ecstasies and heavenly raptures, which allure and draw the heart from earthly vanities, and the soul shuts its eyes to worldly delights, and says of laughter with Solomon, "It is mad, and of mirth, what doest thou? Can it warm its thoughts at the crackling of thorns under a pot, nor be joyful in the house of a fool?" Ecclesiasties 2:2 and 7:64. It is the soul's pleasure to loath pleasure itself. None so beautiful to him as Christ, the chiefest of ten thousand. No sweetness like that of the tree in the midst of the wood, the tree of

life, in the midst of the paradise of God. He sits under it with great delight, while it drops sweeter than honey into his closet, Revelation 2:7 and 1 Samuel 14:26.

3. Its admirable prophecies: prayer stands upon Mount Zion with a divining, presaging spirit. It foretells great things, to the church's joy and its enemies' terror. Elijah, at prayer in Horeb, receives answer of the ruin of the house of Ahab, and bid to go and anoint Jehu the son of Nimshi king over Israel, 2 Kings 9:2. The two witnesses under the Roman defection have power to smite the earth with plagues as often as they will, Revelation 11, consonant to what Tertullian said of old, "The prayers of Christians confounded the nations." And so it will shortly prove when the doom of Babylon comes out of the temple.

When the sanctuary is full of the smoke of the incense of prayer, the seven angels come out with the seven last vials full of the wrath of God to pour them out upon the anti-Christian world, Revelation 15:7-8 and 16:1. Prayer calculates and hastens the ruin of Rome. When the spirit of prayer is once poured out, it brings deliverance to Mount Zion, and gathers the nations into the valley of Jehoshaphat unto judgment, Joel 2:28-32, and 3:1-2. Let us never be discouraged. If prayer fails to work and awakens Christ in the ship of the church, her storms will cease in a halcyon calm, Luke 8:24.

4. Its comforting evidences. Secret prayer duly managed is a notable evidence of adoption. Pray to your Father who is, and sees, in secret, who knows the secrets of your heart. Your groanings are not hid from Him. None but a child of promise has this sweet freedom with God as a Father.

5. Its rewards and reverences: Nothing revives and cheers the spirit so much as answers of love and mercy from heaven. As it feasts the conscience with the royal dainties of sincerity, so it sets a lustre upon every mercy as being the child of prayer. Our closets exert an influence upon our shops, our ships, our fields, and all that we enjoy, so that they smell of the divine blessing. As David said of the precepts, the soul may say, "This I have because I urged the promises," Psalm 69:56.

Pity the miserable blind world that knows not where true comfort, joy, and strength are to be found, who see no beauty in the ways of God and feel no sweetness in communion with Him, who find no pleasure in closets but all in play-houses, which Tertullian called the devil's churches, that cry out with Esau that they have enough, Genesis 33:9. Alas! what enough can be in the creature unless of noise, rattle, and vanity! O how ignorant of heavenly treasures, of that fountain of mercies whereof prayer drinks and refreshes the spirit of a saint, who know not that blessed "enough" whereof Jacob speaks, that ocean of all things to be found in God! Genesis 33:11. Now let Europe be in flames and the very ark in danger, a prayerless man cares not though the one be burnt and the other in ashes. So he is safe, and if his concerns catch fire, he can only repair to Endor of Ekron, 1 Samuel 28:7; 2 Kings 1:2. Such have no acquaintance, no hope from God, no interest in the keeper of souls. The world is a deplorable hospital, the great Lazar house of sick, lame and impotent persons, as Gerson terms it, who have no face nor heart to go to the physician of souls.

But ah! most lamentable is the state of some profligate wretches of our age that are, I fear, almost incur-

ably gone with spiritual ulcers in their lungs, and pu-
trid cancers in their tongues, who breathe nothing but
venom, and openly spit out their rotten atheistical
jeers against the spirit of prayer, and make a mock at
communion with God, who scoff at what God has
promised us as one of the choicest tokens of His love
to the church and symptoms of the glory of the latter
times, Zecheriah 12:10; Joel 2:28,32; Romans 10:13,
when God will turn such Ishmaels into the desert, and
their drunken songs shall expire in dreadful howlings.
Profaner than many heathen, that in the primitive
times had some reverence for Christian worship,
though they persecuted, Amos 8:10. Job 30:31. But
those of this adulterous Roman age, like brute beasts,
speak evil of what they are ignorant, and are in danger
to perish in their corruption, 2 Peter 2:12. Pity such if
there is yet hope, and commend their condition to
God's mercy and to penitent sorrow, that they may
weep here where tears smart, not in hell where they
scald and burn and swell that river of brimstone.

In the mean time, O you that fear the Lord, be diligent to observe and interpret messages after secret
prayer, for the life and joy of a Christian is improved by
it. God has declared Himself graciously pleased with
secret prayer, so as to send an angel, that glorious creature, to fly into Daniel's chamber. Weary with flying, he
moved so swiftly, as the original test expresses it, Daniel
9:21. What a high expression is this, that even angels
are represented weary with hasty flights to bring saints
their answers! And of what great account does the
Lord esteem His praying people, that angels are expressed to be tired in bringing tidings of mercy!

6. Meditate on the glory of heaven, where all our

prayers shall be turned into praises, when every sigh
below shall be an accent.